*The Risen Christ
and the Eucharistic World*

THE
RISEN CHRIST
AND THE
EUCHARISTIC
WORLD

Gustave Martelet

translated by René Hague

A CROSSROAD BOOK
THE SEABURY PRESS · NEW YORK

The Seabury Press
815 Second Avenue
New York, N.Y. 10017

Originally published as
Résurrection, Eucharistie et Genèse de l'Homme
Copyright © 1972 by Desclée & Co., Paris
English translation © 1976 by William Collins Sons & Co. Ltd,
London, and The Seabury Press, Inc., New York

Library of Congress Catalog Card Number: 76-23849
ISBN: 0-8164-0316-3

Printed in Great Britain

Contents

Foreword

At the heart of the Christian faith is the doctrine of the Incarnation, the belief that the un-space-time-conditioned Word of God is echoed on our space-time-conditioned planet. Living a human life, he died a human death and – rose again, to 'return' to the Father whom he had never left. It is, in T. S. Eliot's words,

> The point of intersection of the timeless
> With time.

Christ is, but is so much more than, a man who spent some thirty-odd years in a particular area of the world's surface, in a specific situation. He is that because only so could we come to recognize our kinship with him; he is more than that precisely because our human thought cannot imprison the whole truth which he expresses, which he *is*.

In Fr Martelet's striking description, 'while man is at home with animals and stars, he is also the cosmic neighbour of the Absolute . . .' In the contemporary jargon, man is self-transcendent. That self-transcendence is a sort of reflection of the truth about Jesus of Nazareth. In his divine nature, Jesus expresses the Father's self-transcendence, since he is the expression of the Father's own self-transcendent utterance. In his human nature, in his eucharistic self-giving, in his death-transcending resurrection, he is the expression of man's refusal to be totally restricted to the here-and-now, to the limitations of his individual, earthbound, death-interrupted experience.

In this remarkable study, Fr Martelet singles out these two aspects of our incarnational faith – Eucharist and Resurrection – and analyses their significance in relation to our everyday world. Central to our Christian belief is the conviction that a man who was born in the kingdom of Herod of Judea and was put to death at the order of Pontius Pilate, who ruled over that same Judea in the name of the Emperor Tiberius, was yet alive and seen by his friends within forty-eight hours of his burial. Central to our

Christian practice is the Eucharist, in which we believe that that saving death is commemorated, that risen life communicated.

In an increasingly complex world, the Eucharist is also, as the author reminds us, a recall to the basic simplicities of human life. 'By placing on the table such simple things as bread and wine, even though our world produces so many new and wonderful things, the Eucharist reminds its guests of the essential aim of hominization.' The reality that the Eucharist is is also a symbol – symbol of man's physical condition and physical needs, of his cultural and social activities, his desire for companionship, his links with the cosmic order. For, in the words of Teilhard, quoted by the author, '*my* matter, or my own body, is not a *part* of the universe that I possess *totaliter*: it is the totality of the universe possessed by me *partialiter*'.

Again and again throughout the book, Fr Martelet refers to and quotes Teilhard. But, for all that, the work remains his own – stamped with the mark of his individual genius, his personal interests, his unique insights. Thus, when he says, 'Transubstantiation is not an isolated mystery that could be regarded as arbitrary; it is a direct consequence of the structure of a world created in Jesus Christ', he is carrying further a familiar Teilhardian idea. And when he affirms, 'The eucharistic mystery of the Church is also the eucharistic mystery of the cosmos', he is not merely echoing his master; he is developing his thought.

Inevitably, faced with the mystery of the Eucharist, the believer is baffled in his attempt to try to understand *how* it is possible for Christ to be present in the individual host; he is still more baffled when he reflects that Christ is not less truly present in a hundred million hosts across the world. Yet his bafflement is clearly consequent on the fact that he is here faced with a particularly vivid example of the all-pervading truth about God's dealings with his world, about the action of the Eternal in the temporal.

What is of special value in the book is the way in which the author insists on and enlarges a truth which, though commonly accepted by theologians, is all too easily forgotten by Christians at large. It is a commonplace for preachers and others to proclaim that the body of Christ as present in the Eucharist is the same body as that which walked the streets of Nazareth. True as this is, it is by no means the whole truth. We must ever remember that here is the *risen* body of Christ. Only because he is risen, because, that is, he is no longer hampered by the human restrictions which he had freely accepted, can he be so present, individual yet universal, enriching his Church by vitalizing its members, who are also his.

Suppose that for a moment in our minds we withdraw the risen Christ from the Lord's Supper, what remains of the latter? The table is immediately bare; it has been cleared; no dish remains to supply our needs; there is no Presence; the table is no longer sacred, and we can leave it without regret. This is what we are told by faith; without the risen Lord himself, his supper is *nothing*.

It is not too much to say that a careful reading of this book should lead to an enrichment of the spiritual and sacramental life of any thoughtful Christian. It is also an intellectual stimulus.

THOMAS CORBISHLEY, S.J.

Introduction

The world is changing, and changing fast: but in what direction? It is almost as though we were witnessing a mutation. We can all now see that it is becoming other, but in that other is there a genesis, or is there simply a turbulent chaos? Without being too hasty in forecasting the direction each stage of the process will take, and without denying the tragic ambivalence of each total situation, the Christian answers that our whole world is a process of growth and life. He adds, and this he emphasizes above all, that an unprecedented mutation is at work upon our world: that of the Resurrection to which Christ in person is introducing it, and to which he is already pledging it. Such is the prime evidence contributed by faith; but it is subject to one condition, that faith shall have remained truly faith. In fact, however, the faith that operates in us is often impermanent and adulterated. It is only at its outer surface that it is vigorous; beneath that, it becomes confused with secular affirmations relating to culture, justice, progress, or even revolution. When this faith has to make its way back to its own centre, it evaporates, for there it finds a Christ who, it says, partakes of the nature of myth. The truth is the very opposite – not, indeed, that man is a myth; but he will very soon become one if Christians lose sight of Christ's resurrection, or if it melts away, as seen by them, into a mere product of their own consciousness.

To show that the resurrection of Christ is the foundation of faith because it is the supreme event of history is what unmistakably defines what has rightly been called 'the uniqueness of the Christian'. 'If Christ has not been raised,' says St Paul, 'then our preaching is in vain and your faith is in vain'; but equally vain is the existence of the world. Neither man, nor history, nor the cosmos nor knowledge, nor power, nor anything won by art or by love, nor, we need hardly say, any non-being, nor even 'God' (for he would then be without Jesus Christ) – none of these will ever fill the great void created in the heart of man and in the being of the world by the suppression in history of the risen

Christ. This may well have been the void, for which Christians might become responsible, at the prospect of which Zarathustra shuddered.

There are many ways of showing that the resurrection of Christ is the centre of gravity of world history. The starting-point of our demonstration here will be the Eucharist itself, for the Eucharist is one of the most paradoxical forms in which the Lord is actualized. If Christ is not risen, then the Eucharist is in vain, and its supper is a hollow void. No emphasis on the community can, by itself, fill the gap; nor can any rethinking of the symbols of faith. You find young persons who suddenly give up the Eucharist after being told, for example, that Christ's walking on the waters is simply a myth. And they are quite right; for the truth is that if Christ is not he who in a real sense has mastery over the world and, in his resurrection, has conquered our death, then the Eucharist which depends upon him has no essential contribution to make. It is no more than the rite prac-tised by a human group imprisoned in death, and it will dis-appear as that group disappears. But this does not fit the facts. 'I am the resurrection and the life,' Jesus tells us; and again, 'I am the bread of life.' All that is implied in those words hangs together. The Eucharist is the Resurrection, it is the risen person himself become our food. It is man's nourishment deified by Jesus, the viaticum for us, the supreme mutants,[1] the nutriment of this life which leaves death behind; it is the incorruptibility which Christ gives to this world in the bread and wine which he blesses and so transfigures.

If we are thus to bring together the Eucharist and the Resur-rection, as scripture shows us we can, we shall have to probe man and Christ until we reach the mystery of the body; for what the Resurrection and the Eucharist are concerned with is the body of Christ, and similarly it is with the body of man that we are concerned when we say that Christ assumes it and deifies it. We are sometimes told that the greatest problem of faith belongs to the order of symbol. This is quite true; the symbolic meaning is fundamental and has been too long neglected; but it leaves something even more deeply important unsaid. The bread which nourishes and the wine which quenches thirst are, in the Eucharist, the flesh and blood of the risen Christ. The symbol refers to the mystery, and here the mystery is that of the body of Christ in person. If these statements stand for something real, then their content must produce an anthropology capable of carrying the full weight of love, of glory, of life-through-resurrection, by concentrating attention on the supreme importance, both in man and in Christ, of the body. It is thus, too, that we shall be able to determine the unique significance, as a contribution to this world, of the Church of the Resurrection and of its ministry.

It is this that lies behind a scheme of work which an introduction can do no more than suggest. In the light of eucharistic symbolism, we have first to make our way back from the Lord's Supper to the resurrection of Christ, by the road of the body. We shall then, by the same road, have to come back from the Resurrection to the Lord's Supper in order to see how we can speak of such a supper in the language of body and not merely of substance. When we have grasped the Eucharist in this way, it will serve to introduce us, with a fresh insight, to the ministry of the Resurrection, as that ministry is fundamentally related to man's integral development. Thus there are three stages in arriving at a more exact view of the risen Christ in his relationship with the genesis of man, with a view to a Christian renewal of which both Church and world, we believe, are in urgent need. Any readers who are hopelessly discouraged by discussion of method and other preliminary matters may well move on immediately to the second chapter, always with an eye to turning back later to the first. Finally, may I beg the reader not to demur at any occasional difficulty of phraseology. In spite of some appearances to the contrary, this is not a book for specialists; its aim is simply to help in seeing man and Christ in a new light. Any point about which there is some obscurity can be cleared up by another. What holds the book together is a vision whose essence is concentrated in St Paul's words, 'Christ in you, the hope of glory' (Col. 1 : 27): words that can be realized in every Christian.

Part I

EUCHARISTIC SYMBOLISM AND RESURRECTION

CHAPTER 1

The meaning of symbol

Anyone who has seen the opening of the Olympic Games – the stadium, the flags, the torch – knows just what we mean by symbol. Every day, again, as soon as we go out into the street, the constantly repeated alternation of the traffic lights from red to green and from green to red governs our walking and our driving. At our work, arrangements of figures, presentations of records, 'progress-charts', all these represent, by transposition, the particular part each and all of us have to play, the plans to which we have to work, all our debits and credits. Diagrams and charts, card-indexes, records, chits, memoranda, stand for the circulation of human beings and their goods, their transactions, the use of their leisure, their cares and their troubles. The cinema, too, feeds us with pictures of ourselves and of others. We see ourselves mirrored in the actors and actresses. We live in a world of symbol, and family life, like social life, is the daily untangling of a skein of signs in which love, not without difficulty, gradually transforms our mediocrity. Scientists, too, are caught up in a world of signs. From atoms to stars, they encode, they cipher, they register. The computers on which they rely operationally cannot work without 'symbols', for which they have an insatiable appetite. If we go back in time, the ethnologist is looking for a way of handling all the elements of the world that will again be symbolic. Earth, air, fire, water, the mountain, the sun and the moon, the four cardinal points, the centre, the rainbow, the serpent, trees and birds, everything has served for the passage from one domain to another. Can we point to a single element that has not, some time, made that leap from its 'natural' orbit to express something quite different from what it appears to express by itself? Suppose we turn to the Church? There, too, and there most of all, in a form that some find over-simple, symbol is ready to greet us and enclose us. The cross, the water, the bread and wine, light, song, altar-stone and spoken word, all these are the sign of a world which exists only by being indirectly evoked.

The things at which we have glanced are thus very diverse; and designedly so. Rather than work to a hard-and-fast plan, what we wish first to do is to emphasize that we live immersed in symbols. The symbol is so familiar to us, it is used so constantly, it so determines our daily life and work, that we have great difficulty in detaching ourselves from it in order to define it more exactly. As soon as the simplest form of reflection appears, symbol is already there, presenting world to man, and man to himself. So, what precisely is symbol? What does it tell us about ourselves, from whom it appears to be inseparable? What is its original meaning, and how does the complex way in which it is used gradually build up all that it stands for?

SYMBOL AS UNION

The word 'symbol' comes from the Greek, and it means, etymologically, something which is so broken that when the two broken halves are put together again those who have them in their possession can recognize one another. A symbol is 'each of two halves of a vertebra or other object, which two strangers, or any two contracting parties, broke between them, each party keeping one piece, in order to have proof of the identity of the presenter of the other'.[1] Thus it can apply to the two halves of a token deliberately broken, which by fitting together guarantee to a third person the identity of a person unknown to him. The symbol is therefore an agent of unity. It is broken, but only in order to unite. It divides a single element, but only in order, sooner or later, to overcome confusions or misunderstandings, and lack of knowledge too, that distance or forgetfulness has produced among certain persons. When we turn to the Greek verb, we find this view confirmed. *Sum-ballein* means to throw together. The verb expresses the action of throwing (*ballein*) in order, as the prefix *sum* indicates, to bring together. *Sum-ballein* means, therefore, to bring together, to assemble, to make one, what was originally discrete. Of two contestants who engage one another, the *Odyssey* says that they 'symbolize'; and, again, of the two banks of a river which are joined by a bridge: they, too, 'symbolize', for they are brought together.[2] To sym-bolize is, first of all, to bring together, to unite; so that the primary notion is not of substitution, even though the latter is by far the most frequent and we shall have to explain how that has come about. 'A sign', we already read in St Augustine, 'is a thing which, *over and above* the impression it makes on the senses, causes something *else* to come into the mind as a consequence of itself',[3] and we know how much Freud saw in the symbol an indirect representation and a transference.[4] The sign and the symbol derive, in that case, from substitution: that, again, as we shall see, is true. At the same time, there is a primary and different meaning, of which we must not lose sight. It is in art that we can see this initial meaning that has been lost. In speaking of the sym-bol, art uses a musical idiom of 'harmonics' and 'correspondences'.[5] Sym-bol, in the primary sense of the word, is not originally substitution but rather convergence. It brings together and holds together what seems widely separated. The great poets, Aragon for example, are familiar with this:

> *Femme, vin généreux, berceau ou paysage,*
> *Je ne sais plus vraiment qui j'aime et qui je tiens*
> *Et si ces jambes d'or, si ces fruits de corsage,*
> *Ne sont pas au couchant la Bretagne et ses pins.*

> *... Tant pis si le bateau des étoiles chavire*
> *Puisqu'il porte ton nom, larguez, larguez les ris*
> *On le verra briller au grand mât du navire*
> *Alors Hélène, Laure, Elvire,*
> *Sortiront t'accueillir comme un mois de Marie,*

> *Elles diront Elsa comme un mot difficile*
> *Elsa qu'il faut apprendre à dire désormais*
> *Elsa qui semble fait d'un battement de cils*
> *Elsa plus doux que n'est Avril*
> *Elles diront Elsa que c'est un mois de mai.*

What comfort whence: is it wine's warmth, woman,
    child-lapping cradle, roll of down ?
Whom do I love, tell me, whom do I hold?
Is the flush of gold on limbs, apple-round in breast:
Or does the land's end thrust out
    to Ushant and the sinking sun?

Let the stars' great craft swing and veer
For we read your name gilt on the stern:
Shake out a reef, haul again on the sheet
And see the gleam on the mainmast –
May-month of Mary's loveliness will flock
In greeting: Helen, Laura, Elvira.

Elsa they will spell stumbling,
Elsa the name they shall learn,
Elsa, known by eyelids' flicker,
Elsa more sweet than April,
Elsa they shall name, for in her is
  May-month loveliness.

These shifts from one order to another, from the stars to the mainmast, from the beauties of the woman to the provinces of France, from the flicker of her eyelids to the charm of April, are never effected by the poet by choosing one domain at the expense of the other. He sees everything working as one whole, as in music, in a permanent interchange of forms, of memories, of sounds and values. Everything is simultaneous, is an echo, is in harmony: Helen, Laura, Elvira, the modulation of the days in Mary's month. A real poem is made up of these coincidings which detach the mind from the narrow and the partial. Although the poet starts from things which are disparate and widely separated, he refuses to see in divisions and dispersions the true essence of the world; or he does his best, at any rate, to overcome them by means of the symbol. And that is why he is an artificer of beauty.

Everyday life is also the home of sym-bol. 'As we cross a road busy with traffic, we see the colour of the cars, their shapes, the fresh faces of their occupants; but at the moment we are absorbed in using this immediate show as a symbol for the forces determining the immediate future'[6] and we adapt ourselves accordingly. Looking at it in this way, there must be countless numbers of persons to whom the symbol is what prose was to Molière's Monsieur Jourdain: pavement-prose, one might say, written offhand in the hum of traffic. In fact, if we see our daily life as a continuous adaptation to things and persons, it is completely sym-bolizing, for living means for us first of all looking for and finding, either by conscious effort or by instinct, some way of incorporating ourselves in a given environment which thereby becomes a part of ourselves and of which we become a living element. Since the symbol presupposes the healing of a breach, our life, too, belongs in this sense to the order of sym-bol: there is a gap between others and ourselves, and we are trying to regain unity. The symbol, then, is no longer separate from us. Seeking as profound a harmony as possible with the real, whether cosmic or human, each one of us is initially nothing but a hidden and often heart-rending yearning to symbolize more fully with all others and with the whole of the other. Whether in poetry or in humdrum existence, the sym-bol, therefore, means a hope, but at the same time an anxiety: for it is constantly threatened. Sharing in and even identifying itself here with the order of persons who are trying to establish meaningful and soundly built relationships, it contains in itself the substantiality, but also the anxiety and the danger, of the human world that is sick for unity.

It is not long, however, before the word takes on a much more functional meaning, substitution taking precedence over union. Symbol becomes synonymous with completely objective guarantee of identity. It is true that underlying this there is still the consequent idea of agreement, since the recognition-token, for example, ensures free passage; but it becomes obscured by the functional relationship between the token and the holder. The essential thing in such a symbol is no longer an *act of sharing* between persons, but the *social indicator* which one presents without the other person having to do the same. 'Tickets, please!' The Latin equivalent is the word *tessera*. This is the die used in gaming, the tablet on which the military watchword or countersign was written, or again it is the hospitality-token or invitation card, or the ration-voucher. The relationship of the 'symbol' to the thing or the act has become factitious. We are on the way to the purely functional symbolic chains made up of combinations of zeros and units for use in 'language-machines'.[7] Here the symbol is identical with the abstraction of coded languages. The mind which creates sign-systems thereby displays its freedom in relation to things, whose concrete value gradually disappears. The element of the symbol is distance and separation; and if it nevertheless aims, as do all languages, to *bring together* in the very act in which it *abstracts*, the processes by which the conjunction between signs and reality is effected depend upon techniques of such complexity that these, again, create new distances. Thus the world of symbols operates and stands for the recession of the subjective and the human.

Following another line of its semantic history, the symbol may nevertheless be classed among things which bear a concrete significance and serve affectively to unify. A document which sets out the terms of an agreement between contracting parties, a pact or a treaty, everything which defines the conditions which make friendly relations possible and guarantees peace, all these may be called symbol, and all lead back to the notion of the achievement or maintenance of unity. Once again the word reverts to sym-bol: it serves to indicate a method of coming together and of mutual recognition in the personal sphere. As it did initially, the sym-bol belongs wholly to the order of persons and the harmony we seek to establish between them. In our own day, the United Nations Charter is truly a sym-bol in this sense: and, what is more, it enables us to understand how, long ago, the word 'sym-bol' came to be used by Christians.

THE 'SYMBOL' OF THE APOSTLES

In the Church, the 'Symbol of the Apostles' or Apostles' Creed is an ancient summary of baptismal faith. Its complicated history[8] concerns us here only in order to bring out the reason for the name given to this very ancient Roman 'catechism'. Calling this alphabet of the faith 'symbol' was meant to show that the elements that make up the Christian mystery had been collected, had been 'thrown together'. The legend which begins to become current towards the end of the fourth century supports this interpretation. The Apostles, assembled in *one place*, had (it was said), before dying, assembled in *one document* the most important elements of the faith. The idea lying behind the legend culminates in the alleged 'fact' that each one of the Apostles was the author of one of the twelve articles which make up 'their' Symbol. In this completely fictitious story the word 'sym-bol' was taken in its strongest possible sense, and so the etymology of the word found its most faithful commentary in the legend. Not only was the 'Sym-bol' regarded as the document in which the faith that comes to us from the Apostles is assembled and unified, but it was claimed also that it was the result of an actual historical assembly of the Apostles themselves.

The fact that the 'Sym-bol' is not what the legend maintains does not deprive it of its value and its meaning for and in the Church. It sets out the principal mysteries, and is not simply a comfortable formula, a password that does not commit you. It constitutes an integrating part of the unity into which one is undertaking to enter. Recitation of the Sym-bol presupposes holding to it. It is a *confession* by which one adheres to the faith which brings the Church together. Its *content* is essential to its use. It draws the faithful together, and does so by expressing the *datum* of faith in a unitary order. It is a creed. To recite it is to proclaim how God and men meet in Christ and the Spirit. The Father's creation, the Son's incarnation, divinizing communion with the Spirit, that is basically the content of this Symbol. It is by confessing it *together* that one recognized, and now recognizes, that one is a Christian.[9] The ancient baptismal liturgy included a ceremony called the *redditio symboli* or 'the returning of the symbol'. The catechumen used to give back to the community the formulary of faith which had been given to him: he *recited* it in the presence of the community. Before being completely accepted into the Church he thus publicly declared his agreement with it, as one who held the same things as the Church held, and so professed. The Sym-bol of the faith was the concrete evidence, handed over by one party and faithfully returned by the other, which expressed and set the seal on a profound concord. The formula was truly sym-bol: it forged the unity of the Christians; to proclaim it was a step towards baptism.[10]

The unifying force of the Symbol cannot, moreover, be separated from the mystery of Christ in person. We may even say that it is Christ himself who is the only great symbol, not in the sense that he takes the place of the mystery of God, but in the sense that he is in himself a fully perfected *conjunction*. The Incarnation is in fact the supreme union between God who gives himself and mankind which receives God in his flesh and blood. If sym-bol means coming together across a gap, then there never will be and never could be a better sym-bol than Christ. 'Descended', as the Apostle says, 'from David according to the flesh and designated Son of God in power according to the Spirit of holiness by his resurrection from the dead' (Rom. 1:3–4), Jesus is truly he in whom 'all things hold together'

(Col. 1:17). 'He reflects the glory of God and bears the very stamp of his nature' (Heb. 1:3), and is thus wholly at one with God, of whom he is, in the Spirit, the eternal replica; while, at the same time, in his incarnation, he is wholly at one with man, whose likeness he has assumed. Sym-bolizing with each of the terms of this supreme dissemblance represented by the creature in its distance from God, he is the mediator who reveals to us the *agape*, that is to say the absolute power of the most profound communions. Christ is thus the fullness of sym-bol, for in his incarnation, death and resurrection he is the *fully actualized gatherer-together of God and men*, of the eternal and the passage of time. It is by bearing witness to this mystery that the Church, too, by the power of the Resurrection, must spiritually bring the world into one.

Further, this culmination of the sym-bol brings out unmistakably the initial breach upon which it rests.

THE SYMBOL AS SEPARATION AND AS DIFFERENCE

If the sym-bol unites, it is because a situation exists in which there is division. As we have pointed out more than once, the sym-bol operates within a breach. No doubt it overcomes the breach, or does its best to do so, but in so doing it emphasizes it. A bridge – for example, the Verrazano bridge at the entrance to New York harbour – brings out the width of the estuary which it enables you to cross. In the same way, the sym-bol, which brings things and persons together, at the same time draws attention to their initial disjunction. Associated as it is with separation and standing apart, the symbol thus presupposes the dispersion which it tries to overcome by stimulating in the mind the unitive force of memory and love. We speak of 'the lamp of remembrance' at the Arc de Triomphe, and thereby we show that the symbol can relieve the darkness of oblivion. In France, again, we call a wedding-ring an *alliance*, by which we mean that the sym-bol calls to mind and protects the oneness of the married couple; and yet the flame is not memory in a real sense, nor is the wedding-ring love. The sym-bol is simply a *sign*, it evokes reality but does not communicate it; its relation is to reality, but it is not the real. When what it stands for is effected, it then, in the very accomplishment of its purpose, disappears. When a visit, or an approach, or a meeting, has been successful, we say that it has not been *merely* symbolic; and this is because the sym-bol is not reality itself, and always suffers from being to some degree removed from things; and the first effect which that gap, in turn, produces is upon language.

Our language, which debouches into the world and enables us to give a name to it, rests, in fact, upon a gap and a vacuum. I am neither the things of which I am speaking, nor the other person to whom I address myself when I speak. Moreover, even if my language is my own and I have no choice but to adopt it, it is far from being merely identical with myself. Things which do not come from me are introduced into it, be they initially no more than phonemes and syntax. The signifiers – that is, the language itself – are given to me, but there is an interval, there is a certain amount of play, in their relation to the signified, which is the meaning I wish to convey.[11] Although language is fundamentally an eminent act of the mind,[12] it suffers from an innate weakness, which prevents it both from being a pure image of each one of us and from being identical with pure reason itself. In short, language transmits a considerable degree of contingence and of personal and social opacity. A further result of this is a new scepticism: it takes pleasure in this gap or 'fault' (in the geological sense) which, we are told, ineluctably cuts off the subject from his speech, and his speech from a true relation to the absolute.[13] The facts, however, are more complex and more profound, and a visual image may indicate their nature. In *The Gold Rush* Charlie Chaplin invites a girl to dinner, and she never turns up. He waits and waits, but nobody comes. Finally, he gives up. He then takes a couple of rolls, sticks a fork into each, and with these little clogs he gives a performance on the tablecloth of the absent girl's dancing. Here we have, surely, the symbol of an essential aspect of language. In man, language is in fact the first structural repercussion of a lack, an appeal to what is absent, the first reaching out towards what is different from self – things and persons – and therefore an acknowledgement of absence which prepares us for meeting greater-than-self. It is thus that language resembles sym-bol, which also makes us aware of our distance in relation to the ultimate reality of our own selves and of things; and this is how it introduces us to the sphere of religion.

It is impossible, the Bible tells us, to look on God without dying. Without dying – that is to say, without emerging from the empirical domain inhabited by our human possessions, powers and knowledge. The supreme Other, which is in fact more us than we are ourselves,[14] must necessarily always elude their grasp. No doubt, as St Paul says, 'ever since the creation of the world his invisible nature, namely, his eternal power and deity, has been clearly perceived in the things that have been made' (Rom. 1:20), but the universe in which he expresses his presence obscures as much as it reveals him whom, the Apostle also says, we find only by 'feeling after' (Acts 17:27). Shut up in the world, we cannot do much more than guess at the identity of the hidden Responder who invisibly holds the universe in his hands and offers it to us as a vast visible sym-bol of himself. The tally or recognition-token of the cosmos presupposes, there-fore, an absence on the part of God, who nevertheless passes through the world in order to make himself known to us. That is why, when man discovers God in the universe, he nearly always does so first from a foundation of distress which religious consciousness is not afraid to acknowledge. While man is at home with animals and stars, he is also the cosmic neighbour of the Absolute, but as such he remains on the finite and mortal face of the world. It is from that side that he calls out and prays. He sym-bolizes with God, but, as with a presence which stays uncertain, remains, we might almost say, no more than suspected. He launches himself towards God, like the arch of a bridge which leaps across to the farther bank, but he does so without seeing, or even really being able to guess at, exactly where he will come to rest and find peace in that supreme Other, in whom, he feels, there is something of an absentee.

> *L'animal naît, il passe, il meurt.*
> *Et c'est le grand froid.*
> *– C'est le grand froid de la nuit, c'est le noir.*
>
> *L'oiseau passe, il vole, il meurt.*
> *Et c'est le grand froid.*
> *– C'est le grand froid de la nuit, c'est le noir.*

Le poisson fuit, il passe, il meurt.
Et c'est le grand froid.
– C'est le grand froid de la nuit, c'est le noir.

L'homme naît, mange et dort. Il passe.
Et c'est le grand froid.
– C'est le grand froid de la nuit, c'est le noir.

Et le ciel s'est éclairé, les yeux se sont éteints.
L'étoile resplendit.
Le froid en bas, la lumière en haut.
L'homme a passé, le prisonnier est libre.
L'ombre a disparu.
– L'ombre a disparu.

Khmvoum, Khmvoum, vers toi notre appel.
– Khmvoum, Khmvoum, vers toi notre appel.[15]

Animal is born, animal goes, animal dies.
And the great cold comes
– the great cold of night, the black.

Bird goes, bird flies, bird dies.
And the great cold comes
– the great cold of night, the black.

Fish hides, fish goes, fish dies.
And the great cold comes
– the great cold of night, the black.

Man is born, man eats, man sleeps. Man goes.
And the great cold comes
– the great cold of night, the black.

Brightness has come to the sky, darkness come to eyes.
Star's blaze is beacon.
Low lies cold, high shines light.
Man has gone, prisoner is free.
Shadow clears.
– Shadow clears.

Khmvoum, Khmvoum, hear our cry.
– Khmvoum, Khmvoum, hear our cry.

Nevertheless, belief in God's personal entry into our world does not of itself entail enjoyment of the bliss communicated by his presence. 'Even if we believe that Christ has overcome death, that he is living, present and active in this world, it yet remains true that, in some way, he *is still dead for us*. We shall not meet Christ in a relationship of the same sort as we find in simply human intercommunication. We are deluding ourselves if we claim to "feel" the presence of Christ or his activity, and to place them on a plane other than that of faith, as though they could be included in the field of human experience in the same way as is the presence or the activity of one of our own kind.'[16] It is true, as we shall see, that the risen Christ symbolizes only imperfectly with our universe. The absolute Living Being of Glory seems to us to be absent, not because he is really absent, but because his life, which excludes all death, is not *empirically* apprehensible in a world in which death still has the last word in reply to life. If our world is to be brought into harmony with the Resurrection, it will first have had to be reorientated so that it is wholly directed towards the mystery of God in the glorious body of the Lord. Thus the risen Christ himself is still subject, in the Church, in the world, and in the Eucharist, to what one might call the interregnum of sym-bols and signs. It is not that Christ is unreal or mythical, but that he is still dependent upon a form of the world which he has not yet completely assimilated to himself. So he remains an absentee, not from inability to communicate himself or because he has nothing to say, but because he respects the historical structures of man's world and accommodates himself to the world's genesis-phase, which is not to be supplanted by his glory but perfected. History, therefore, is never the parousia; we live history as a deferment of glory, in which deferment Christ, never ceasing himself to grow greater, is really given, but given only in signs.

A paradox of union and separation, the sym-bol thus reaches in faith the climax of its ambivalence. In fact, as we have just seen, Christ is as much the *one expected*, who makes us appreciate his absence, as he is the *one who gathers*, who unites us to himself and to others in that very same expectation. And this means that if we think of sym-bol in Christian terms we sacrifice neither aspect of its ambivalence.

Two related points should be noted as we conclude this introductory sketch: sym-bolic condition reaches down to an immense depth in the human, and it is in that condition that the Lord's Supper finds its place; it is therefore impossible to understand such a supper without understanding how its symbolism is in harmony with man's condition.

CHAPTER 2

Eucharistic symbolism and man's condition

The symbols in the Eucharist have a dominating tone of food and drink, and it is in that key that they relate to man and, in their own way, throw light on his condition. In the very act by which they communicate Christ to us, they signify and recall that man is compounded of culture, community, body, and mortality in a way which we must now define by gradually allowing the eucharistic symbolism to unfold its immense richness. Even if our faith is in other respects fully alive, we are often hampered in our appreciation of the Eucharist by the lack of an alert and reasonably confident sense of symbol. The eucharistic symbols often do not mean very much to us. Is this perhaps a cultural or temperamental allergy? They are trivial, banal, we are told, they are ill-adapted to our world or at any rate to our age. Those who feel that such comments or criticisms are superficial hardly care to express their surprise; they are afraid of appearing over-ingenuous, and yet they would be the first to ask what, just as much today as in earlier days, conveys more, humanly speaking, than food and drink. We must, therefore, bring out once more the depth and simplicity of the eucharistic symbols. Nor will this be, as some might allege, a waste of time, but rather a saving. We must dig down into the meaning of the symbol until we reach the meaning of man, and into the Eucharist until we reach that of Christ, if we are to get past certain feelings of reserve about eucharistic symbolism and the reality for which those symbols stand. This may be difficult, but it is by no means impossible, and to do so is today an essential condition for the understanding of our faith. We shall quietly examine some elementary things and see how it is the whole man, seen in his most authentic genesis, who is reflected in them and so enclosed in them.

BREAD, WINE AND CULTURE

Bread and wine as symbols of nature

That bread and wine symbolize primarily man's work is an elementary fact that has not always been understood. To a man who is still hardly aware of the surplus-values his labour contributes to the world, bread and wine, which are so dependent on wheat and the vine, are primarily the fruit of the sun and the seasons. He shuts his eyes to his own work with plough and sickle, pruning and vintage, kneading, with oven and wine-press, and seems to see in bread and wine nothing but what is independent of his own manual powers. 'As for the *earth*, out of it comes *bread*,' says the book of Job (28:5)! True enough, without arable land there is no wheat, and without wheat no bread! And yet between earth and loaf there are the many forms of man's labour, ploughing the field, sowing, harvesting and threshing, grinding, kneading, and baking, before he can call it 'his' bread. Wine calls for man's intervening with even greater nicety and frequency. All this work is practically dismissed, so modest is the part it is allotted in comparison to that played by nature, which human labour assists but does not replace.

As the man in question thus obliterates himself in favour of the earth, he is filled with wonder that this should all be God's handiwork. The earth comes to him with the spiritual impact of a gift. It is always there, he can walk on it, he can see it. It is creation itself. Day after day he finds it again and accepts it. It has been put there by someone who has obviously entrusted it to him. It is to him the sign of an invisible love. The power that man asserts over the earth when he ploughs or gathers the grapes still cannot take away its mystery. When he makes use of the potentialities of the earth, he does not withdraw it from God's domain, for it is God in person who assures the relation of seasons to harvests. 'He will give rain', says Isaiah, 'for the seed with which you sow the ground, and grain, the produce of the ground, which will be rich and plenteous' (30:23). All will be well. What ultimately counts is not so much man's work as God's providence. It is God's gifts that plump out grain and grape, and man's husbandry has little effect on the growth. 'Man', says the Evangelist, 'should sleep and rise night and day, and the seed should sprout and grow, he knows not how' (Mark

4:27). In such a cultivation or 'culture', God is always the supreme artisan.

> From thy lofty abode thou waterest the mountains;
>> the earth is satisfied with the fruit of thy work.
> Thou dost cause the grass to grow for the cattle,
>> and plants for man to cultivate,
> *that he may bring forth food from the earth*,
>> and wine to gladden the heart of man,
> oil to make his face shine,
>> and bread to strengthen man's heart (Ps. 104:13–15).

Man's part is clearly indicated (in the sentence we have italicized), but it is included in, if not swamped by, God's creative initiative, and it is God who is the dominant interest of the poet's contemplation. If such a man, then, gives thanks – and this he will surely do, for he is illuminated by the love of God – he may well compress his thanks into phrases in which God will appear to be the only person active in the bread-cycle. 'Blessed be thou,' such a man will say, 'our God, King of the universe, who bringest forth bread from the earth.' And similarly with wine, 'Blessed be thou . . . who dost give us this fruit of the vine.'[1]

The same will be true of Christian prayer: 'As this bread that is broken was scattered upon the mountains, and gathered together, and became one, so let thy Church be gathered together from the ends of the earth into thy kingdom.'[2] It is only God who is referred to as the subject of a transitive verb; man's work, which makes possible the passage from hillside to wheat, and from wheat to table and loaf, is merely glanced at as that of an unnamed passive spectator. 'Just as', we shall find the commentators saying, 'the many separate grains of corn are brought together, ground and kneaded into a single loaf, so we must realize that in Christ, who is the bread of heaven, there is but one single bread which embraces all our plurality.' Here it is the bread which grinds and kneads the grains – man is not mentioned. This is what Cyprian of Carthage says,[3] and we find the same in many later writers.[4] They are only too ready to include bread and wine in a symbolism of God working through nature, and have little, if any, desire to include them in a symbolism of man working through the arts of cultivation. In our own age the relationship is reversed, and it is only man that matters. Ideally, we should effect a synthesis of the two and so restore the balance. This is what the new liturgy of the Mass does. 'Blessed are you, God of all creation; through your goodness we have this bread (this wine) [to offer]: which earth has given *and* human hands have made.' However much, in fact, nature may precede cultivation in history – a priority which so impressed our ancestors – nevertheless wheat and bread, vine and wine so clearly depend upon the work of human beings that it has become impossible for us to offer them to God without saying that they are *also* the fruit of cultivation and of man's free decisions;[5] for this is the simple truth.

The components of culture: a brief summary

For man, eating is never a mere enslavement to nature. Even when he has simply to go out and pick what he wants, he still prepares it, and, whether he cooks it or leaves it raw, he humanizes it and dresses it to his requirements. What he does when he eats, he does also when he sleeps; and so we find huts and caves, and gradually we come to proper houses. How does this apply to his procreation? In that act man asserts an emancipation which again belongs to the order of culture and spirit. Sexuality ceases to be appetitive anarchy, and its impulses become humanized in institutions. 'Each human society', we read, '*conditions its own physical perpetuation by a complex body of rules*, such as the prohibition of incest, endogamy, exogamy, preferential marriage between certain types of relatives, polygamy, or monogamy – or simply by the more or less systematic application of moral, social, economic, and aesthetic standards.'[6] We may even say that 'man is a special case as a creature',[7] for he crosses the frontier between the kingdom of nature and that of spirit. His position as 'spearhead' is not a mere fact, something given to him and passively accepted. It is an act, and, as Teilhard says, a 'breakthrough'.[8] He crosses a threshold by creating for himself humanly liberating prohibitions which are for him what has been called a 'schooling of desire' which no 'libidinal deflection' can replace.[9] But of all the new things that make up culture, language is both the most profound and the newest.

In spite of certain appearances to the contrary, human language is still 'without significant analogue in the animal world'.[10] It is

R.C.E.W.   C true that the mechanisms of speech play an extremely important part in this, and none of us could dispense with them and yet speak. In that respect language is something that is given to us. Nevertheless it is given to beings who are capable of making use of it and thereby acquire knowledge of self, contact with others, scientific knowledge of the world and the most profound forms of invocation and prayer. Only human speech implies the word, that is to say the power to express self and what is other than self, and to call things and persons, including even God himself, by their names. If style is the man, the word is mankind itself! It is the starting-point, certain if not always easy, of spiritual development for human beings, and is the justification of our saying of man that 'he is born not in nature but in culture'.[11] Or rather, if man, who is flesh and blood, is still necessarily born in nature, he is so born from within a culture which, from his very birth, introduces him to the irreplaceable heritage of history and the human.

'By what mysterious labour of groping and selection has it been in formation', asks Teilhard, summarizing the very points we have been emphasizing, 'ever since man's most distant origins, this *additive* and *irreversible* kernel of institutions and view-points to which we adjust ourselves at birth and which we each contribute to enlarge, more or less consciously and infinitesimally, throughout our lives? What is it that makes one invention or idea among millions of others "take on", grow and, finally, fix itself immutably in man's cultural heritage or general *Consensus*? We cannot insist too often . . . that *there are* technical discoveries (Fire, nuclear energy . . .) and *there are* intellectual revelations (the rights of the individual, the reality of a cosmogenesis . . .) which once made or experienced are man's for ever . . . No, it is certainly untrue that, as is still said, the human starts again from zero in us with each new generation. The truth is, on the contrary, that by the accumulated effect of co-reflection, it takes off again each time at a higher turn of the spiral, in a world constantly more ordered and better understood.'[12]

Bread and wine as symbols of the human
In the light of this cultural growth we recognize in the world, can bread and wine, which have for so long been apprehended as elements belonging to nature, *truly* symbolize the order of culture and introduce into our eucharists a faithful, highly

concentrated, reflection of what we are and what we do? We can have no hesitation in answering that they can, and for two reasons. Bread and wine are in themselves, and therefore for us too, part of *humanized nature*. They are linked not to the time alone of their first appearance – the neolithic age – but to man's *act* from which culture continually springs. It is man in his entirety, and not only his manner of growing wheat or dressing vines that is signified in our eucharists by bread and wine as fruits of culture. Bread and wine stand not only for the conquest of the grain-bearing plants from which, seven or eight thousand years ago,[13] man produced cereals, but also for the *contemporary annexation by man's genius of the world's resources*. As true products of the work which, historically, is characteristic of man, they contain in themselves the symbolic loading of man and his world; they are an unpretentious summary of the earth's cosmic and cultural Odyssey; in their own way they are a diagrammatic representation of the human. And that is the second reason for their authenticity as symbols.

Bread and wine mean that nothing man has accomplished in history has any value if it does not foster, gladden and develop man's very *being*. Let us go straight to the heart of the matter. God did not make himself steel or nylon; he made himself flesh and blood, food and drink, word, love, presence and gift of self, source of communion and life. In his incarnation and his eucharist God is strictly inseparable from love and bread. That is why we cannot speak correctly about man's material progress until we have fully appreciated the inestimable value of the human fact itself, which bread and wine symbolize with such disarming simplicity. What are cyclotrons, rockets, telstars, skyscrapers and aircraft, if they do not exist solely to serve the human? And what does 'the human' really mean? Every historical age has to ask itself this question if it is not to betray it. And what we can say of our own time is that many hearts are deeply disturbed by realizing how far we have travelled from the human.

By placing on the table such simple things as bread and wine, even though our world produces so many new and wonderful things, the Eucharist reminds its guests of the essential aim of hominization. In symbols, without words, it tells us again that, for all the range and brilliance of its achievements, culture acquires no true value except by becoming for man a food that sustains life and a drink that fosters love. The purely 'rustic' simplicity – to use a word that is sometimes applied in rather a patronizing way – of the eucharistic elements thus brings to mind a spiritual need which man cannot afford to forget. With the whole world caught up in a scientific and technological mutation, the eucharistic symbolism proclaims in its own way that nothing in culture can be of real service to men unless it remain faithful to the infinite depth of love which sheds radiance on life by the very simplicity of its gifts.

TABLE AND COMMUNITY

Bread and wine cannot exist in ordinary life, any more than they can in the Eucharist, independently of a community which produces them for its own use and makes them its own at the common table. There is today great emphasis on the fact that the Eucharist is centred on the table and not solely on the 'altar' in the narrower sense of the word.[14] It is true that the Eucharist is sacrifice, but it is so as 'the Lord's Supper'; it reproduces the Last Supper and, not without a recalling of the meal shared with the risen Christ,[15] it also anticipates the *marriage-feast* of the Kingdom.[16] Such a unity of symbol presupposes an anthropology upon which it rests. While the Eucharist does not exclude *invitation* (for this, like every human table, it implies), what it primarily entails is *meeting, sharing, commensalism* and *union*.[17]

The need to eat and drink is common to the whole of mankind; but, what is more, it is a need which the individual cannot meet satisfactorily except in *association* with others. 'As yet,' we are told, 'social anthropology has been little concerned with the elementary phenomenon of feeding, so that we are more familiar with traffickings at an apparently elevated level than with the normal and everyday, with ritual dues than with commonplace services, with the circulation of marriage portions than with that of vegetables; we are much more familiar with the thought of societies than with their bodies.'[18] And yet it is just here, with marriage itself, that we meet the most vital of human exchanges, which enables us without any doubt to understand the very earliest forms of human society. Rejecting out of hand 'the old picture of the primitive wandering "horde" as certainly false',[19] Leroi-Gourhan sees in the primitive human

group a 'subsistence-unit' made up of a 'restricted number of
individuals of both sexes, functionally specialized and occupying
in a periodic cycle the territory which corresponds to the correct
balancing of their needs'.[20] It would appear that the whole of
society is thus based dynamically on these elementary needs in
which men and women recognize that they are complementary,
not only from the sexual point of view but also in the specific
nature of the functions which each of the partners undertakes
when they face the basic needs of life: the man being more
concerned with hunting and the defence of the group, and the
woman with the production and preparation of food and with
the constant care of the child.

Nevertheless, if today we seek to estimate precisely what is
included in the fact of eating, we must go beyond these primitive
descriptions: we have to look at things as they are now, and our
analysis will have to be extended to a planetary scale. It has been
well said that 'when we eat, we share in all the processes of
production and distribution which cover the globe . . . All that
we are permitted to do is to choose (to some, very small, degree)
the link in this net by which we wish to be caught – for caught
we are in any case. And man has no more complete form of
acquiescence to the whole which imprisons him than the act of
eating. It is the human way of saying yes, human because the
yes comes from both body and soul. It is thus that we fulfil in
common mankind's common destiny: its affliction, its service,
and its mistakes . . . with no escape possible!'[21] That is why the
Eucharist, which to bring men together, still lays a table and
shares food and drink with them, cannot escape from the world
problems that the provision of food forces upon mankind.

'When you meet together,' writes St Paul to the Christians of
Corinth, 'it is not the Lord's supper that you eat. For in eating,
each one goes ahead with his own meal, and one is hungry and
another is drunk. What! Do you not have houses to eat and
drink in? Or do you despise the church of God and humiliate
those who have nothing? What shall I say to you? Shall I
commend you in this? No, I will not' (1 Cor. 11:20–2). He then
gives an account of the Lord's institution of the Supper. What
called for remonstrance, then, in the Corinthian eucharist was
the lack of due proportion in eating and drinking which accompanied or preceded it. It is true that the Apostle appears to say
that private domestic rules are independent of the demands of the

Lord's Supper, for he seems to accept that one may do at home what is condemned 'in the church of God'. But this is only apparent. In fact, the Lord's Table, being bread and wine offered and shared without distinction between rich and poor, is incompatible with *any* table which would be an insult to the poverty of a part of the world. What is needed, as the Apostle says, is 'equality', that is to say justice, and that the abundance of some may supply the want of others (2 Cor. 8:14, 15), thus securing a balance which was encouraged by the 'distribution' and 'collection' in the Apostolic Church.[22]

Paul's attitude is still valid today. The behaviour, a scandal to Christians, which was condemned at Corinth is no more acceptable today, when the problem of hunger in the world has immeasurably increased disparities of eating habits. The Lord's Supper, celebrated throughout the world, can no more be reconciled with 'mankind's table',[23] groaning with food for some, hardly laid, let alone supplied, for others, than it could be with the extravagant contrasts found at the Corinthian 'eucharist'. There have, no doubt, been many changes since such writers as Josué de Castro began to awaken the public conscience.[24] At the same time it is apparent that there is no need seriously to revise the judgement expressed by the FAO in 1965, that in thirty-five years it would be necessary to quadruple the food resources of all the countries of the Third World if their inhabitants were to receive the minimum essential ration of calories.[25] Nor can Paul VI's suggestion to the nations of the world be dismissed, even if it does not touch the heart of the problem, when he said that they should 'devote even some part of the money they spent on armaments to a world fund, in an effort to solve the many problems faced by millions of the have-nots: food, clothing, housing, medical care'.[26] 'The problem of the poor', as François Perroux says, 'is a challenge to the whole of our society, handed down to us as it has been from its origins in Greece and Rome, and impervious to the cleansing influence of the living waters of Judeo-Christianity.'[27]

I know a housewife who, once she had learnt about the unequal distribution of world food resources, could never lay a meal without feeling that she was incurring the blame of two-thirds of the world. That was going too far, for to feed one's own family is an obligation sanctioned by the Eucharist. It is nevertheless true that the eucharistic table judges households just as it does nations, for every mouthful of *bread* is in a way a mouthful of *world* which we are prepared to eat. Who can say where his own table begins? And who, therefore, can excuse himself from earmarking some fixed contribution from his own budget, from his own expenses, which proclaims his absolute determination to help others to obtain enough to eat?

This is the sort of social problem which the Lord's Table raises for us today. Just as the symbolism of the Creator in nature must not be allowed to obscure the symbolism of man in cultivation, so the assertion of the unity of the Church which is brought out by the eucharistic meal should not blind us to the demands it makes in relation to the common good of mankind. As, therefore, the bread and wine bring to the table of Christ the symbolic loading of the world's culture, so we must accept that they evoke, too, the world's distress; for the food and drink which the Eucharist uses as though they were available to all as a matter of course are still an unsolved problem for the majority of the world's inhabitants. And that is why, wherever the Lord's Table is set up, it ought to be the most solid foundation for the work of justice which every society is obliged to undertake.[28] Moreover, this work of justice, which modern life has made of worldwide urgency, has its roots in man's corporality, of which we are constantly reminded by the Eucharist.

NOURISHMENT AND CORPORALITY

When the Eucharist offers food and drink to its participants, it is on the assumption that they are all, men and women, beings with needs, rooted in the world by their bodies. This in itself inexhaustible question of corporality is first brought to our attention by the Eucharist from the angle of hunger.

The body as need
'*Hunger*', explained Marx in 1844 as a refutation of the wholly abstract anthropology of Hegel's *Phenomenology*, 'is a natural *need*; it requires, therefore, a *nature* outside itself, an *object* outside itself, in order to be satisfied and stilled. Hunger is the objective need of a body for an *object* which exists outside itself and which is essential for its integration and the expression of its nature.'[29] Food and drink, prepared and offered in their most

speaking forms, signify that man cannot do without nature if he is to live. A vast number of men, we have seen, are unable to satisfy this need; but, wherever we look, whether in destitution or in luxury, food and drink are an inevitable necessity for all. Culture and love transform it in the glamour of the feast or in the domestic celebration, but the basic need still remains.[30] Even the technical effort itself, which seeks to release us so far as possible from enslavement to nature, cannot get rid of man's biological conditioning; and the problems presented by the pollution of air and water, with all such 'nuisance' problems, derive from this situation.

There correspond to these needs which govern human life certain sacred rights and duties, strongly emphasized by the last Council. 'Furthermore,' it says, 'whatever is opposed to life itself, such as any type of murder, genocide, abortion, euthanasia or wilful self-destruction, whatever violates the integrity of the human person, such as mutilation, torments inflicted on body or mind, attempts to coerce the will itself; whatever insults human dignity, such as subhuman living conditions, arbitrary imprisonment, deportation, slavery, prostitution, the selling of women and children; as well as disgraceful working conditions, where men are treated as mere tools for profit, rather than as free and responsible persons; all these things and others of their like are infamies indeed. They poison human society, but they do more harm to those who practise them than to those who suffer from the injury. Moreover, they are a supreme dishonour to the Creator.'[31] The infamy denounced here does not attach to the corruption of *souls*, which is how some would express it; it consists in the attack on *man* himself and plundering the treasure he represents, body and soul together, by an abuse, in his person, of his necessitude and vulnerability. 'Therefore,' says the Council, 'there must be made available to all men everything necessary for leading a life truly human, such as food, clothing, and shelter; the right to choose a state of life freely and to found a family, the right to education, to employment, to a good reputation, to respect, to appropriate information, to activity in accord with the upright norm of one's own conscience, to protection of privacy and to rightful freedom in religious matters too.'[32]

Such demands coincide with, and give a wider application to, those which are emphasized in the Lord's Supper. While the Supper brings out the glaring incompatibility of its celebration by Christians with the injustice of the world's food distribution, the phenomenon of eating and drinking brings out that man is the very basis on which these rights are built because, through his body, he has an innate relationship to the universe.

The body as relationship to the universe

Palaeontology and genetics have shown us the processes, both phyletic (relating to species) and individual, which shed new light on the appearance of the human body and its structural relationship to the cosmos. Progressively built up from the stuff of the world, in an evolutionary development which runs from the clumsiest form of tetrapody (walking on four feet), as illustrated by the huge reptiles of the Secondary era, to the most perfected form of bipedalism, which relieves the fore-limbs from any concern with locomotion, the human body emerges as preadapted to a certain domination of the world. The ancients already understood this. 'Man stands upright,' says St Gregory of Nyssa, 'reaching towards the sky and with his eyes raised aloft. This posture fits him for command and signifies his royal power.'[33] And in our own day we read: 'Upright posture, by freeing the hands and allowing them to use weapons, as well as tools for cultivation and protection, made man the king of the jungle and enabled him to lift his eyes skywards and to look for the causes of what he found happening on the earth.'[34] While man is organically one with the universe by genesis and structure, he is at the same time related to it by his intelligence and finds nourishment in its cultivation. Teilhard has a fine passage on this point, in *Le Milieu Divin* (*The Divine Milieu*): 'If even the most humble and most material of our foods is capable of deeply influencing our most spiritual faculties, what can be said of the infinitely more penetrating energies conveyed to us by the music of tones, of notes, of words, of ideas? We have not, in us, a body which takes its nourishment independently of our soul. Everything that the body has admitted and has begun to transform must be transfigured by the soul in its turn. The soul does this, no doubt, in its own way and with its own dignity. But it cannot escape from this universal contact nor from that unremitting labour. And that is how the characteristic power of understanding and loving, which will form its immaterial individuality, is gradually perfected in it for its own good and at its own risk . . . The labour of seaweed as it concentrates in its tissues the substances scattered, in infinitesimal quantities, throughout the vast layers of the ocean; the industry of bees as they make honey from the nectar distributed among so many flowers – these are but pale images of the ceaseless working-over that all the forces of the universe undergo in us in order to reach the level of spirit.'[35]

Man is so well harmonized with the world only because it is from the world that he comes. Since he is corporeally a product of the earth, it is not by accident or by compulsion that he is of cosmic stature, but by genesis and identification. This does not mean that everything is smoothed out in advance and that there is no tension. Man's relationship with the world is often dramatic – it includes diseases and earthquakes, not to mention death. But this relationship is necessary; he feels it, even, as a vital requirement. Man cannot become himself without drawing from the cosmos not only his food and drink, but also his knowledge, his power, his art, his religion and his language: in one word, all his truth. Being a man means integrating in one's self the meaning of the world and occupying a cosmic situation. As Teilhard again explains, 'The consciousness which we are gradually acquiring of our physical relationship with all parts of the universe represents a genuine enlarging of our separate personalities. It is truly a progressive quickening of the universality of the things surrounding each of us. And it means that in the domain external to our flesh our real and whole body is continuing to take shape.'[36] This obviously presupposes our seeing the body as an effective relationship with this world. '*My* matter, or my own body,' writes Teilhard, even more profoundly, 'is not a *part* of the universe that I possess *totaliter*: it is the totality of the universe possessed by me *partialiter*.'[37]

Nevertheless, while our body is thus co-extensive with the universe, it is not annihilated or dispersed as though the efflorescence which spreads it breaks it down to vanishing point. Even though it is a true relationship with the entire universe, the body is nonetheless an entirely personal act of expression.

The body as expression

The most elementary *analytical* knowledge would prove to us, were any proof needed, that it is fundamental to man to express himself, or, as it is also put, to objectify himself in and through his body. Freud has shown that the interior universe which we reject, or which we think it convenient to ignore, continually appears, it comes to the surface on the skin, in speech, in the form of involuntary slips or *lapsus*, nervous tics or word-plays or meaningless insistent tricks. What is repressed is like 'a sentence which forms itself unbeknown to the subject, and which, being unable to use the method of explicit speech, finds its way through the mesh of defence and censorship mechanisms'; nothing can stop it from objectifying itself. This writer speaks of 'the symbolic surreptitiousness of half-completed gestures, of dream-allegories, of metaphors used in speech or in the arts, or again of neurotic syndromes'.[38] In short, anything which we think we can or should tuck away always, in the end, betrays itself; and so it is impossible for the human being to try to exist and at the same time refuse to show himself. The human body, even when it is silent and still more when it speaks, be it only to disguise itself, is a permanent give-away; and to reject this is to be sick. Curing the person who destroys himself in the belief that he is hiding himself comes down to giving him the power and the right – the happiness – of expressing himself as he is and so sym-bolizing with himself in his body.[39]

Man, then, is indeed that animal who, if he is to exist, has to come out into the open for himself and for others. He is a being of expression, of self-manifestation – in a word, of language and therefore also of body. In man this body is not a *thing*, but is always fundamentally the very sign of a *subject*. While the body is *generic*, that is to say similar from the structural point of view in all individuals, it is also so *personal* to each man that if he is not to be false to its truth he must, in one way or another, speak of it in terms of *own body*.[40] The body is accordingly defined as 'the soul's field of expression'[41] or as 'the symbolic reality of man'.[42] It is the first word that every man pronounces; it belongs in fact to 'the order of language'.[43] We may go further and, as Jousse suggests in his re-insistence on the prime importance of *gesture*,[44] we may say that it is language itself, found at its very source. Inasmuch as it is that *by* which and that *in* which man, both *Homo sapiens* and *Homo faber*, stands in relation to the world and expresses his individuality, the body asserts itself also as the nicest of all instruments.

The body as instrument

There are some who look askance at this idea: it seems to

disguise a certain dualism. 'By men', says Origen incidentally, 'I mean . . . souls that *are located* in bodies!'[45] The use of this concept to clarify the paradox of corporality goes back at least as far as Plato.[46] There we find it in the context of a somewhat cut-and-dried treatment of man as doer and maker, which was gradually superseded by the much more organic interpretation put forward by Aristotle and the Stoics. Christian thought was to adopt this idea which ancient philosophy used in expressing man's subtle unity. The very first defenders of the faith were to make use of it to describe – in the light of the Prologue to the Gospel of St John – the relation of the Logos or Word to the created universe: for them, the creative Logos is expressed *by means of* the world, rather as the soul is *by means of* the body. Later we find this idea of instrument used to comprehend the mystery of Christ, in whom humanity appears as the instrument of his divinity. Here the idea comes close to that of mediation, which is strictly scriptural.[47] This is the highest point in the application of the idea, and the source of later uses. We meet the same idea in Edouard Le Roy.[48] Gabriel Marcel holds that the body can be described as absolute instrument, if it is seen as a means fully integrated with the unique growth in being of the subject.[49] It is in this sense that developmental neurology also uses it, and so allows us to appreciate its most profound significance.[50]

When we are dealing with man and speak of the body as an instrument, we must remember that it is not like a scalpel or a violin, which remains unchanged when it is used: as the body is used, so it develops. It is an instrument only in the sense that it is in itself the exercise of effort, of invention, of trying, of 'praxis'. And for that reason we cannot attribute to it any superficial kinship with the family of other instruments; it constitutes a genus in itself. Initially indeterminate and never a prisoner within the series of tasks it undertakes,[51] the body is capable – through education, it is true, but nonetheless capable – of increasing and even multiplying its skills to an unlimited degree. Man's childhood, therefore, is not concerned with an instrument which has been assembled earlier and into which *entry* has to be made, as cosmonauts enter a space-capsule. The body is never external to the subject which learns how to use it. Apprenticeship is to an instrument which is itself in process of genesis and development. Everything keeps in step, student, class and lesson. Every day the child is initiated into a body which every day grows into new powers: powers which – speech, to take an eminent example – are the secret of spirit. Spirit, too, is equally included in this slow maturing of the body's capabilities: it never arrives nor asserts itself 'from outside'.[52] For man's spirit, the body is the soil in which it grows; as body ripens, so does spirit come into flower. One cannot exist without thereby providing the genesis of the other. Everything is linked and synchronized in development and growth; spirit appears *through* body, and body *through* spirit, in a single emergence in which magnitudes, often mistakenly thought to be opposed, are united and harmonized. Thus man is formed dynamically by a long and arduous effort of *integration*, in the course of which body and soul disclose, confirm, and accentuate their inseparable unity.

We can see the human body, then, as instrument and programme. It is an instrument, strictly unique in its kind, and so linked to spirit that it is spirit itself in somatic form. When we say this, however, we mean more than that it is a mere fact or resultant: it is a complete programme, since it is the determining condition of our authenticity. So long as we retain the dualism of body and spirit, we deny mankind its true nature. That dualism suggests itself to us spontaneously and is almost universally accepted, but it is nevertheless arbitrary. It brings about a disintegration of man, who is reduced, controversially, either to matter alone, which he calls body, or to a perishable abstraction, which he calls spirit. In either case he destroys himself, since he dissociates that whose nature it is to 'sym-bolize'.[53]

The body as symbol

The fact that my body is sym-bol means, then, that I exist for myself and for others (for God, too) only as *thrown* (*ballein*) into a constitutive relationship *with* (*sum*) the universe. Just as I am not myself without world, neither am I myself without body. My body, as innate relationship with the cosmos, determines my identity as person and my whole power of expression.[54] This begins in a very simple way, since to exist is initially to enter into organic and vital relationship with those most universal elements represented by water, air, earth, sun or fire. Gaston Bachelard has said this time and again in connection with dream and imagination,[55] but it holds good, too, from the very fact of existing. No longer to be aware of being in the world, no longer to feel one's body as presence, relationship and encounter, is no longer to know self, no longer to be able to say who 'others' are; it is to lose one's wholeness just when one expected to obtain complete fulfilment by stepping beyond matter.

'You thought,' says Teilhard, referring to the cosmic state of spirit, 'you thought you could do without [matter] because the power of thought has been kindled in you? You hoped that the more thoroughly you rejected the tangible, the closer you would be to spirit: that you would be more divine if you lived in the world of pure thought, or at least more angelic if you fled the corporeal? Well, you were like to have perished of hunger . . . Never, if you work to live and to grow, never will you be able to say to matter, "I have seen enough of you; I have surveyed your mysteries and have taken from them enough food for my thought to last me for ever." I tell you: even though, like the Sage of sages, you carried in your memory the image of all the beings that people the earth or swim the seas, still all that knowledge would be as nothing for your soul, for all abstract knowledge is only a faded reality: this is because to understand the world knowledge is not enough, you must see it, touch it, live in its presence and drink the vital heat of existence in the very heart of reality.[56]

How is it that Western thought has so often had little or nothing to say about the body's mediating the genesis of spirit, or the universe's mediating the spiritual authenticity of man: why, in short, has it been silent about the essential function of the body? The reasons for this are complex and as yet by no means clearly worked out. Many factors have been at work, unobtrusively but decisively: the considerable weight of our Platonic heritage, with the added burden of Neoplatonism, the wiping out of our Semitic legacy, the insignificance of the dogma of the Incarnation as a real influence on Western anthropology . . . If we believe, with Claude Bruaire in particular, that 'the body is understood as God is conceived',[57] we shall understand also how spontaneous association of the Transcendent with depreciation of the sensibly apprehended could hardly encourage an awareness of the value of the body. There have been exceptions, but they have come too late and have not been followed up sufficiently.[58] And yet, the Christian man, with whom God comes together through incarnation and, in the Eucharist, by symbolism, is essentially a being embodied in, 'on the strength of', this world. Did not Christ recognize this, did he not admit it – I was on the point of saying 'proclaim it' – by setting up for us a table at which he makes contact with us only through the 'shorthand' of those things which are elemental to the world? Thus the Eucharist in no way renders our human condition suspect, inasmuch as it is corporeal; rather does it approve it, and it should, if necessary, be sufficient to enable us to rediscover its beauty.

Or is all this a dream? For this man, whom we say that it is essential for him to symbolize with the truth of the world, is the same man who is robbed of the world by death. Thinking to serve man, have we not in fact compromised his transcendence and his greatness? I do not think so. If it is the eucharistic symbolism which makes us recognize in man the greatness of his body, the same symbolism, which implies the gravity of death, will introduce us to the profundities of resurrection.

THE BREAD OF LIFE AND MORTALITY

Part and parcel though man is with the world, he does not enjoy an historical relationship with it that will never decay. Man depends upon a universe which seems to be able to do without him. Death triumphs over life. The bread that brings us life does not prevent us from dying, and laying the table does not obviate digging the grave. Nourishment, finiteness and mortality are all one. It is to the man so situated that the Eucharist purposely offers a meal which releases him permanently from death. 'I am the living bread,' says Christ, speaking of himself in the eucharistic discourse. 'If any one eats of this bread, he will live for ever' (John 6:51). Nothing in the Eucharist seems at first to reflect the fact that it is thus the meal of absolute Life. The elements it uses appear themselves to be still contained within the life-system which is dominated by death: the bread we eat in the Eucharist comes from our fields, the wine we drink comes from our vineyards. There is nothing there which is not human. Nevertheless, the respect and veneration, the cult, and what one may in one word sum up as the worship, directed to the consecrated bread and wine in a liturgy worthy of the name, mean that for the faith which offers them, consecrates and consumes them, they are something much more than mere symbols of human brotherhood in death. They are in a real sense the food and drink of the Resurrection, the body and blood of the risen Christ; and the attitude of believers is such as to make it clear that this is how their faith does indeed look upon them.

It is seldom, however, that *culture* appears to come to terms so readily with death. We may turn to Freud to find a particularly striking example.[59] And he will make us understand what this man-of-death is to whom the Eucharist offers the bread of life.

Freud and the death instinct

It would appear, says Freud, that it is the pleasure principle which sheds most light upon human behaviour. Does not the individual act with a view to achieving the best possible balance between himself and the *external* world, and still more between himself and his own *interior* world? 'Analysis', however, gives a very different answer: it shows that in the majority of neuroses the individual looks for things and adopts behaviours which entail his own destruction. In man, accordingly, there is not only a sadism which drives him to inflict pain on others, but also a masochism which drives him to inflict pain on himself. Moreover, this masochism is simply a sadism directed against himself, for no apparent reason. For no reason? – unless it be for some reason which we must try to discover.

In fact, if we look at the pleasure principle more closely, we shall see that it is based on a system of the least possible effort, itself akin to the instinct of self-preservation. The sole purpose of the latter is to maintain a balance which shelters the subject from the 'new' and different. If I am concerned to avoid undue pain, then I am most easily adapted to what conforms with what I am already, with what I am most accustomed to and is the least different from myself. For this reason, a readiness to accept the *identical* and the *same* markedly predominates, in the instinct for self-preservation, over every impulse to seek the *other*. There are further complications which are not at first apparent. Thus the sexual instinct works in a contrary direction, as a drive of ego towards other, as a venture into the objectivity of the world, a call to the different, a decided zest for structural situations which introduce something new into life. Whatever may be the way in which the two tendencies or impulses are harmonized in the ego, Freud believes that a double contradictory instinct can be recognized in man: the life instinct, the Greek *eros*, a deep-seated desire for what is different from the ego, of which sexuality is the pre-eminent form, and the death instinct, which represents in man the lure, disguised but nevertheless recognizable, of the homogeneous, the identical, the primordial, and the repetitive – in one word, of death.

If we are fully to understand this death instinct, or these death instincts, Freud tells us, we must not overlook the lessons of biology. Biology teaches us that life is different, real even though incomplete, from the root condition of the world, which is inorganic. Life is never completely distinct from this primordial inorganicity, because it is to that that it returns. Death, therefore, is an integral part of life. What is more, in spite of the potential immortality of the *germen*,[60] death appears to have the upper hand of life, over which it always triumphs in the end. Proceeding then to identify the term of life with its true finality, Freud sees in death an *omega* which brings us back completely to our *alpha*. Extending this initial view to a general picture of the world, he not only posits the inorganic at the historical beginning of things but sees in the inorganic their irrevocable final end, and he makes life into an enforced return to the formless state of the world, which thereby becomes the universal principle and target. 'If we are to take it', says Freud, 'as a truth that knows no exception that everything living dies for *internal* reasons – becomes inorganic once again – then we shall be compelled to say' (and the italics are Freud's): 'that *the goal of all life is death*, and, looking backwards, that *what was inanimate existed before what is living.*'[61]

From this it follows that the instinct for self-preservation which causes us to avoid the heterogeneous and the differentiated, both of which are essential to life, ultimately coincides identically with the death instinct. 'Seen in this light, the theoretical importance of the instincts of self-preservation, of self-assertion and of mastery greatly diminishes,' writes Freud. 'They are component instincts whose function it is to assure that the organism shall follow its own path to death, and to ward off any possible ways of returning to inorganic existence other than those which are immanent in the organism itself.'[62] Thus death is not 'accident or chance' but a 'remorseless law of nature'; it is '*ananke*', from which no living being can escape.[63] And this is true, so long as we do not take 'nature', understood in this sense, as the final word. From this point of view, again, the pleasure principle is, we are told, only a principle of economy, a way around whose purpose is to involve the subject in the least expenditure of energy and to reduce to the minimum in him the costly hetero-geneity of life. The pleasure principle, therefore, is 'a tendency operating in the service of a function whose business it is to free the mental apparatus entirely from excitation or to keep the amount of excitation in it constant or to keep it as low as possible . . . the function thus described would be concerned with the most universal endeavour of all living substance – namely to return to the quiescence of the inorganic world.'[64] In short, *our real pleasure is death itself*, for life is always dominated by a fascination, never fully got rid of, with its opposite; it is a re-finding of death after having been for a moment, and inadvertently, an avoidance of death. This instinct is, therefore, regressive by nature, and we should include it, Freud tells us, among 'the myrmidons of death'.[65]

Freud admits that he is conscious of the hypothetical element in such a view: and that is all to the good. He even appeals to anyone who could help him to understand men other than through this 'dualism' which he himself is determined to main-tain at all costs against Jung,[66] but which swings the whole system over to the side of our death instincts. At the same time he rejects all theories, he tells us, 'which are contradicted by the very first steps in the analysis of observed facts',[67] even though he suspects that biology is the great normative science which may bring his ideas tumbling down like a house of cards.[68] We believe his fear was justified. At the very moment when, as he says again, he was abandoning himself to this 'often far-fetched speculation',[69] and so laying the foundations of a 'metapsy-chology'[70] which was in fact to become immensely successful, Teilhard, starting also from the general sciences of man and life, was marking out a completely different road. Freeing himself not without difficulty, he tells us, from the bewitchment he found in the 'Nirvana principle',[71] he was arriving at the spheres of irreversibility of spirit through the paths opened to him by evolution.

'In order to escape from the remorseless fragility of the multiple,' Teilhard tells us when he is explaining his reaction to one of his great temptations, 'why not take up our position at an even lower level, beneath the multiple, we might say?

It was in this insidious way that there tended to take root in me a concentration upon and a leaning towards – both, for all their scientific garb, completely Eastern – a common stock under-lying the tangible – element of all elements, support of all substances – directly attainable through relaxation and diffusion, *beyond* every determinant and every form. I dreamt of possession of the world through complete surrender, through passivity and disappearance within a boundless amorphous; a movement of "centrifugal communion" inspired by the instinct to extend and distend one's own self, at a lower level than all plurality and all particulate compartition, to the dimensions and homogeneity of the total sphere . . . In order to be all, to be lost in all.'[72] There is a strange agreement between Teilhard's language and that which Freud at the same time was using from his own angle, when, attributing value to what Teilhard dismissed, he was systematizing the death instinct.[73]

Teilhard's faith, it is true, enabled him to keep his balance, but it did not work like a charm. It gave him profound illumina-tion, and in particular allowed him to understand the danger of relying on a scientific technique which confuses real knowledge of the world with an analytical working-back towards the most homogeneous.[74] What justification is there, in fact, Teilhard wonders, for treating the pure multiple, the inorganic or the undifferentiated as the supreme value? If we are to remain faithful to the movement which is most typical of life we must reverse the 'scientistic' course and, while retaining the importance of the essential analytical effort which makes knowledge possible, we must look for the true significance of the world in the direction of the ascending series of life's syntheses.[75]

The two sides of the universe

Obsessed by what he calls a 'neo-anthropocentrism of move-ment',[76] Teilhard seeks for a physics or, to use another of his terms, an 'ultra-physics',[77] to which man 'would contribute his own value of serving to interpret and provide the necessary key'.[78] 'The true physics', he writes at the end of the foreword to *The Phenomenon of Man*, 'is that which will, one day, achieve the inclusion of man in his wholeness in a coherent picture of the world'[79] while still retaining his uniqueness. Teilhard was stimulated, but not satisfied, by Pascal's image of the two infinities which make man a cosmic exile,[80] just as he was dissatisfied by the materialism which makes man a living prisoner of nature and death; he emphasizes, therefore, a third infinite in man and so modifies the usual picture of the world. 'Traversing', he says, 'the rising axis from the infinitesimal to the immense, another branch appears, rising through time from the infinitely simple to the supremely complicated.'[81] With '*quanta*' of energy in the infinitesimal,[82] with generalized 'relativity' in the immense,[83] we therefore have, in the order of centricity, the phenomenon of man, 'on whom and in whom the universe enfolds itself',[84] and his irreversible passage into spirit.[85]

'The universe', Teilhard was writing as early as 1930, 'may not be as simple as we think; it may not be gliding down a single slope towards homogeneity and rest. The whole of its primordial excitation may be divisible into two irreversibles. One, by the accumulation and conjunction of confused movements, might lead to a progressive neutralization and something like complete disappearance of activities and freedoms: this is entropy. The other, by directed explorations and growing differentiation, might bring a freedom with no scientifically ascertainable limits (but no doubt in the direction of some new change of state analogous to that marked by the appearance of the phenomenon of man) to the truly progressive portion of the world.'[86] One can no longer, therefore, define the structure of the world by a single law. Once we apprehend the phenomenon of life as crowned, transposed, and brought to fulfilment by the phenomenon of man himself, then we find a double law governing the world. To the energy which is materially *dissipated*, there corresponds another energy which is spiritually *incorporated*, and of which man is the living visible expression. Here we may turn to Teilhard himself, writing in a way not uninfluenced by the Bergson of *Creative Evolution*.[87]

'The i is dotted (if I may put it so) by the fascinating case of man – evolution's *latest arrival*, in whom extreme cerebralization (or "cephalization") of the organism is accompanied by a staggering increase in psychic faculties . . . For my part, I can see only one possible intellectual attitude to this vast fact which a general convergence of all branches of science is gradually forcing us to accept. This is to recognize that the universe is literally *twice* what we thought it was. Until now we used to look on the mass of the cosmos as being animated by a single global movement, the movement that produced the slow dispersal and dissipation of its energies down the gradient of the more probable and the less demanding of effort. Now a second current is appearing, running in the opposite direction from this first descending current (and yet generated by it): this, too, is cosmic, but in this case it is directed upwards, in the direction of the less probable and the more demanding. It is from this that there gradually emerge, with the passage of time, progressively richer forms of association, forms that are in consequence progressively more organically centred – and, concomitantly, more vitalized. That is what I mean by noogenesis' – by, that is to say, the truly cosmic ascent of the human.[88] This ascending current, which determines the structure of the world, too, is what is now meant (to use a word that is somewhat baffling at first, but highly significant) by the phenomenon of *neg-entropy*.

What in fact is life, from the point of view of energetics, but a way of climbing back up the slope, down which all energy slides automatically, towards those states which are the most probable and the most homogeneous? Life makes its way up again either by storing up programmes of constructive action in the form of chromosomic guidance data, or by building up extensive molecular structures whose energy will cover muscular or nervous expenditure which would otherwise be impossible, and which, again, are creative. While entropy, that is to say increase of disorder, automatically grows more powerful, life insists upon and effects 'an increase of order',[89] and thereby represents a negative entropy. Schrödinger appears to have been the first to use the expression 'negative entropy';[90] Costa de Beauregard speaks of 'structural neg-entropy';[91] Lwoff of 'structural negative entropy'[92] and Joël de Rosnay, again, of 'structural neg-entropy'.[93] All these scientists and thinkers are undoubtedly agreed on one point: that in determining the cosmic importance of life we must regard it as a counter-current in the loss of the world's energy. If, then, death presents a problem – one, indeed, that is only too real – it presents it within and not outside this counter-current.

So we come to man, 'the abyss of synthesis',[94] where, Teilhard explains, 'consciousness has flowered upon complexity'.[95] Is he not in himself, and without prejudice to other possible peaks, the culminating point of a vast process of negative entropy – might we not say that he is a cosmic victory won by the structures of life over the dissolving probabilities of death? Man's cosmic stature, to which we referred earlier, here stands out with its full import. First life, and then still more man, where life unfurls itself in reflection and so in invention, represent in sober fact the world's structural neg-entropy. Man's special character, which has appeared evolutively in the universe of which it is thus the crown, is in no way alien to the cosmos. Linked to the cosmos, as the flower or the fruit is to the bough, man, through his spirit, is the supreme emergence of a world which becomes unintelligible without him.

No doubt there is still much to be dug out and illuminated in this notion of neg-entropy, for it has not been very deeply explored so far; nevertheless we know enough about it to understand that life, and man still more, represent in themselves a decisively *informative fact* about the structure of the universe and the human problem of death.

The individual importance of death
By attacking a man in his body, death issues a terrible challenge to that man. It is an existential, and not a purely theoretical challenge, for it attacks the individual in the very act of existing. It is in his body that man is a living being, and it is in his body, too, that death strikes him. The astonishing thing, accordingly, is not that there should be a problem of *personal* death, but that we should think it possible to avoid it with so little difficulty. 'A non-objective being', i.e. one which is not embodied experientially in history, 'is a non-being' is Marx's peremptory assertion.[96] The individual human being who dies, and so loses all objectivity as he loses all power of expression in the world, thereby loses, too, all reality; thus the death of the individual man does not, according to Marx, raise any real question. 'The particular individual is only a *determinate species-being* and as such he is mortal.'[97] There is, in fact, no more to be said. It is true, no doubt, that the whole of this new contribution which man imposes upon nature – through thought, speech, action, love, and culture – always retains a constitutive relationship with nature. Man's historical existence is so bound up with that of his body that when he dies he seems to lose irrevocably everything that makes him stand out: while his body lived, he *exercised* at least a partial *dominance*, but now he becomes completely *dominated* by nature in death, where all forms of passivity take over. Thus what is new in man seems to disappear never to return, and man, we shall find it said, 'differs from nullity only

for a certain phase'.[98] True: I am not mankind, and so I can disappear without *ipso facto* entailing the loss of the whole human species. But, since I am certainly *a* man, my death is in consequence the death of an element which is constitutive of mankind itself. My own case is also that of countless millions of other men without whom the human species is a mere abstraction whose value I must reject in my recognition of the effective value of the actual man.[99]

The nullity of man in death, and the nullity of man during life
That death is the historical suppression of man is a fact, and, in some respects, it is *the* fact. But if man stands out from nature, as he is said to do – if he represents an emergence from within nature – then can we simply say that when his appearance is historically wiped out, man is absolutely nothing? In order to be able to answer that question with a categorical affirmative, we should have to prove that *nothing* in man's historical existence imposes on the subject in question an affirmation of *absoluteness*. The providing, however, of such a proof would amount to deny-ing the *human* character of history: and to assert that death leads man into nullity is to jeopardize, in history itself, the real emergence of man; for this *improper* affirmation, which is used as applying to *man's nullity in death, is found to rebound, necessarily and disastrously, upon the value of man in life.*

In the domain of action, we have seen, there is the formidable danger of denying the greatness of man by concentrating on the profit that can be derived from his body. It is that which the Council refers to as 'infamous'. In the domain of thought, the alienation of man consists in a complete surrender to the question of death by *affirming* that man's death consigns him to nullity. To speak in such terms is again to deny man's greatness on the ground of his fragility. This is often forgotten today. In fact the age-old way of speaking of human emergence in terms of *immortality* seems to have become philosophically out of date.[100] And so, indeed, it is, precisely in so far as the immortality of the *soul* implies an unacceptable dualism. Nevertheless, the *substance* of the problem of man in relation to death still remains intact, even if the *way* in which it is expressed is incorrect. The highly questionable phraseology of *the immortality of the soul in the body* covers and disguises, in fact, the question, which anthro-pology must necessarily answer, of *man's irreducibility in the world*. If, when we criticize a dualism that we cannot accept, we fail to understand that point, we compromise the trueness of man on the plane of *thought*, by overlooking the basic demands to which *action* must give validity.

Human action and man's absolute emergence

To have said, and, for lack of a better answer, to have had to repeat, that the soul is immortal, can only mean, in my view, that *man*, and not simply his *soul*, is *never* reducible to nature, from which, at the same time, he can never be separated. His inseparability from nature has already been sufficiently demonstrated. The real problem is that this man is *never reducible to*, and yet can *never be dissociated from*, the universe. If those words mean anything at all, it is this: that neither in life (that goes without saying) nor, even more certainly and even less, when faced with death, can we either leave out of account the world to which man *is related* or (again even more emphatically) allow the world to eclipse the man who *emerges* from it. Relationship to the world and man's emergence from the world are in fact one, but *emergence* must govern *relationship* or man is annihilated. In this fundamental domain of structural affirmations, life and death form a single whole with respect to which human transcendence is affirmed or denied in its entirety. If there be a day when man emerges, then that day either never draws to a close or has not yet dawned. Unless man's value be *absolute* – unless, that is, it assert itself *for ever* – then that value is *nil*: in other words, it will *never* appear. It is here that the law of all or nothing operates: it insists, in its own way, that when man appears in the universe something completely new comes into it. Thus, to maintain that in death man ceases to raise any question, on the ground that he will be completely reabsorbed into the molecular cycle of the world, is in fact to deny man's *effective emergence*.

If, indeed, we hold that in death man ceases to be anything at all, we shall have to admit that we are mistaken when we speak of the *absolute* respect we have to accord to this man so long as he lasts; for we cannot give *absolute* respect to a value which is only *relative*. We shall therefore have fundamentally to revise the ethics of the action we discussed in the preceding section. If, on the other hand, we believe that historically man truly deserves the *boundless* respect which is *the only measure of his greatness*, then we shall have to follow up that line of thought to its full conclusion. We shall have to say that in himself man is *always* something which *nothing* and *nobody* may or can ever do violence to or destroy. 'Man is always something', I wrote; but I should have said 'someone', some person whose emergence in relation to this world from which he comes and to which he is essentially linked is strictly irreversible and, in virtue of that irreversibility, governs the true value of the world. Man's significance must extend as far as that, or else it has not even begun to exist. The appearance of man means to me a being to whom I owe *at all times* an *absolute respect*, one, that is, which knows no limits and cannot be shared. I can *never* treat that being in a purely *relative* way, whatever the non-being assumed, in my eyes or in his own, by his outward *semblance*. Initial weakness, physical infirmity, terrible spiritual downfall, mental degradation, every form of affliction, whatever be man's appearance – even if, so far as I can see, that appearance is annihilated in death – I shall *never* deny that it has belonged to or still belongs to *some-one* to whom I am bound by the never-to-be-rescinded respect that I owe to every human individual. No power in the world, no power in nature or in history, can dispense me from the duty of absolute allegiance that the absolute in man unceasingly demands. Even that desperate, heart-chilling, situation which causes nature, which at first is man's cradle, to become sooner or later his tomb, cannot really destroy a greatness to which we give unique recognition *by rejecting the absolute dominion over that greatness which death seems to exercise over the man*. And I find myself obliged calmly and deliberately to affirm that death, which reduces all men to *silence*, does not reduce them to *nothing*.

Such an affirmation, it will readily be understood, does not imply any suggestion about what goes on *beyond*; its sole concern is with what happens *on this side*. It expresses, *in relation to this world*, the imprescriptible transcendence of man – of even the mortal, and even the dead, man. Love of man, which recognizes the duty of *humanizing* the world by action, finds itself obliged also, and for the same reason, to *express the problem* of death on the plane of *thought*. It therefore refuses, without irrefutable proof, to identify man's *historical* end with the absolute victory of nullity. When it comes to these fundamental questions, the love of man rightly rejects the lofty dogmatism of certain forms of despair; on the contrary, it sym-bolizes completely with the indomitable demand of the ever-fresh opportunities to be found in life's human greatness.

The Christian point of view

Is there any point in denying that the way in which Christians have sometimes treated death has not made matters easier? Since the soul is immortal, one felt they were saying, death can ulti-mately affect only the body – so why the heart-burning? And yet, by attacking men through their body, death brings crashing down the only support in the world that we recognize. If, in fact, man comes to light, as we have seen, through *the fact of his body*, then to find himself deprived of the conditions of his *appearance* is to suffer an attack, penetrating deep into his very self, which strikes at the historical reality of his *being*. No one can go through and think about so distressing an experience without having understood what is the real framework within which absolute questions are properly asked.

Whatever anyone may say, belief in God is a most valuable stand-by in this context; yet when the non-believer is faced with this extreme expression of the problem, he too can be brought to a similar frontier and so find a valid transition into faith. Teilhard was so convinced of this that he was constantly trying to demonstrate it to others. 'I think,' he was writing in 1926 to a correspondent in New York who was too inclined to allow herself to be persuaded of the sovereignty of nullity, 'I think you have submissively accepted the fatal prophecy of your dramatic shepherd: "And there is nothing, nothing." If this were true our human life *would have to* come to an end immediately, and this is impossible to accept: that the immense resources of goodness, light, and love enlisted in the world are condemned to disappear *by the very fact of* their being perceived. What is true is that for a thinking person it is "all or nothing". If it is not "nothing", as I just said, it must be "all": which is to say that our hopes are insatiable and require a divine end.'[101]

Rejection of nullity, precisely in virtue of man, who emerges consciously from it, is a most certain road towards the reality of God. Once that rational act has been made, the Christian can truly agree that he would never hold so firmly to *man's irreduci-bility as against the modern axiomatic acceptance of death* were he not supported by his faith in resurrection. Resurrection does not mean that he can dispense with an anthropology of man's greatness within his wretchedness; it gives him the assurance, when he has to face the terrifying paradox of death, that the relationship with the world which conditions man's historical existence can be redrawn in an entirely new way by him who, in his own person, establishes a universe from which death is excluded.

It is, in fact, the first-fruits of such a universe that the Christian partakes of when he assists at the Lord's Supper. In Christ he looks for and finds the perfect man who has passed through death and has emptied it of its content, and who, sym-bolizing eternally in his renewed body with life that knows no death, invites all men to draw nourishment from his resurrection.

If the Eucharist is to invigorate such a hope, it is clear that Christ, who gives himself as the bread of life, must be entitled to be acclaimed truly as the conquerer of death, and as history's only risen-from-the-grave.

Thus our view of man starts from the symbolism of the Eucharist and ends with a question which concerns Christ himself, from whom that Eucharist draws our nourishment. That question is the question of a possible anthropology of the Resurrection. It demands a completely new effort on our part, in which the meaning and, in consequence, the exegesis of the New Testament texts cannot be divorced from anthropology.[102]

CHAPTER 3

The anthropology of the Resurrection

'But if there is no resurrection of the dead, then Christ has not
been raised; if Christ has not been raised, then our preaching is
in vain and your faith is in vain' (1 Cor. 15:13–14). In this
respect the Eucharist is like the preaching of the Apostle and
like faith itself: if Christ has not been raised, the Eucharist, too,
is 'in vain' – it is emptied of its substance. The eucharistic table
sym-bolizes so closely with the Resurrection that to suppress the
latter is to clear away the former, so that Christians who still
wished to take food from it would find that what they were
eating had no existence, and they would be, not the most unfortunate of men, but the most foolish. 'But in fact', continues
St Paul, 'Christ has been raised from the dead, the first fruits
of those who have fallen asleep' (1 Cor. 15:20). The words which
Christ spoke over the bread and wine are therefore 'spirit and
life' (John 6:63). 'I am the resurrection,' he says to us again, as
he said to Lazarus' sister; 'he who believes in me, though he die,
yet shall he live, and whoever lives and believes in me shall
never die. Do you believe this?' (John 11:25–6). It is of us that
that question is still asked, just as what follows is also addressed
to us: 'Truly, truly, I say to you, unless you eat the flesh of the
Son of man and drink his blood, you have no life in you; he
who eats my flesh and drinks my blood has eternal life, and I
will raise him up at the last day. For my flesh is food indeed,
and my blood is drink indeed' (John 6:53–5). That is why, as
St Ignatius of Antioch comments, the bread we break 'is the
medicine of immortality and the antidote that we should not die
but live for ever in Jesus Christ'.[1]

In our own day, doubts about resurrection have invaded the
minds of Christians. A cultural change brought about by the
spread of ideas that used to be confined to small groups of
intellectuals, a general awakening to a certain critical sense, an
irrepressible trust in man's scientific claims, an emphasizing of
the prime importance of questioning anything that is accepted,
a widespread lack of religious culture, the difficulty of finding

valid answers or of obtaining any answer at all, and still more perhaps, the absence of any overall diagnosis of the reasons for the rather muddled condition in which we find ourselves – all these, no doubt, explain how it is that the gospel witness to the Resurrection is received more often with suspicion than with confidence. And the suspicion derives, it would appear, from the general feeling that *the direction the human mind takes* has so changed that we can no longer think as the Apostles thought, nor accept without qualifications what they, nevertheless, offer us as the essence of our faith.

This is no new difficulty; in many respects it is the same as that of the modernism which shook the Church at the beginning of this century. It is, in particular, the difficulty associated with a man whose influence, for lack of an exact study of his historical position,[2] it is difficult to estimate, but some of whose views are a curious anticipation of what is most open to criticism in views we hold today: I mean Edouard Le Roy, and his *Dogme et Critique*, which was published in 1907, and immediately placed on the Index. The purpose of the book was to establish that dogma cannot be a proclamation of truth which ties the intelligence to a determined content of faith. Rather, held Le Roy, is it a code of behaviour, expressed in terms of a mystery which goes beyond, and even contradicts, all the theories built upon it. This would accordingly apply to the resurrection of Christ, which Le Roy offers as a proof of the ideas he puts forward. Without claiming to say the last word on the question of the relation between today's crisis and modernism, we can even so begin to see that when we set out Le Roy's views on the Resurrection, we bring to light in the most surprising way most of our present difficulties – particularly if we realize that they all share a common basic problem.

PRELIMINARY PROBLEMS OF METHOD

Hermeneutics and evidence of the Resurrection

We often hear it said today that the fundamental difficulty raised by the gospel account of the Resurrection is one of 'language', and that the great problem is one of hermeneutics. Hermeneutics was much practised by the Fathers of the Church and in the Middle Ages in relation to holy scripture,[3] and, inasmuch as it is a 'disclosing of meanings',[4] it is an integral part of all true exegesis before it becomes, as it is more precisely defined today, 'the theory of the understanding and analysis of texts'.[5] 'Truth is proposed and expressed', teaches Vatican II, 'in a variety of ways, depending on whether a text is history of one kind or another, or whether its form is that of prophecy, poetry, or some other type of speech. The interpreter [i.e. the hermeneutist] must investigate what meaning the sacred writer intended to express and actually expressed in particular circumstances as he used contemporary literary forms in accordance with the situation of his own time and culture. For the correct understanding of what the sacred author wanted to assert, due attention must be paid to the customary and characteristic styles of perceiving, speaking, and narrating which prevailed at the time of the sacred writer, and to the customs men normally followed at that period in their everyday dealings with one another.'[6] In other words, a scriptural writing is a dated writing, and must be understood in terms of its own time. This holds good for the New Testament too. If we are to understand the New Testament writings, we must take into account not only the literary type of each one – the Gospel of St Mark is not a Pauline epistle – but also a universal cultural sensibility which is no longer necessarily our own. Obvious examples are St Paul's statement about women veiling their heads and his views on angelic Powers.[7] Here questions of language are of prime importance, and they are the key to the discovery of meaning. Nevertheless, however justified all these points of view may be, they still do not reach the heart of the problems we have to face.

The fact is that the great difficulty we meet in the New Testament writings, and in particular in the accounts of the Resurrection, is not in the first place a difficulty of language. In one sense, we can see only too clearly what they wish to tell us, and it is against this perfectly plain meaning that objections are raised. When I reject the authenticity of a particular miraculous story, such as the healing of the paralytic, the quelling of the storm or the raising of Lazarus, for example, it is not so much because I am not sure what these stories mean as that I cannot accept what they tell me. A more basic problem than the *meanings* expressed by the text is their *plausibility* in the eyes of the reader who comes across them and can either accept them or push them to one side. Thus the meanings which are the starting-point of exegesis imply a prior acceptance without which they simply do not exist for the reader. What in reality are the accounts of the appearances of the risen Christ for me, if I think that Christ *could not* have appeared, as the gospels evidently tell me he *did* appear? The discovery of meanings presupposes the existence beforehand of the power to assimilate them, and in consequence the absence, at the very least, of preconceptions that prevent me in advance from appreciating their validity.

Bultmann is therefore raising an essential question when he asks, 'Is exegesis without presuppositions possible?'[8] He answers that it can be, but subject to a condition which is a fresh challenge to this fully justified initial affirmative. 'The historical method', he says, 'includes the presupposition that *history is a unity* in the sense of a closed continuum of effects in which individual events are connected by the succession of cause and effect.' This does not mean that there is no freedom in history. On the contrary, for Bultmann history consists in discovering the 'motives of actions', all of which 'have their causes and consequences'. However (and it is here, to my mind, that the mistake comes in), 'historical method presupposes that it is possible in principle to exhibit these [causes and consequences] and their connection and *thus to understand the whole historical process as a closed unity*' (our italics). This is to lay down as a principle what Guitton rightly calls the barrier of an 'initial impossibility'.[9] This means that historical method, or rather *such* an historical method, has the strange effect of *forbidding* history to present in its *empirical build-up of history* evidences of any action which cannot be reduced to the purely human order. Were that to be allowed, in fact, the concatenation would no longer be infallible, since a force would be at work in history in a way that, in relation to man, is without precedent. That this is what Bultmann thinks is apparent from what follows:

'This *closedness* [and it is I that italicize to draw attention to the phrase which so well expresses the *empirically* closed character of such a conception of history], this closedness means that the continuum of historical happenings *cannot be rent* [my italics again for the rejection of any such possibility, in principle] by the interference of supernatural, transcendent powers and that therefore there is no "miracle" in this sense of the word.'[10] Nothing could be more clear, or at the same time more arbitrary. I do not mean that the question of 'miracles' is an easy one; nor is it simply that Bultmann is denying to God the right to 'intervene' or to the mind of the believer the right to speak of 'miracle' – otherwise faith, which consists in *affirming* both those rights, would no longer be possible. No, what Bultmann persists in rejecting is that God's 'intervention' has *in itself* some experiential character and that the 'miracle' is anything but a *meaning* we construct for ourselves; for Bultmann it is never a *fact* that we are presented with.[11] God's intervention, as accepted by Bultmann in the name of 'historical science', has therefore in itself *no* reality that can be located in the objective order of facts. Historical method 'as science cannot perceive such an act and reckon on the basis of it; it can only leave every man *free to determine* [my italics again] whether he wants to see an act of God in an historical event that it itself *understands* in terms of that event's immanent historical causes'. Historical method, therefore, *allows* the believer to call 'divine' events which, in its own eyes and in themselves, are and can only be *purely human*. This amounts to saying that it *tolerates* what is to it, historically speaking, the *purely arbitrary* affirmation of faith. 'It is in accordance with such method as this', Bultmann continues, 'that the science of history goes to work on all historical documents. And there cannot be any exceptions', he concludes, 'in the case of biblical texts if the latter are at all to be understood historically.'[12]

So there the matter rests: for 'historical method', understood in this sense, faith is a pure *structure* produced by the mind; it cannot depend upon a transcendent event made plain in history . . . The fact that there is nothing new about such an attitude,[13] the very fact that it is accepted today by some Catholics,[14] and above all the fact that it claims to be scientific although it rejects that absolute openness to the real which is the mark of true science[15] – none of these, and nothing else, can justify the dogmatism which makes a method into the *a priori* standard of reality itself. What right have we, in fact, to deny to God the power of entering our history in a strictly personal way, and of introducing into the experiential course of things signs that are sufficient evidence of his own presence? If we reject in principle the historical possibility of a more than human action, and one which operates, as scripture says, only *for us* and never *against us*,[16] then we are basing our hermeneutics not on the *meaning* of the texts but on the *ideas* in the reader's mind. Recognizing this situation, we should therefore distinguish two forms of exegete, whom we may refer to (with a reminiscent glance at Kierkegaard) as exegete A and exegete B.

Exegete A and exegete B
Exegete A meets in the documents the difficulties which are inherent in all historical evidence. They arise (and this applies particularly to the Resurrection) from the uniqueness of the presumed event, from the complexities of the experiences which characterize it, and from the diversity of the accounts we have received of it. The questions that arise are numerous, and their solution is certainly most difficult. Who was the witness? Whom and what did he witness? In what circumstances and subject to what limitations? How often and in what order? Where? What traditions underlie the accounts we now have? What was their original purpose? How were they transcribed, and with what end in view? What influences, theological or other, operated on their final version?[17] Nevertheless, exegete A is not troubled by the difficulties produced by a rejection in principle of all transcendent intervention. It is not that he accepts everything in the Gospel without question, but that, when he is faced, for example, by the whole body of stories which make up the gospel evidence for the Resurrection, he does not think that he can *a priori* reject the coherence of a series of 'facts' which, left to himself, he would never have imagined to be possible.

It is a different matter for exegete B. He shares, it is true, all those problems which we have just ascribed to exegete A; but in addition, he has the specific difficulties raised by his decision to reject *a priori* as impossible any historical manifestation of God. While this principle would appear at first to release him from all the 'supernatural' and therefore, in his opinion, from all 'myth', this same principle, *his* principle, nevertheless proves a considerable hindrance to him. The fact is that the New Testament writings with which he is dealing are completely ignorant of the axiom which defines for him the objectivity of history. He is continually, therefore, meeting facts and ideas, expressions, a whole store of symbolism, which, for the author, belong to this divine intervention that our modern hermeneutist rejects *a priori* as non-historic. Exegete B is obliged accordingly to dodge any number of stories, allusions and expressions, or to 'explain' them in his own way: he has to what is now called 'de-mythologize' them. Very well; but in any case, from the point of view of the text he is asked to work on, he accepts or rejects, rearranges or cancels what he would call 'his' documents but what are in fact *ours*, in a way that is completely alien to the 'historical science' for which he so loudly expresses his respect. Thus, still as a matter of method, he creates a formidable ambiguity.

The difficulties encountered by exegete A are only too real, as we have seen; but our exegete B proposes to use them as evident *confirmation* of his own principle, whereas they are just as well, if not better, explained by the reality which his principle excludes. If, in fact, we admit – as we must (a point to which we shall return later) – the possibility of a divine manifestation in history, it is hardly surprising that the events relating to such a manifestation should constitute, for the historian, a *paradoxical* and basically *unique series*. Presented with these unique events, B does not look for a reasonable meaning in them, but declares without hesitation that none of this *is* historical, because for him it is *a priori impossible* for it to be historical. He accordingly rejects things or statements as 'made up or told by the community' simply on the ground that they deal with the type of 'facts' whose possibility he denies *beforehand*.

This means that what goes by the name of hermeneutics amounts to pushing aside stories or sayings whose sole fault is that they belong to a type that has been pronounced *a priori* inadmissible. The difficulty lies no longer in the deciphering of the scriptural *language*, but rather in the actual *reality* to which that language is applied and which, we are told, it is no longer 'possible' to accept. What then governs exegesis is not so much the *text*, which we 'are obliged' to contradict or 'rehandle', as the *ideas* which cause its rejection. This accounts for the awkward position of those who think that by means of hermeneutics they can bypass negations which exegesis expresses but itself provides no basis for. As they read the text, in fact, a negative *a priori* is constantly intervening; and it is this *a priori* that it is of the utmost importance to detect, if we wish to leave behind the destructive hermeneutics which abolishes the transcendence of what is signified and, instead, practise the constructive hermeneutics which restores it.[18] Once we have understood such a problem, which reaches back, through exegesis, to anthropology itself, we can also understand the importance of a critical examination of Edouard Le Roy's ideas on the Resurrection.

EDOUARD LE ROY'S THOUGHT
ON THE RESURRECTION

Exegesis and anthropology

Le Roy had no intention of casting doubts upon the fact that 'after Jesus Christ had passed through death, he came back to life';[19] all he wished to do was to criticize forms of representation which are associated with that statement. As described in current speech, Christ's resurrection, he thought, is identified with a 'reanimation of the dead body' which makes Christ into a second Lazarus (161). If the Resurrection is understood in this way, it cannot stand up against criticism, and, what is more, it loses all significance for history. The whole trouble is potentially present in that view, and it derives, Le Roy tells us, from a mistaken anthropology. Forgetting that 'the identity of the body does not reside in matter' (170), we establish a physical link between 'the possibility of the Resurrection and some unspecified material residue . . . some indeterminate minimum of corpse', detracting from the spiritual magnitude of the mystery by a false view of the *body*. 'Why', asks Le Roy, 'should the Resurrection, which is a transcendent fact, be subject to conditions that belong to the physical order? Why should it necessitate a hiatus, a sudden break in the continuity of our possible perceptions: by that I mean why should "some particular thing" be suddenly withdrawn from the natural phenomenal order? . . . A moment's thought will show that the continuity of corpse with glorified body – which, it would appear, is what it is sought to establish – is to all intents and purposes meaningless except for the imagination' (171–3). The real problem, therefore, comes back to working out an anthropology worthy of the Resurrection, one, that is, which is freed from a formidable burden of 'realism'. And this, Le Roy believes, we are far from achieving, since we try at all costs to cling to some objective element.

What, asks Le Roy, gives rise to this 'desperate wish for the Resurrection to have a physical support in a physically observable fact?', to this 'almost openly admitted fear that if such support be withdrawn from it, the Resurrection will disappear into legend?', whereas, in his view, this attempt supposedly to preserve it does nothing but rob us of it? The reason is that there is an eagerness for 'positive findings, in the material sense

of the word, from which, it is thought, there will later emerge
an irrefutable apologetical argument' (173). Once we give up
this vain concern, it will become possible for us to understand
the meaning of the Resurrection. If we examine things more
reasonably, in faith, we find that the Resurrection cannot be
known in the way that 'the existence of Alexander or Caesar can
be known'. It cannot be separated from the faith which bears
witness to it; it is therefore included among those realities which
'cannot be contained in purely rational arguments nor, similarly,
in purely positive findings' (178-9). 'Revealed rather than
observed',[20] as St Thomas himself says, the fact of the Resurrection is 'not so much proof as sign' (226); it is not so much a
reason for believing as an object of faith, the greatest of all such
(183). We must therefore at all costs get back to the traditional
meaning of the Gospel, as Augustine, for example, already understood it, and see in it 'rather a witness of faith than an historical
writing to be taken as a purely documentary summary of evidence'
(190). It is in this way that we can rid ourselves of the obsession
produced by a false historicism which claims to find a 'photo-
graphic document' in the text (195).[21]

The empty tomb and the appearances of Christ

While recognizing that the story of the empty tomb has only a
'negative and indirect' meaning (189), Le Roy regards it for that
reason as undoubtedly suspect. He sees in it the wish to *insert*
the Resurrection *into* the experiential stuff of the world and to
make it into 'an event that is apprehensible outside faith' (199).
This enslaves the Gospel to an extremely crude anthropology,
which makes the Resurrection a reanimation of a corpse in order
thereby to be in possession of a proof. If we are to make any
progress, we must dismiss this story.[22] On the other hand, we
can 'admit as a general datum that appearances did occur, the
most important and best attested being those recorded by St Paul'
(218); but their true meaning has to be understood.

This is a point we, too, can accept without hesitation: the
appearances imply that the risen Christ was seen only because
he made himself visible.[23] This presupposes a special dispensa-
tion, in virtue of which Christ was made manifest 'not to all the
people but to us who were chosen [in advance] by God as
witnesses' (Acts 10:40-1). Le Roy, however, again sees things
quite differently. In his view, the appearances lie in the strange

borderland which divides, or maybe separates, perception and hallucination. From hallucination they draw the fact of being 'effected by the mind', and from perception the fact of establishing 'contact with a reality properly so called', which possesses 'an intrinsic consistence, even though men do not, generally speaking, attain it in ordinary life' (222). 'Ordinary', however, is precisely what the life of the Apostles was not.

Ever since Christ's public ministry, 'a dynamic principle', a 'germ of living faith', had been alive in them. The time of trial was to be its ground of election. Christ's death was to act for these men, unexpectedly but most providentially, as a shock and a stimulus that opened their eyes.[24] The *certainty* of Christ's death introduced the Apostles to the *corresponding certainty* of his resurrection. It was not a victory won in a pure moment of reason; rather was it a progressive victory, in which faith, already received, came to maturity and so ensured the conditions necessary to its complete triumph. Christ's appearances were therefore his *interior* answer to the *spiritual* step the Apostles took in refusing to believe that *everything was finished*. [25]

The question obviously arises: Did the Apostles see because they believed, or did they believe because they saw? Scripture tells us that Christ was made manifest to those who believed (of what use, indeed, would it have been for Christ to appear to a person who was unwilling or unable to 'assimilate' his new presence?), but at the same time it not only does not recognize, but formally rejects, the first alternative. It is at pains to let us know that Christ's appearances found the apostles Peter and John (John 20:8-9) incredulous – as, of course, was Thomas (John 20:25), and similarly, we may be sure, all the others (Luke 24:24, 37). They believed (and even then with difficulty) *only* because they had seen. Otherwise, had it been their faith which produced their vision, they would, surely, have themselves been in some way the creators of the object of their faith. Le Roy was well aware of this objection. He anticipated it by saying that 'we must not conclude from the fact that a faith recognizes its object, that it creates it' (225). True; but the fundamental question still remains – was it the faith of the Apostles, sustained by the grace of God and 'the reading of the scriptures' (226), which of itself produced the 'fact' of the appearances; or was it, as the Gospel clearly tells us, the *fact* of the appearances – a fact freely granted by Christ – which produced *faith* in the risen Christ and so transformed the Apostles' lives? It is clear that for Le Roy the appearances depend essentially upon the faith of the Apostles – a completely 'supernatural' faith, it is true – since in his view that faith is not merely the *condition* but *the cause* of the 'appearances' of Christ which they witnessed.

Laberthonnière well appreciated Le Roy's mistake and exposed it. 'Historically and psychologically', he writes, 'the appearances are only the proof that the Apostles believed in the Resurrection; it was in that way, too, that their faith was expressed in concrete form. There is nothing, it is true, to prevent the appearances from being metaphysically at the same time an answer given to their faith, as the sign of the deep reality whose action initially aroused this faith in their souls and then made it explicit and justified it, using a means adapted to their mental condition. That, however, is a way of regarding the appearances which has nothing to do with history. *From this point of view, the appearances are evidence of faith, not evidence of facts. And it is as a believer and not as an historian that one would so accept them.*'[26]

Le Roy on the nature of the Resurrection

'Even if we knew', continues Le Roy, 'exactly what the appearances were, we should still have to separate the pure objective fact as given from the more or less contingent and inadequate form in which the witnesses clothed it in order to perceive it' (229). Here the double relativeness 'psychological and historical', of the witnesses' world creates a further and almost insurmountable barrier between them and us. We may recognize and appreciate that barrier, but can never cross it completely; and it allows us to do no more than risk an affirmation of existence bearing upon 'something', without being able truly to 'define' it (230). This 'something', moreover, is 'a law rather than a fact' (232), by which we are to understand: a principle of action rather than an event. This 'mysterious object' is not verbally expressible 'in itself'. We reach it in a practical way, 'not through its directly apprehended intrinsic determinants and its ontological content . . . but through the vital reactions it produces in us and demands from us' (254).

So the Resurrection is immediately forced into the purely subjective experience which the Apostles made it to be, and can reach us only in the form of an experience which, itself too, is found to be irrevocably deprived of every precise definition as soon as it tries to emerge from within the pure boundary of the subject. Anyone who attempts to put such an 'experience' into words does so at his own risk. However apt the suggested method of expression may be, it will never be more than a 'pure theory', necessary, indeed, but purely interpretative of a content that remains strictly inexpressible if it has to carry the weight of history (225-57).[27] 'I would be prepared', says Le Roy, 'to define the dogma of the Resurrection in the following terms [the italics are his own]: *the present state of Jesus Christ is such that if the attitude and conduct called for from us are to correspond to its inexpressible reality they must be such as would be appropriate in the case of a contemporary of our own*' (225).

Le Roy, in fact, is so afraid of seeing Christ's resurrection being *naturalized* in a reanimation of corpse, that, anticipating by forty years Bultmann's paper on demythologizing,[28] he annihilates the 'objective' import of Christian speech and reduces the Easter event to nothing but the *fact* of the disciples' *faith*: 'There are plenty of reasons', Le Roy explains, 'for holding that no particular observed event occurred on the morning of the third day . . . What that Easter day was from the phenomenal point of view is something which is today indefinable historically and moreover, as we have seen, physically unimaginable also. We are obliged, therefore, to fall back on a pragmatic interpretation. The Easter date relates less to truth in itself than to the practical reflection of that truth in man. It is a date that relates to the history of mankind's religious attitudes and approaches' (252). Easter is therefore a *date* which primarily concerns *the Church in its faith* and not primarily *Christ in his being*. Le Roy goes on to ask, 'What can be the meaning of a temporal relationship for a being who has entered into his glorified life?' (252), thus, without realizing what he is doing, destroying the significance of the very fact of the Incarnation.[29] However we look at it, Le Roy, in following a strictly logical line of argument, has completely removed the Resurrection from history as an *event* which concerns Christ himself in history.

'The criticism which leads Le Roy to the conclusion that dogma cannot be expressed either in *ideas* in our mind or in *facts* in nature . . . produces this result, that the stories according to which this transcendent reality took place in the historical fabric of events, so to become in some way an object of sensible experience, are therefore no more than *myths*.' It is Laberthonnière again who points this out;[30] and we could hardly find a better way of summing up Le Roy's attempt: The Apostles did not see, and could not see, the risen Christ. If they speak of the *reality* of such a fact, and if we believe in it, then we are both completely mistaken. What they described and passed on in all good faith as *facts* were no more than an *effect*, inspired by their *faith*, but *without any true historic content*. Their *faith*, which was *real* enough, projected *imaginary facts*, which we now at last know to be no more than *myths*.

A CRITICAL ESTIMATE OF LE ROY'S POSITION

Le Roy's bold experiment is at once impressive and instructive. Starting from what would appear to be a perfectly justified criticism of a faulty representation of the Resurrection, he is gradually led into contradicting the gospel testimony, even while protesting his own profound belief in the Resurrection. What happened? and what is still happening if it be true that Le Roy's case is not exceptional? There are many who, like him, quite rightly refuse to reduce Christ's resurrection to a reanimation of corpse, and who in consequence find they can no longer accept the gospel evidence: as though loyalty to the witnesses' accounts entailed an unacceptable conception of the Resurrection, while on the other hand getting rid of a false idea was to jeopardize the story and fact of the Resurrection! Were we indeed faced by this dilemma, we would be in a serious and, indeed, hopeless situation. In order to maintain the authenticity of the Resurrection given to us in the gospel teaching, we should have to accept conclusions that are manifestly absurd. We cannot, in fact, believe in the existence of such a dilemma. The mistake made by Le Roy and those who, wittingly or unwittingly, imitate him or derive from him, is not that they saw there was matter for thought; still less was it that they criticized what is not open to criticism; it was that they appreciated only the *negative* aspect of the problems raised by the Resurrection. For it is not enough to deny that the Resurrection is a reanimation of corpse; we have to go further and say what it is, *without rejecting as 'mythical' or 'popularized'* the gospel testimony which *alone* enables us to speak of it.

An initial unfortunate simplification

An eloquent example of the way in which Christian thought has often built up for itself, as it still does, an unacceptable picture of the Resurrection may be found in the following quotation: 'If you doubt that Christ rose,' says a well-known preacher to a perhaps dumbfounded congregation, 'come to the sepulchre, as you might have done two thousand years ago. Roll back the stone that blocks the entrance. Make your way into the cave. Look at the rigid corpse, swathed in the linen cloths, and wait . . . Suddenly there is a slight movement. The wrappings loosen and fall away. Jesus stands erect. We can see him, brimming with life. Tell me, who roused him? Who? One of the Apostles?'[31] There is no need to quote further; there can be no mistaking the process to which Le Roy objected: in order to carry more conviction, to 'prove' the case more completely, the speaker embroiders the description or demonstration, in spite of the completely contradictory evidence of the Gospel.

When the women or, according to St John, two of the Apostles go to the tomb, no one is mentioned as having witnessed what occurred. All, men or women, stood before an empty tomb: the least we can say is that they were presented with a *result*. The words of the angel, which in St Mark express the transcendent significance of the fact, refer to something which *has happened*: 'He is risen.' Whoever profited from, or was the cause of the fact, is said to be absent. 'He is not there.' The first witnesses of the Resurrection found it *already over*, if I may so put it, and not *happening*. No one will ever claim later to have been a witness of the *event* itself. For the Apostles, it belonged to that inexpressible happening which scripture, speaking of Christ, calls his 'entry into glory' (Luke 24:26). Thus the story of the tomb found empty means that, even for its most privileged witnesses, the Resurrection is *an act that remained without witnesses*, because it is, in truth, an act without any sort of visible *image*: and in that it differed from what a reanimation of corpse, similar to that of Lazarus, could have been.

The soundest patristic tradition, that of St Gregory of Nyssa for example, fully confirms this gospel account, and it is this account which should govern all correct thinking about resurrection. Although he is convinced that resurrection, inasmuch as it presumes the recovery of the unity of soul and body, entails *also* what we may call a reanimation of the corpse, St Gregory does not urge his audience to go and observe the *act* of resurrection. All he asks them to do is to precede the women to the tomb, not in order to *see* what they did not see, and what cannot be seen, but to *believe*, even before the women, if possible, in the vastness of the mystery which they were the first to witness.[32]

Nor, in fact, could it be otherwise. If Christ resumes life experientially – with a quivering of the eyelids – then it is clear that he is not *rising*; he is *waking*, like a Lazarus doomed once again to death, since he is resuming a body; he stirs a little, stands up, and moves away . . . But Christ's resurrection, for all the verbal similarity,[33] is not an emotionally moving return to mortal condition. It is something quite different: it is the decisive, absolute detachment from this mode of 'life' in which death has dominance over us through the medium of a body, which St Paul calls 'this body of death' (Rom. 7:24). 'For we know', teaches St Paul, 'that Christ being raised from the dead will never die again; *death no longer has dominion over him*. The death he died he died to sin, once for all, but the life he lives he lives to God' (Rom. 6:9–11). Or again, we have Christ's testimony in Revelation: 'Fear not, I am *the first* and *the last*, and the living one; I died, and behold I am alive for evermore, and I have the keys of Death and Hades' (Rev. 1:17b–18).

There is something, therefore, in the Resurrection which transcends the world's experience, since it relates to a human existence which has been divinely *transfigured* by the abolition of the dominion of death. It is this that is overlooked in a naturalistic view of the Resurrection. Le Roy is more than justified in rejecting such a view, but he himself also simplifies the mystery. From the necessary rejection of the misunderstanding, which he wrongly attributes to scripture, he passes without warrant to dismissal of all somatic continuity between death and the Resurrection. It is here that he oversimplifies and goes astray by failing to see that to underestimate the importance of what happens in history to Christ's empirically apprehensible remains is to contradict the Gospel; and, what is more, is tantamount to envisaging the mystery of the Resurrection either as fitting into some theory of immortality or on the model of our own resurrection. In both cases we have a misunderstanding of the nature of Christ's resurrection.

Resurrection and immortality: their difference
from the point of view of the body

'Precisely what happened to the body we shall never know', writes Dr J. A. T. Robinson. 'The New Testament is silent . . . Some will find it possible and natural to accept a literal vanishing or transformation of the atoms that composed the flesh of Jesus. But even if the corpse was somewhere around, as the cocoon is somewhere around when the butterfly has flown, it was as nothing to his friends any longer.'[34] Loisy thought that Christ's body must have decomposed 'in a common grave'.[35] There were some who said that it had been stolen by his disciples or by his enemies.[36] Others hold that the Resurrection goes so far beyond what happened to the body that one could have found Christ's remains in the tomb and still have believed unhesitatingly in his resurrection.[37] Some again, without going so far, wonder whether 'the historic fact of the empty tomb was in itself necessary'.[38] 'Why should we not suppose', a more recent writer asks, 'that there was a miraculous acceleration in the decomposition of the organic body so that nothing was visible when the women arrived?'[39] Nevertheless, this attitude to what happened to Christ's body, whether over-anxious or over-careless, when it is still his resurrection which is supposed to be under discussion, is *anthropologically* unjustifiable.

It is only, in fact, a doctrine of immortality that can so over-look the *body* and yet speak of *life*. For such a doctrine, the body, *soma* – in the ancient pun quoted by Plato – is always more or less a prison, *sema*;[40] the less we speak of it in decisive access to the Absolute, the more, we are told, do we reach the basic reality of things. But if the announcement that 'Jesus who died is today living'[41] is indeed the announcement of the Resurrection, it is because the dominion of death has been really destroyed in Christ. To claim *in history*, as a full historical fact, that Christ has been removed for ever from death, presupposes that this victory has been won *over the battlefield itself*, and that it is in the actual *body* itself, in which death at first won its victory, that life in turn is to win its own everlasting victory. It is impossible to *say* that Christ has *truly* risen from the dead, and at the same time to *display* his *corpse*.[42] The theory which Le Roy, for example, and so many others after him are prepared finally to accept – the theory of a resurrection so 'spiritual' that it ceases to have any relation to the contents of the tomb – is, in fact, *in the case of the Lord*, the very negation of the Resurrection. On that theory the Resurrection evaporates into a startling representation of immortality. In fact, only 'immortality' in the most dualist sense of the word is really compatible with such a neglect or disregard of the body or, at least, of its 'remains' in death.

While it is true, then, that the Gospel does not recognize a 'resurrection' of Christ which is reduced to reanimation of the corpse, it is equally true that it knows nothing of a 'resurrection' in which the remains of Christ are not, in some unspecified and inexpressible way, *transmuted* for ever. The transcendence of the Resurrection passes through the humility of the tomb and transfigures the sign of death in its own glory. Thus the Resurrection ceases to be concerned with a corpse, and completely rules out that aspect. It makes the empty tomb the *negative record of the glory*,[43] the scorching from a transcendent touch, the vestige of a past that has been destroyed in its work of death. The testimony of the Apostles, which is so clear about the *fact* that death has been conquered on the field of its own triumph, probably reaches its greatest height, in relation to the *meaning*, in the Gospel of St John. For him, rood and glory constitute one and the same event (John 12:32) and therefore concern one single Lord, glorified in the flesh in which he was crucified. Thus the only resurrection to which the Gospel bears witness affects Jesus Christ in the *fullness of his body*, just as death did. By transfiguring his body without destroying it, it removes from it all relationship with the world of death. In the gospel accounts the risen Christ is therefore at the very least the remains of Christ withdrawn from the hitherto inviolate dominion of entropy and death. Any hesitation on this point makes the 'Resurrection' 'a myth pure and simple symbolizing immortality'.[44] Le Roy rejected at all costs such a minimizing of the Resurrection; and yet, without realizing it, he supported it by claiming the right, in the teeth of the gospel evidence, to reduce what happened to Christ in his resurrection to what will happen to us in ours.

The problem of 'the residue' in our resurrection and in Christ's

There is, without doubt, 'a deep and intimate connection between Christ's resurrection and our own', and 'one is the exemplar of the other'.[45] We can therefore clarify our view of Christ's resurrection by trying to reflect on our own – as Paul himself did[46] – but only if we are careful never to reduce the uniqueness of the former to the common conditions of the latter. Now, for all his anxiety to remove from Christ's resurrection the 'residue' which, he believes, leads Christians into taking the risen Christ for a second Lazarus, Le Roy minimizes the originality of Christ's resurrection by reducing it to the general pattern of our own – of which, indeed, he gives an excellent explanation.

At the opposite extreme from an over-simple materialism which seeks to reduce the body to being merely a *thing* whose experiential reappearance is ensured by resurrection, after death has subjected it to a temporary disappearance, Le Roy sees in the human body, pledged to resurrection, a profound reality. In close agreement here with the most modern views on the *own body*,[47] he defines the body as 'our point of insertion into matter'. As Teilhard was later to say in a phrase already quoted,[48] my body is not a part of the universe which I possess totally, but the totality of the universe which I possess partially. Le Roy expresses the same idea, but less strikingly. In the human body, he tells us, 'we should see not a portion but an aspect or a way of looking at universal continuity'. The body is 'a centre of perception and initiative', and, finally, since it enables us to be open to the totality of the world, 'our true body is the entire universe, as experienced by us'.[49]

From this point of view, death is severance of contact or relation with the world; it is putting out of action the machinery which the soul had, so to speak, constructed and which, with death, 'gradually dissolves into the common mass of anonymous mechanisms which function by inertia'. This does not mean that the soul is thereby disembodied. It is in itself inseparable from the cosmos into which the body inserted it.[50] Moreover, continues Le Roy, 'whatever may happen to the eliminated corpse' – and this phrase is important for the line he later develops – for each one of us there is and there can be 'a resurrection *in carne propria*' which resembles a 'second birth'. 'The soul', Le Roy explains, 'had already for a first time made itself a body; it begins again, and the body that it makes again, being its own work and its own instrument, its own viewpoint and centre of action, must once again be called *its body*, in the same sense and for the same reason as on the first occasion. It is even correct to say that it is the same body, and that it is what fell that rises up again.' It rises up again transfigured, for 'the glorified body is the body completely liberated from the automatic and unconscious; it is the body that has realized the complete fullness of its life, the perfect unfolding of its potentialities and latent riches. It is therefore the whole universe lived by us, not in mechanical inertia and subliminal penumbra, but in light and freedom.'[51]

Allowing for this idealism, whose negative side we shall shortly indicate, Le Roy gives a very plausible philosophic account of our own resurrection – *provided it exist*: for it is clear that what Le Roy has in mind here does not establish the *grounds* of our resurrection, but describes what happens to those *who experience it*. It takes for granted that there exists and can exist a universe in which *death is left behind for ever*, and from a starting-point in which the soul (as Le Roy would put it) or (as we would prefer to say) *man* can construct himself what I might call an *eternity-body*. In reality, however, who can guarantee us the existence of such a world and assure us that it is not mythological? No one, it is obvious, except the risen Lord himself, the first-fruits, in history, of a new universe from which, as the scriptures tell us, death is excluded for ever.[52] Le Roy is well aware of this; but he is led astray by the fruitful idea that *our own resurrection* is not to be effected from a 'residue' other than the universe itself,[53] and so believes that he is entitled to leave behind the gospel evidence of *Christ's resurrection*. In Le Roy's view, we know, that evidence is characterized by the still popular picture (161, 235) of a resurrection that is reduced, he believes, to a reanimation of corpse; and the simplest way to extricate ourselves from this error is to attribute to Christ what is best in ourselves. As our resurrection, therefore, must imply no individual 'residue', the same must be true of Christ's. That most awkward of all questions, Christ's corpse, is suppressed and we can *reconstruct* the gospel testimony, leaving aside the empty tomb and its allegedly mythical implications. Very well; but apart from the fact that once again an *objectively solid* element in the gospel testimony is rejected,[54] in addition the strictly unique originality of Christ's resurrection in *history* is reduced to the level of our own resurrection in *eschatology*. A grave error, indeed.

Eschatology and history in our resurrection and Christ's

Our resurrection, in fact, belongs entirely to eschatology; in other words it is identified with the end of all time. Since it is related to the glorious transformation of the world in the Lord's parousia, it is not to be thought of in relation to the historical course of the world of which it reaps the fruit. The problem of 'residue', accordingly, does not arise, at least in the form of the individual remains of any particular person. Our own remains will ultimately become the universe itself to which, as the liturgy suggests, we shall have been 'committed' without it being possible ever to say that we are annihilated.[55] When, therefore, the cosmos has finished serving man's genesis and has completed its gigantic circuit, as scripture says of the sun (Ps. 19:6), it will be eschatologically relieved from the forces of death which will have been its constant burden. The whole of creation, St Paul tells us, 'will be set free from its bondage to decay and obtain the glorious liberty of the children of God' (Rom. 8:21). In a magnificent blaze of energy, eternally released from the claims of entropy, the world will thus enter into Christ's personal glory; Christ will permeate it with a life that has shaken off the servitude of death and will make it sym-bolize for ever with the new mankind of the Resurrection. Making his way into the furthest recesses of every galaxy and every atom, and *reversing* for ever and ever the structures of death so that they become structures of life, the Christ of the Resurrection will himself appear as the 'true solution of the antagonism between man and nature'. Then we shall *see* what we must now still be content to *believe*, that the risen Christ, transfiguring a universe which exists only 'through him' (1 Cor. 8:6), is alone 'the solution of the riddle of history and knows [himself] to be this solution'.[56]

As for ourselves, since our 'residue' is the cosmos itself, into the molecular current of which historical death returns us without annihilating us, our having had the *type of personal relation with the cosmos which determines our own body*, will be sufficient to ensure that such a relation will be transfigured by the transfiguration of the universe itself to which we shall have been physically returned. This is what Le Roy, rightly, calls 'a second birth'. This indeed, if anything can have earned the name, is a cosmic birth – a birth wholly made over to life, over which death will never again have any hold, since it will rest upon the Lord's absolute sovereignty over the universe and death. While Le Roy, then, thus gives us an idea of Christ's resurrection in its *effects upon us*, he still tells us nothing about that resurrection *as it takes place in Christ himself* and as we can speak of it in faith. As we shall soon see again, the Christ of the Resurrection appears at least as the potential transfigurer of the world, but he will be so at the end of history only because he will have revealed that he was so *in the very heart of time*. He signifies in the unfolding of time itself, whose passage he thus transcends without halting it, what men will, through him, receive only at the end of time. He gives faith its object at the very same time as he gives mankind its salvation. 'If you confess with your lips that Jesus is Lord and believe in your heart that God raised him from the dead, you will be saved' (Rom. 10:9).

To believe in this way in the eschatology of the Resurrection calls for a proper understanding of the significance of the historical signs of it that we have been given. Without this, we should have to say that 'the Resurrection was no more than a disappearance from our world, a separation of Christ from amongst us'.[57] We would search the scriptures in vain for justification of such a concept of Christ's resurrection. For scripture (and here St Paul is an eloquent witness), faith in the Resurrection means intellectual adherence to the testimony of the Apostles; and this tells us that in Christ 'upon us the end of the ages *has come*' (1 Cor. 10:11), and that history has been transformed by the transcendent and yet historical *fact* of Jesus Christ risen, and, most particularly, having 'appeared to more than five hundred brethren at one time'.[58] To remove, therefore, from history the *signs* of the completely unique fact of the Resurrection is to detach the message of faith from its roots in time and to attribute to it the initial structure of a myth.

A re-examination of the problem of the 'residue' in Christ's resurrection

That is why Christ's resurrection is essentially such that it cannot dispense with these *signs* which weave its uniqueness into the real stuff of the world. One of these signs (not the only one, but the one without which Christ's resurrection could be so reduced as to fit into the general pattern of immortality) is, as we have already seen, *the humanly inexplicable absence of Christ's mortal remains*. It is only this absence, we saw, that really authorizes the witnesses to *state* that, in Christ, death has been conquered on its own ground. What *is going to happen to us* in our own resurrection, therefore, is no standard for judging what *must have happened* in Christ's. Our resurrection, being *eschatologically* related to Christ, has no need to produce specific signs of its reality which we can recognize visually; but Christ's resurrection, existing in our *history* as the foundation of our own resurrection, must provide, in that history, a sufficient *sign* of its own truth. In Christ, we know quite certainly, 'something happened to death'; and that is why the problem of the 'residue', apparently so petty and even ridiculous, is in fact essential. It is an historical 'cut-out'; and its suppression and relegation highlights, in a way that is negative but yet real, the flooding in of a glory whose effects it would otherwise be impossible to gauge.

Harnack, then, was quite right when he said: 'Whatever may have happened at the grave and in the matter of the appearances, one thing is certain: this grave was the birthplace of the indestructible belief that death is vanquished, that there is life eternal.'[59] The spontaneous concern for Christ's mortal remains that we find in the gospel testimony is in no way what Le Roy called a 'popularizing' of the event; it is an integral part of the profundities that make up the Resurrection; it belongs to the merely historical aspect of the event, while the other signs – Christ's appearances, and the Church itself which was to be born of the Spirit – can neither be reduced to that aspect nor make it superfluous.

That the kerygma is normally silent about this sign in no way weakens its value, for the silence has a satisfactory explanation. There was, as it happens, no need to mention such a fact either in Jerusalem, where it could be ascertained, or elsewhere, where it could not be checked.[60] On the other hand, its mention in *all four gospels* early in the morning on the very day of the Resurrection does not mean that it was gradually invented;[61] it is simply that in the Gospel Christian memory reconstructs the whole sequence which first led the women, the Apostles and the first disciples from Christ's death to faith in the Resurrection, a sequence which should lead us, us too in the Spirit, to an identical certainty.

We may conclude that the real problem raised by the gospel

evidence of Christ's resurrection is not how we are to alter the text nor what is questionable in it; it is to try to understand it in the form in which we have it. This we cannot do if we start from an anthropology which is such as to oblige us to reject the only witnesses we have of the events of the Resurrection. On the other hand, the gospel evidence becomes eminently clear if we are prepared to effect, or at any rate to complete, with that evidence for our guide, the emergence from dualism (and in consequence, the complete recasting of our fundamental anthropology) which has been outlined in all that has been said above.

ANTHROPOLOGY AND RESURRECTION

Understanding the Resurrection, and the primary role of the body

The first and inescapable content of the Resurrection, then, is that it removes death from a life over which death has always triumphed. Death, we have seen, breaks the sym-bol between men and their world; it de-structures them without their being able either to consent to or, still more, repair this violence done by history.[62] If we are to see how Christ can obtain through his resurrection the power so to transform the universe that he becomes in it the cosmic pruner of death's ill-governed powers,[63] we must revise our view of the body. Le Roy did well to understand this, but the body still remained for him a *viewpoint* upon the universe (238), which would make the risen Christ into *pure beholding*. He is indeed this inexpressible beholder and should we ever forget it, the Byzantine Pantocrators are there to remind us – but he is much more than that. As St Paul tells us, he has 'the power which enables him even to subject all things to himself' (Phil. 3:21), and thereby to raise us up again, rooting out from the world the structures of death. Thus we believe that Christ, *through* his *risen body*, is the principle of a life so absolute that it embodies on the cosmic plane the ultimate hope of a world that has been created for the Resurrection.[64]

That Christ's resurrection can thus affect the cosmos in its utmost depths implies, therefore, that resurrection operates directly upon the *body* and transfigures it; for the body is man's organic root driven into the heart of the universe, which makes possible at one and the same time his victory as a living being and his defeat as a mortal. It is in and through this body that man is both the *structural neg-entropy*[65] of the world and at the same time the most spectacular check to that neg-entropy, because in the end the de-structuring forces of the universe over-power man just as they do every other living being. In his body, then, man is inseparably both *action* and *passion*: passion that dominates and action that is dominated.[66] That is why, speaking in terms of energy, man is always equivocal: while no bounds can be set to the scope of his projects, he nevertheless remains mortally conditioned in history by his relationship – vital relation-ship though it is – with the universe. Through the life that animates him and through the spiritual power that is incarnate in him, he is *structural neg-entropy*; and yet, since death finally swallows him up, he stands to the world only as a *relative neg-entropy*. Death is therefore the sign, written into the cosmos, of man's historic finiteness. Through death, nature triumphs his-torically over man, without anybody being able, humanly speak-ing, radically to modify, in history, death's assertion of its claim on the cosmos.[67]

Christ's resurrection as absolute neg-entropy

But if it is indeed true that there is resurrection, as faith, relying on the testimony of the Apostles, asserts of Christ, then the whole picture is certainly modified. As we have seen, resurrection does not mean that the *relationship to the world which defines man's body is annulled* – were that so, we would not have resurrection but immortality – it means that the relationship is *reversed*. In history it is seen to be both positive *and* negative; by death it becomes *entirely negative and passive*; and then it reappears in *purely* positive form in resurrection, from which death is by definition entirely excluded. 'Christ being raised from the dead', the Apostle tells us again and again, 'will never die again; death no longer has dominion over him.' Christ's resurrection, then, is *neither* mere reanimation of a corpse, *nor* abandonment of the body in so far as it is *relationship with the world*; on the con-trary, it is the radical transformation of that relationship, or, again, its absolute *metabolism*.[68] In the Resurrection, *the relation-ship to this world* which defines Christ's body, as it defines man's, remains *the same in absolute value*, but it undergoes *a change of characteristic sign*. During his life it was ambivalent; inseparably both dominant and dominated; in death it became purely dominated and negative; then, finally, it becomes, and asserts itself as, entirely positive and purely dominant in his resurrection. We then see the Resurrection as the *radical reverser* of direction at the level of death, and as the beginning of a completely new relationship which revolutionizes man's real development in his *world* and thereby in his *body*.

Seen in this light, Christ risen from the dead can no longer be regarded as a second Lazarus. In his body, and therefore for the universe, he becomes literally a *'mutant'*, the *supreme 'mutant'*, or, more precisely still, history's only 'Transfigured'. He alone, in all the world, is the complete transgressor of the iron law which sets an inexorable term to all life's successes and imposes upon every living being the initially beneficial but at the same time annihilating yoke of the laws of nature. If Christ's resurrection has a real meaning from the cosmic point of view, it is that it is the decisive revelation, in history, of what we can henceforward call *absolute neg-entropy*. This is no longer a *relative* neg-entropy, proper to the living being which momentarily deflects the laws of matter to suit its own purposes; it is *absolute neg-entropy*, imposing on the world-system, where life can never exist without death, an entirely new type of existence in which *life is for ever and ever without death*. The Christ of the Resurrection represents such a revolution in the development of the universe that he is in very truth a new origin from which all things are born again; he is a second creation, he is entry into new times, which are transformed beyond recognition even though passionately awaited; he and he alone is truly the potential transfigurer of the world whose full revelation will be the parousia. He who inaugurates in himself such a condition of the universe is indeed the man who is unique in his species, he is the Messiah, the First-born of every creature, the Beginning; in a word, he is 'the Lord'.[69] Far, therefore, from Christ's resurrection being reducible to ours, it is ours which is based on his. His is the pre-eminent artefact which reveals to us what, in the promises which at last 'find their Yes' in Jesus Christ (2 Cor. 1:20), is the very Spirit of God.

Resurrection of Christ and revelation of Spirit

St John goes to the heart of the matter when he says of 'the Spirit' during Christ's public ministry that as yet it 'had not been given, because Jesus was not yet glorified' (John 7:39). St Paul had the same in mind when he spoke of Christ as 'descended from David according to the flesh and designated Son of God in power *according to the Spirit of holiness by his resurrection from the dead*' (Rom. 1:3–4). The message of the whole of the New Testament is that the outpouring of Spirit which establishes the Church in the world is directly related to the Resurrection, which makes definitively manifest the incomparable existence and uniqueness of the Holy Spirit himself. It is upon this relationship between the Holy Spirit and the Resurrection that everything hinges, it is to this that our attention should now be turned.[70]

Through Christ's resurrection the world-system, we now see, is dethroned, not relatively and within the cosmically tolerable limits that are applied to life's successes, but absolutely, through complete transcendence of the laws of nature. At the same time, this transcendence is not arbitrary, nor uncontrolled. It is perfectly reasonable, since it is effected for the benefit of the human kind which represents a completely unique point on the world's evolutive curve. Has not man, ever since his most distant origins, been the bearer, on his own behalf and on that of our universe, of infinitely encouraging promises, which the inexorable grasp of death always prevents him from fulfilling? And now these promises are suddenly seen to be realized, to be realizable, in the Resurrection. In Christ there is an amazing, instantaneous detachment from entropy and death, which simultaneously affects Christ, mankind and the world, and so establishes through one man who lives for ever the hope of 'a new heaven and a new earth' (Rev. 21:1).

Such a feat, supposing it to have been accomplished, cannot be attributed to man's power. However great the strength of the spirit he contains, which explains the existence of his body and the high degree of his culture, his own power flinches and succumbs when it has to face the de-structuring factor built into the universe. In spite of all his triumphs, man is then incapable of asserting his freedom from the ultimate defeat inflicted on him by entropy and death, and he dismisses as 'mythical' every testimony which claims to assure him that the barrier on which he comes to grief has really been crossed. There would obviously be good grounds for his doubts, if one could succeed in proving that God or the Absolute, or whatever name is given to the foundation on which the world rests, does not exist and cannot therefore present himself to history and so effect in history what man so earnestly demands and yet can never give himself. Denial of 'God' and 'demolition of the transcendental signified',[71] which is its intellectual preliminary, may well appear necessary to one who thinks that God is an 'indestructible and monumental substance';[72] but God is no such thing, and those who argue for this 'overthrowing of every kingdom',[73] which, in their view, is what the abolition of such an idol means, are, in fact, using the phrase to designate the true Absolute. When they speak of a 'kingdom' purged of every false transcendent – one, that is, in which no idol remains but from which some 'trace' or semblance insists on emerging, indicating the presence of being – then, no doubt in a still negative way, they are evoking the true frontier of being. Can we, then, doubt but that what we reach at the peak of the most subtle negations is anything other than the Absolute itself, even though extreme reluctance to use the name is still predominant? In any case, in our view 'God' is *still* or rather *already* there. Disguised and buried, he can still be discerned and is still living under the rubble and ruins as 'the dimension of the unconditioned in being and spirit'.[74]

Since 'God', by whatever name we call him, is so indestructible that he reappears in the very act that should, we are told, abolish him, his manifestation in our history, however *paradoxical* it may be and must be, is in every way *plausible*. It is absurd to 'forbid' this 'God' to make himself manifest, when his existence re-emerges structurally the very moment we *say* that we are abolishing him. If, in fact, we believe that we can deprive the Absolute of the power to exist by making itself manifest in a way that is *significant* for us, it is still not the Absolute itself of which we are speaking, but a caricature or, at any rate, a shadow of it.[75] That Absolute contains in itself, in virtue of being and reality, the power which we were denying to it, and it is already making use of that power by giving itself to us. In consequence (and this is the point we have been trying to establish) the hypothesis of a *sign* which says that 'God' has revealed himself, himself overstepping man's at once cultural and cosmic finiteness, as the gospel testimony of the Resurrection implies, is not in itself 'mythical'. On the contrary, it is completely plausible, and if the sign which tells us of it is given, it will say that Infinite Love, 'master of the impossible', has been at work in history.

The Spirit of the Resurrection

While the cosmos constitutes the boundary that cannot be crossed in history, and while man, culturally speaking, breaks himself on death, the fact (if it be a fact) that death is conquered presupposes a dynamism, an energy or a love, which no longer derives from man's endemic finiteness and his insurmountable impotence before death. The Spirit and the Power[76] which are at work here in no way contradict man's spirit and power, since it is from those that, when history 'cuts out', they take over. They differ, however, in an absolute way, from man's, since they are supreme in their operation at the very point where every individual finds himself historically 'undone', and where, because of the system's structures, mankind will sooner or later find itself in the same case. Christ's resurrection is thus, in history, the anthropologically determinable revelation of a Spirit, quite other than man's spirit, enclosed in death and yet not reducible to death. It is a trans-cultural power, if I may hazard the word, an energy that is not merely 'cosmic', which extends beyond, and includes, the world's structures, and refashions them without annihilating them; it is Love without conditions and so without limits, Spirit really and entirely other than all human spirit, Spirit in one word that is infinite and specifically divine; it is what scripture rightly calls *Holy* Spirit.

We need hardly labour the point here that the Spirit of which we are speaking is not an idea, a concept, a mere eminent power of thinking, the absolute form of knowing. The Spirit of the Resurrection is not identifiable outside the Resurrection itself. It makes itself manifest by *effectively* surmounting what nothing and nobody apart from it has ever been able historically to go beyond: the power of death enclosed in the universe.[77] Every other identity we might attach to the Holy Spirit, which did not in the first place come to it from the Resurrection, which came about *historically* in Christ and from the Resurrection, which was *eschatologically awaited* for men and their world, would still not be its own identity, even if it were presented in the light of the most sublime theories. That is why the incontrovertible sign of the Holy Spirit is not in the first place dialectical skill and speculative power, for all their value, but rather *confession of the faith*: confession that the Son 'has come in the flesh' (1 John 4:2), and that in this flesh he is glorified as being the Lord

(Rom. 1:4), *already* the first-fruits (1 Cor. 15:20), *still* the promise (Col. 1:27) of a universe and a humanity really transfigured by the mastery over entropy and death which Christ alone has assumed.[78]

Holy Spirit and body of risen Christ

That the *Spirit* is thus the transcendent operator of the Resurrection does not alter what we have said about the mystery of the *body* of the risen Christ; it simply confirms it. The absolute emergence from the cosmos which Christ's body acquires does not destroy the *relationship* between body and cosmos, but it refashions it completely. Whereas Christ, in his public life, was still *contained* within a world dominated by death, his resurrection shows that in the power of the Spirit the humanly insurmountable misfortune of mortality has been fully overcome in the person of Christ. Far from the risen Christ being henceforth contained in the world and therefore ultimately *subject* to the world, we now have to say that the world and all its depth are really contained *in Christ*, in a way which the Eucharist will enable us to define more closely.[79] For Christ, then, the glory of the Resurrection is not a matter of position or place but rather, if I may put it so, a matter of *relationship to this world transfigured by the power of the Spirit*. This radical transfiguration, which is effected not by *suppression* but by *reversal* of the relationship to this world, does not annihilate Christ's body, because, as we have seen, his body is *the relationship itself*.

Although Christ is bound more closely than ever to this world, he is so bound in a way which is still independent of history. The apparent paradox is simple enough to grasp. Through his resurrection Christ inaugurates for the universe a type of deathless existence, of which man and the cosmos, both imprisoned in entropy and death, can have no *immediate* experience. No one could obtain a share in the new character of the universe which necessarily emerges from the Resurrection without thereby being transformed into the glory of a life completely enfranchised from death. The total and experiential entry into Christ – Christ as transformed by the Resurrection in his world-relationship – would already be the parousia, that is to say the glorious transformation of the world by direct, open, contact with the Supreme Mutant. That is why the Resurrection, in its actual realization and as a direct consequence of its reality, cannot be contained within the experiential scheme of history: if it were, it would annihilate the very historical sequence which, in fact, it seeks to fulfil and preserve. At the same time, although the resurrection of Christ cannot appear in history precisely as it is in itself, it is in a real sense *signified* in this history which could not tolerate a larger measure of glory without a premature and definitive fulfilment. So, while the Resurrection, as *parousia*, stands outside history, by the *economy* it establishes it enters into history. While *met-experiential* and *trans-phenomenal* by structure, the event of the Resurrection is nevertheless *historical*, with a real and unique historicity that we must now define more exactly.

THE HISTORICITY PROPER TO THE RESURRECTION

German has the advantage of being able conveniently to distinguish several separate notions in the make-up of every event: the *Geschehen* or *Ereignis* (that is, the real, effectively occurred) or, to describe the event as such, the *Erfahrung*, or again the *Erlebnis* (that is, the *experience* I can have of it) and *Historie*, which is the *scientific knowledge* of past events.[80]

As we use the word, 'history', in the light of the distinctions which German develops, covers a complex tissue of meanings: it means *both* the event itself as having really happened (the German *Geschehen*) *and* the experience I can have of it: the *Erlebnis* and also the *Erfahrung*. What is more, our 'history' includes the event as scientifically discoverable by empirical methods, the German *Historie*. It is this that accounts for the ambiguities that attach to our adjective 'historical' as applied to the Resurrection.

In its *act* and its *Geschehen*, the Lord's resurrection is the absolute Real of history: it is, as we have seen, the parousia inaugurated in Christ, just as the parousia is the Resurrection fulfilled in the world. In consequence, it is not a *fact* empirically determinable in itself, for no person could have witnessed it without thereby being torn away from this world. That is why we can say that the Resurrection, occurring in Christ, is not *historical* in the *documentary* sense of the word. In fact, since, by structure, it cannot be contained within the world's experiential store, it cannot, as such, become the *possible object of an immediate observation* that bears upon this event in itself.[81] Had the presumed witness been present in the tomb at the 'moment' of the Resurrection, he would have seen nothing but an erasing flash, if I may use the phrase, which suppressed the death-relationship that still defined Christ's remains, by converting it into a glory-relationship.[82] If, then, we confine the word 'historical' to the *scientific observation* of a fact in its actual occurrence, we shall say that the Resurrection, considered in its *act* and *as occurring*, is certainly not historical in that sense, since it is by nature cut off, in its origination, from every possible witness. That was already Le Roy's view, and it is shared, I believe, by every exegete worthy of the name. 'The Resurrection is not simply the miraculous reanimation of a corpse, apprehensible by historical criticism from the evidence of those alleged observers.'[83] However, we must be careful, in thus removing one ambiguity, not to produce another.

For us, 'historical' denotes not only what is in itself knowable by a documentary approach, but also what *has in fact occurred*. Here the same word expresses two completely distinct ideas, which can very well exist together. An event can be perfectly *real* (from the point of view of the *Geschehen*) without it being possible for us to establish its features scientifically (from the point of view of *Historie*). If we say that Christ's resurrection is not historical, we may mean two things which are not mutually exclusive. The first, obvious, meaning is that Christ's resurrection is not empirically observable *in itself* as a *fact*, since it is neither more nor less than 'Christ's entry into glory'; and the second, unacceptable, meaning is that the Resurrection itself did not really *occur* or that we are without any *objective sign* of its reality. Now, whether we intend it or not, the mere affirmation that the Resurrection is not 'historical' in the first sense of the word – i.e. that it is not *empirically verifiable* in its origin – often brings with it the idea that it is also not 'historical' in the second meaning, in other words that it did not *really occur* or, at least, that its only apprehensible content is the faith of the witnesses who believed in it.[84]

It is true that the event of the Resurrection would be nothing *for us* without the witnesses who speak of it in the light of their experience (their *Erlebnis*) as believers. Empirically unattainable in its origin and at the same time transcendent in its content, Christ's resurrection nevertheless, *from the point of view of history,* impresses on the universe of the Apostles, and so upon our own, the double and incontestable mark of its reality: the first, negative, mark is that of the tomb found empty, which gives credibility to a message relating to the Resurrection; the second, positive, mark is that of Christ's appearances, which gives to those who witness them the experience, *included in their objective world,* of the Christ who calls for their faith. In the *Risen* they have as it were grasped the ungraspable character of the *Resurrection.* In this sense, the *experience of the Apostles is an integral part of the event of the Resurrection.* Nevertheless, the essential part played by the Apostles does not mean that the *event* of the Resurrection could be reduced to no more than their *faith.* It simply means that *the transcendent fact of the Resurrection, if not signified to men who could understand and communicate it in the Spirit, would have been nothing for us.* So the Apostles' *experience* of the *risen* Christ, inexpressible in himself in his *resurrection,* is not for us the *only reality* of that resurrection; it is the *historical* approach to that supreme event, which cannot be reduced to the experience; for what the Apostles *experienced* concerns *something in existence,* which, now that it exists, *is binding* on us.

To reduce the *fact* of the Resurrection to nothing but the birth of the Apostles' *faith* is therefore to contradict the Gospel, by presenting their *evidence* on the Resurrection as the *only* historically certain *content* of the Resurrection. What the Apostles intended to bear witness to was not a faith which governed the existence of a fact, but rather a fact which gave birth to their faith. If we are to see the faith of the Apostles as exclusively the fact of the Resurrection, we shall have to adopt exegete B's position and assert that the Resurrection could not have been *signified* in history, nor could the risen Christ have convinced the Apostles of the original evidence of its reality.[85] Unlike Le Roy, then, who spoke of Christ's resurrection *in terms of the genesis of a fact from a starting-point in faith*[86] – which is how myth is made! – the Gospel speaks of *the genesis of faith from a starting-point in a fact,* which is the event of the Resurrection apprehended through its initial historical indications. Although the Resurrection cannot be reduced to those indications, nevertheless it reaches us through the account of them which the witnesses have left us. And that evidence, which can never be isolated from the witnesses themselves, relates entirely to the *reality of a fact*, without which their statements would have no object to be attached to, either for them or for us.[87]

It may perfectly well be said that 'if Christ is risen, he is no longer of this world', or that the Resurrection 'is Christ's emergence from space and time',[88] if by that is meant that the Resurrection is a fact transcendent in itself. But we must immediately add that, for all the transcendence it possesses and we must accord to it, the paradoxical fact of the Resurrection touched history *in itself*, and still so touches it, in which it is unmistakably *signified as an event which concerns the Lord himself and not only the witnesses of the event*. In a word, Christ's resurrection is truly *historical*, not in the sense that its originating principle is *experientially* apprehensible inside our history, but in the sense that, while it is in itself completely *met-experiential*, it is objectively signified for us by its *effects* – negative, like the empty tomb, or positive, like the appearances – not to mention the faith of the women and the Apostles and the birth of the Church itself. In putting it in this way, we do not underestimate the greatness either of historical science or of faith: we pay full respect to both, to the former by recognizing its ability to record the evidenced indications of the greatest event to set its mark upon history,[89] and to the latter by accepting the sublime realism which characterizes the event of the Resurrection as the foundation on which our whole structure rests.

It is in this belief that the gospel witness takes on its whole value. Completely sym-bolizing with the Real which it can reveal to us, and which it is seeking to reveal to us, it represents what has been well called a phenomenology of the Resurrection,[90] a consideration of which brings us to our conclusion.

A PHENOMENOLOGY OF THE RESURRECTION

The empty tomb

'As an *awakening*, the Resurrection is without witness and remains known to God alone. Further, it presents itself as being on the road towards a fulfilment which the New Testament calls the Exaltation; so much so, that we must never reduce the mystery of the Resurrection to the single dimension of awakening from death, but disclose in it the upward movement which prevents this awakening from being a return to terrestrial life.'[91]

This is what is meant by the finding of the empty tomb. That was not in itself the fact of the Resurrection, though it depends upon the fact and therefore bears witness to it in its own way. It confronts the first witnesses, the holy women, with a hard fact whose meaning has to be interpreted. Peter and John do this for themselves, St John tells us (20:8–9), but it is explained to the women. 'He has risen,' the angel, the sign of the Transcendent, tells them. Even so, in each case, the Resurrection is apprehended as a *fact* and a *realized* fact. 'Why do you seek the living among the dead?'[92] No one gives an exact explanation of the transition, and with good reason. If it is real, then it is specifically inexpressible; and the Gospel is silent except for the statement that it was 'an entry into glory', in other words an act completely divorced from human experience, anticipating our own eschatological transfiguration by the same act.

The appearances

If, therefore, the risen Christ appears in this world – and he will appear, in order to assure his own people of his identity – he will not do so in a natural way, obeying, that is, the laws of space and time. As the Risen, is he not the eschatological restructuring of the world – for in his body, that is in his personal relationship to this world, he has become the Principle of a Life which excludes all death. That is why our world, in which life is by definition involved in death, could not without explosion contain a Christ whose life in relation to this world – whose body, that is to say – is without shadow of death. The risen Christ, principle of an *absolute* neg-entropy for the world, cannot therefore be perceived, as such, in the system of merely *relative* neg-entropy unless he transforms the system to his own scale. This transformation will be effected at the end of time, and it will be the parousia, which coincides with the hope of life contained in and founded upon history's one single risen person. If, then, the risen Christ wishes to show himself, and so confirm his faithful in their faith, in a world whose continued existence he has at heart (since what he came for was to make sure of its *direction*, not to halt its *course*), then he will appear only within the limits this world can tolerate; and that means keeping very close to what *he was* and with no more than a discreet hint or adumbration of what *he is*. It will be something between the two, quite unambiguous in itself, and yet necessarily impermanent. This is what Christ does in an almost shadowy way, or, we might say, with *economy*: that is to say, it conforms *to the rules of the household*, which is still the world of entropy and death.

Nevertheless, it is completely untrue to say that it was the faith of the Apostles which made Christ appear in some sort of 'mystical' process. On the contrary, it was the very fact that *he showed himself*, in a way that we have to call 'historical' (that is, objectively included in the universe of the witnesses and therefore in ours), which produced *the Apostles' faith in the Resurrection*. The account they give of these appearances is in no way a 'popular version' in the pejorative sense of the phrase: it fits in perfectly with the profound paradox of a 'spiritual' body,[93] which, let us emphasize once more and finally, has nothing in common with a reanimated corpse. The risen person who shows himself to the witnesses is, in very truth, none other than the crucified person enthroned transcendentally upon the life which, in comparison with the still death-enshrouded life of this world, can never fade.

The Ascension

The Ascension, therefore, is not a 'take-off' which makes Christ 'the first astronaut'.[94] It is simply the end of the *economic* (in the sense used above) phase of the appearances. And similarly it opens out into the phase of the Church which, as history unfolds, is the place where, as we await the parousia, we can read the significance for the world of the life of the risen Christ.

CONCLUSION

With this phenomenology of the Resurrection, we have reached the absolute foundation which allows us to speak meaningfully of that eucharist of which we said earlier that, if it was not the eucharist of the Resurrection, then it was 'empty'. That meant inevitably that we had to find out whether we could speak of the risen Jesus Christ in terms that are acceptable today. This we can certainly do, provided that we work out a commensurate (if I may be allowed the term) anthropology of the body; for it is this that the exegete most frequently lacks, and without it he is bound to regard his texts with suspicion. This accounts for the hesitancies we find in exegesis, and the way in which it disseminates or lends authority to views on the Resurrection which derive not from the texts it studies but from presuppositions which, sometimes unwittingly, it sanctions. If we are to rid ourselves of such ambiguities, then exegesis and theology must work together, for, as we have seen here, each is needed to complete the work of the other. If this is done, again, we can once more have an idiom for the Eucharist, since that idiom too depends directly upon the Resurrection.

What the Eucharist does is to actualize in signs the risen body of Christ, that is, of the Lord himself in his relationship, at once transfigured and transfiguring, with the world and with ourselves. We must never wait for the Eucharist to sym-bolize with a Christ other than the Christ of glory, even if it does so with the memory of the cross in mind. Already, however, a completely different target can be distinguished: our efforts must be directed now not to rising from the eucharistic symbolism to the reality of the Resurrection, but to understanding the Eucharist from a starting-point in the mystery of the Resurrection.

Part II

FROM THE RESURRECTION TO THE LORD'S SUPPER

The symbolism of the Eucharist has introduced us, we now see, to a view of the body which allows Christ's resurrection to assume in our minds the fullness which scripture reveals to us. The next step is obvious: to allow the same process to continue, and to look to the Resurrection, understood in this sense, to illuminate in turn, if not the whole of the eucharistic mystery, at least the particular point of the *Presence*; for this stems, in a very special and legitimate way, from the mystery of the *Body*.

In method, then, this second part will differ considerably from the first. While exegetical questions are without doubt of prime importance in the case of the Resurrection, they play a lesser part when we turn to the Eucharist. Efforts have been made, it is true, to find in St Paul's reference to 'the *cup* of the new covenant' and Mark's '*blood*', an indication of a radical change in perspective. In St Paul, we are told, the mention of the cup is a sign of the preponderance that still attaches to the idea of a pre-paschal community, a living community eschatologically open to sinners; whereas in Mark the explicit mention of *blood*, side by side with that of *body*, indicates a *sacramental* force, which detracts from the preponderance St Paul attaches to the table or the meal.[1] Whatever be the truth about these differences in emphasis, the New Testament knows but *one* Eucharist, and, as even the most radical critics agree,[2] it is in practice impossible to put forward a convincing *genealogy* of the texts.

Here, moreover, the true problem is not in the first place one of exegesis. It is one of dogma, and centres on the way in which we are to understand the relation between the Eucharist and the

Body of Christ. Accordingly, just as anthropology has illuminated the Resurrection for us, so, we believe, it may do the same for the Eucharist by enabling us to connect two mysteries which are too often kept separate. In the light of the Resurrection, we should be able to reach a convincing, while at the same time transcending human logic, understanding of the Eucharist itself.

The first thing, then, that we shall try to do is to draw up a quick balance-sheet covering theological research in the field of the Eucharist during the last half-century. This will enable us synthetically to present from the correct angle the intellectual movement which has led the West to speak of transubstantiation, and the essential significance which the East has always attributed to the epiclesis.[3] We shall then be able, in a third part, to bring out the illuminating relationship which, from the point of view of dogma, links together Resurrection and Eucharist.

In view of the necessarily technical character of this second part, many readers may well be satisfied with a very general look at the problems of which it treats; and so quickly, or even immediately, pass on to part three, which restates, in a more spiritual and less technical way, the conclusions reached in part two.

CHAPTER 1

The present theological position

If we are to draw up a rapid summary of present-day theological speculation in the eucharistic field, the correct starting-point, to our mind, is the German liturgical movement. With Guardini and Casel, attention is concentrated again, and first of all, upon *man*, who must enter liturgically into the mystery, and upon the *act* spiritually performed in the Church. From this 'theology of the mystery', as Casel says, there will gradually emerge a new view of the *Presence*; and that, in turn, will lead to a flexible interpretation of the Council of Trent and a better theological answer to the fundamental demands of eucharistic realism. From the same source is derived a praiseworthy emphasis on the profound reasons determining such a Presence, which in its use of such neologisms as 'trans-finalization' echoes a spiritual concern that is truly patristic. Nevertheless, although eucharistic thought is in a general way receptive of an eschatological colouring, there is still too little emphasis on the relation between the eucharistic *Body* and the mystery of the Resurrection: a lack which modern writers will have to remedy.

THE LITURGICAL REVIVAL IN THE
SECOND QUARTER OF THIS CENTURY

When Guardini said in 1923, 'The Church is waking up in the souls of the faithful', and described this awakening as 'an event of great importance',[1] it was primarily the liturgy that he had in mind. The liturgical movement, initiated before the Great War in the two Benedictine abbeys of Beuron and Maria Laach, had recently become fully organized in Germany. The Abbot of Maria Laach was bringing out a series of books of which the first, *The Spirit of the Liturgy*,[2] was by Romano Guardini himself, and the second by Casel. As early as 1921 the latter had started a scholarly periodical[3] which was to guarantee the scientific basis of the movement, just as Guardini, through his personal reputation as a writer and Catholic thinker, was ensuring its popularity among young people and the whole Catholic public.[4]

Guardini's inspiration

For Guardini, the essential characteristic of the liturgical movement was its educational aim. The task was to recreate a Christian sensibility, which had been destroyed or at least blunted by modern individualism and a certain mechanization of life. Deprived of a sense of community, and unaware of the profound harmony that ought to be effected with God, with other men, and with the universe, the Christian was threatened by a sort of anaemia and, in times that were particularly difficult, he was in danger of losing the feeling for, and appreciation of, a Life of which he should, on the contrary, be the witness. Through the richness, difficult to convey in English, of the German word *Bildung*, which sees in culture an almost architectural *informing* of the human, the liturgy must become, or rather must again become (said Guardini) *formative* of the whole man, and once again give its participants a spiritual *style* or *order* – in the architectural sense, again – which will be able to permeate their whole being and, we might say, rebuild them in their very existence. For the liturgy teaches us again to say 'we' and not simply 'I', and to live as 'Church'.[5] Thus it brings men back to the awareness of a personal value, independent of perishable output or gains. 'The practice of the liturgy', says Guardini, 'means that by the help of grace, under the guidance of the Church, we grow into living works of art before God, with no other aim or purpose than that of living and existing in His sight; it means fulfilling God's word and "becoming as little children".'[6] This plea for gratuitous existence, still effective in our own day, did not fall on deaf ears.

The liturgy was no longer a matter of rubrics; fundamentally, it never had been; it was seen once again as a form of life whose origins reach back into the centuries, driving its roots deep into the heart of God, thence to draw nourishment for men. There was, of course, the alleged danger of aestheticism – a danger that is always with us – but the reality was very different. In the liturgy, as J. A. Jungmann says in connection with the history of the Mass, we are always presented with 'this organic beauty that we admire in a tree in blossom: for all the irregularity of

branches and twigs, leaves and flowers, a noble harmony reigns
in them, a principle of life; a soul governs their growth'.[7]
Throughout history, the liturgy, which has been knitted together
and unravelled so often and in so many ways, represents in
truth what is most profound, most pure and, spiritually speaking,
most educative in the life of the Church. It is the part which
we cannot reject without shutting ourselves out, to our eternal
death, from the most secret depths of man and faith.

'In liturgy', said Guardini in the introduction to his little
book on *Sacred Signs*, 'we deal directly not with thoughts, but
with actualities. And not with past actualities, but with those
now present.' 'We must help ourselves', he continues, 'to read in
the outward form the inner state: to read from the body what
is in the soul; to read from the earthly process what is spiritual
and hidden.'[8] Passing then to the order of faith, he asked questions which are still relevant for us: 'What will become of our
soul, if it can no longer picture to itself the realities of salvation?
If it pronounces words which have no meaning for it? If it
makes gestures without understanding their meaning? Tell me,
what do we think lies behind the words "God", "grace",
"Christ"? What does the sign of the cross mean, or a genu-
flection? What are all such gestures? A revelation of supernatural
realities or an empty shadow? To believe', he continues, 'is to
be in contact with the realities of a higher order; to believe is
to bring invisible realities into one's life: have we this faith?
That is where reform must start!'[9] A start had been made;
Guardini wrote as a teacher – the liturgy could, and must, become
in the Church the eminent centre of education in faith.

Casel's views

It was left to Casel to demonstrate scientifically what this *mystery*
of Christ was, at the very root of the Church's existence and
the spiritual education of Christians. '*Mysterium* means for us',
he wrote, 'what it means to St Paul in his letters to the Colossians
and Ephesians, the great fact that Christ is a hope of glory'
(Col. 1:27).[10] God himself for us in Christ, that is what the
mystery is in the first place. It is also, in a more technical sense,
to which Casel devoted his work and gave his name, *the way in
which Christ effects for us in worship his permanent operation
of grace*.[11] In the first number of the review he founded in 1921,
Casel chose as the subject of his first article the liturgical notion

of action.[12] The *actio*, in liturgical language, means the Mass as
a thing which one *makes* and from which one benefits only by
participating in it. The Mass, as *actio*, is at the same time a
feast and a *drama*; it is a *mystery* in the Hellenistic sense of the
word, and so an *initiation* which secures admission into the very
being of Christ and the Church.

'The Word's nuptial approach, when seeking his bride,'
explains Casel, 'was without parallel. She was lost, but he
followed her and lowered himself to her level. In order to wed
us, the Word took on our nature. The bride was infinitely
beneath him: he stepped down to her, took on her likeness, and
put on her raiment. He went further: since she had fallen into
sin, he even put on the garment of sin, the *similitudo carnis
peccati*, the flesh like unto the flesh of sin. He set this garment,
his human body, upon the cross, out of love for the bride, thereby
restoring her original splendour. Thus he became her "bridegroom of blood" (Exod. 4:25). By his death he swept away the
impediment that prevented the marriage. Once the Lord was risen
from the tomb, the wedding could be celebrated. As a wedding
present he sent from on high the Spirit, the breath of God. Then
this love, this divine kiss, fused the Spirit of God and the spirit
of man into one inseparable unity. And yet the final union will
not be consummated until the world that lies beyond our own.'[13]

Again: 'The Church, the new Eve,' Casel tells us, 'was born
from the rib of the new Adam, Christ, when he fell asleep on
the cross in the paroxysm of suffering. From his blood and
wounds he created his bride, now for ever purified and sanctified:
washed of all sin in the blood of his love and sanctified by his
breath of life, the Holy Spirit. She is Spirit of his Spirit, and
the two together form *one single* Spirit, for the Spirit of Christ
dwells in her. The two make up "Christ", as St Paul says (1 Cor.
12:12). It was for her that he shed his heart's blood, and that is
why he loves her, and she, in her great gratitude, returns his love
with all her strength. Now, the two act together, as *one single*
being: for he has raised her up to himself in an act of wonderful
condescension.'[14] Without going into Casel's detailed treatment
of the Church's heavenly kingdom, we may well try to understand how this Church, at first immersed in Christ, to whom she
is spiritually indebted for her birth, gradually emerges into an
awareness of her own self in this act of love which consists in
worship and, more precisely still, the Eucharist.

Here Christ does not offer himself merely as a spectacle, any more than he did in his incarnation and on the cross; the liturgy is not a drama confined to the stage. The action takes place in the auditorium too, if I may put it so. The oblation has to pass into the Church and not remain in Christ alone, since love resides in him only in order to pass into her and possess her entirely. No thing nor person in the Church may be withdrawn from Christ's offering; everything must become in her the act of self-giving and of entering into the operation of a perfect communion. 'Mystically engrafted into Christ as his body and spouse,' Casel explains, 'the Church joins herself by the most intensive self-giving to his offering, so that she becomes one sacrifice with him.'[15] Church and Christ form one body, and the bride's liturgy is a pure recalling of the bridegroom's love.

The Fathers whom Casel cites had long ago explained that 'it is evident to all those who have been initiated into the things of God that we do not offer any other – any new – sacrifice: all we do is to celebrate the memory of this unique, salvific, sacrifice. For the Lord himself told us, "Do this in memory of me", so that when we see the representation we may remember the passion he suffered for us.'[16] 'The celebration of the Mass', adds Casel, 'is the remembering of the redemptive death. The remembering itself consists in the ritual celebration of the redemptive work, modelled upon the Last Supper. It is at the same time the sacrifice. It is not a subjective memory but an objective reality underlying the rite. In other words it is symbol, image, mystery. So the anamnesis imprints upon the whole of the sacred action the mark of a real memory: under the veil of ritual, the redemptive death becomes reality.'[17] There is nothing in the Eucharist that impairs the strict uniqueness of Christ's death. On the contrary, everything is derived from that death, in virtue of the fullness of an act which, while concerning the whole of history, also communicates itself to the individuality of each of its stages or phases. The memorial is a meal, the remembering is communion, the altar on which Christ continues to offer himself is precisely the table at which he himself is served. 'Through Christ,' Casel was writing over fifty years ago, in 1922, 'man's petition flows constantly to God, wave after wave, and God's grace similarly flows back to man. In this lies the deepest meaning of the phrase "the memorial of the Lord" which is applied to the Eucharist. Through and in the Eucharist, the Lord lives in the Church. When Christians celebrated their commemorative meal, it was not a mere remembering of something that had happened earlier: no, it was Christ once again seating himself among them, eating and drinking with them, giving himself to them as nourishment. So we can understand how, for the first Christians, the Lord's Supper, the *fractio panis*, took on the form of an eternal feast, in the heavenly banqueting-hall, where the Lord moves to and fro, waiting upon his guests and giving them their fill of delicious foods.'[18]

Apart from the technical problems that such a line of thought raised,[19] it involved a radical restatement of doctrine, affecting not only the notion of *sacrifice*, understood as a true memorial, but also, maybe, that of *Presence*, seen as a *mystery* with many aspects, and not simply as a *miracle*.

A NEW VIEW OF PRESENCE

'To accomplish so great a work [the entry of the Church into the paschal mystery],' the last Council explains, in language that echoes what is best in Casel's thought,[20] 'Christ is always present in his Church, especially in her liturgical celebrations. He is present in the sacrifice of the Mass, not only in the person of his minister, "the same one now offering, through the ministry of priests, who formerly offered himself on the cross," but especially under the eucharistic species. By his power he is present in the sacraments, so that when a man baptizes it is really Christ himself who baptizes. He is present in his word, since it is he himself who speaks when the holy scriptures are read in the church. He is present, finally, when the Church prays and sings, for he promised: "Where two or three are gathered together for my sake, there am I in the midst of them" (Matt. 18:20).' 'Christ indeed', the Council continues, 'always associates the Church with himself in the truly great work of giving perfect praise to God and making men holy. The Church is his dearly beloved bride who calls to her Lord, and through him offers worship to the eternal Father.'[21] Regarded, then, as *mystery* 'in the old sense of the word' in which mystery is 'more an action than a thing',[22] the Eucharist is no longer only a, so to speak, instantaneous prodigy: it takes on a body in a liturgy. The presence of Christ takes on also the dynamic character of a love which seeks to arouse a human *responder* as loving as Christ himself.

No one, of course, has ever denied that the presence is a mystery of person in the Eucharist itself; but if this is not stated as clearly as the liturgy presupposes and demands, its full import may be overlooked. On the other hand, once so elementary a truth has been emphatically brought to our notice, we have a strong obligation to reread what the Council of Trent had to say; and in so doing not to confine ourselves to an academic theology which is not a true reflection of the Council.

A new understanding of Trent

'If anyone shall say that in the most holy sacrament of the Eucharist the substance of the bread and wine remains present with the flesh and blood of Our Lord Jesus Christ, and shall deny this wonderful and unique changing of the whole substance of the bread into his body and the whole substance of the wine into his blood, while the appearances of bread and wine still remain, a changing which the Catholic Church most appropriately calls "transubstantiation", let him be anathema.'[23] The decisive clarity, which allows no appeal, of the conciliar statement covers a subtle doctrine which allows us to examine it more closely even while we retain its substance.

Normally, a triple affirmation is read into this passage.[24] The first reminds us that the bread and wine are the body and blood of the Lord; the second asserts the total changing or, if we prefer the word, the real *conversion*, of the bread and wine into the body and blood of Christ; and the third says that the Church gives to this changing the apt name of transubstantiation. It is at once apparent that the three affirmations are not all of the same order. The first is truly scriptural; the second is a restatement of tradition; the third, on the other hand, introduces as normal, or sanctions, a word whose origins, we shall be seeing, are medieval. When we come to define more exactly the significance of this third affirmation and its relation to the first two, we shall be obliged to introduce qualifications which must lead to a playing down of the dogmatic use of the vocabulary relating to substance.

Take the word 'substance', in the first place. In spite of its distinctly technical overtones, the word is surely used in an ordinary sense which avoids as far as possible systematic implications. This is proved by the fact that the Council does not use the word 'accidents', even though, in sound scholastic language, it is complementary to the word 'substance'. While retaining the word 'substance', with its evocation of the realness of things, the Council associates with it the word 'appearances' or 'species'. The advantage of these words is not that they lessen the solidity of the signs, but rather that they describe the road to be followed by faith in its profession of the mystery. To speak of 'species' is simply to denote 'the reality of the bread which will be converted into the body of Christ'.[25] Relying on the Word whose power exceeds, without ever doing violence to, my weakness, I profess of this bread, of this wine, what Christ himself says of it, 'This is my body, this is my blood.' Starting from what I can see, I go beyond the evidence of my eyes, and affirm of it something which I do not then *see*, but which I nevertheless recognize I am justified in *believing*. In itself, the verbal pair 'substance-accidents' might well lead this movement of faith astray by attaching it to metaphysics. But when the word 'substance' is deprived of its habitual partner (represented, in the technical language of the time, by the word 'accidents'), it is detached from the philosophical universe in which it normally moves; and thereby it returns to an order of more restricted significance and simply means the *basic material* of things and their real *identity*. This illuminates the sense in which the Council speaks of transubstantiation.

That word was by no means unanimously favoured at the Council of Trent. In fact it gave rise to vigorous discussion.[26] It was, even so, retained, but its use was clarified by saying that it was an apt term for expressing the *conversion* without which the real presence could no longer be justified. Thus the word plays a subordinate part; it is primarily functional; it enables us to attach a name to a transforming act which lies beyond our grasp, but whose effects are known to us by faith: this bread is no longer bread but the body of the Lord, and this wine is his blood. What matters, then, is not the *word* as such, but the *thing* it envisages, the content of faith which it enables us to profess. Just as 'consubstantial', affirmed for so many years of Christ, enables us to proclaim the equality of the Son with the Father, should anyone be inclined to doubt it, so 'transubstantiation' means that in the eucharistic mystery we cannot leave out the *radical reversal* of things which causes the bread and wine

to have passed wholly and in their very *being* into the mystery
of the Lord, and obliges us to say that they *are* in truth his body
and his blood.[27]

We see, then, that the word 'transubstantiation' is a sort of
gloss, something one can fall back upon,[28] at least as a formula
to end discussion: it has a purely practical purpose. It is chosen
to prevent a shift of meaning which other words, less inexact
or indeed ambiguous, might encourage.[29] 'It was not a rational
explanation of the mystery, but a categorical affirmation of the
reality of Christ's presence.'[30] What Trent wished to do,
accordingly, was to guarantee the existence of something inexpressible, without exhausting its potentialities: it gave no legal
sanction to any metaphysical system that might be associated
with it. All it did was to lay down what we must assert if we
are not, by the language we use, to compromise the *absolute
originality* of the mystery.[31] It does not provide, at the invisible
core of things, what I might call an advanced observation post,
which would allow us to see what the Lord does, or (even more
impossible) *what he must metaphysically do*, if he is to be truly
present. The *conversion* of the bread and wine into the body and
blood of the Lord is as completely *original* as the transition of
Christ's dead body to its state of glory – but with this added
paradox, that when the bread and wine are converted into the
body of the risen Christ, *they still remain elements that are
immanent in this world*. While the Resurrection removes Christ's
body from the experiential structure of the world, the Eucharist
allows the elements it uses to remain intact in it, so that they
thereby become signs of a reality which still eludes us. This
means that, compared with the Resurrection, which enables us
to hope for the transmutation of the world into glory, transubstantiation does not belong to the order of even metaphysical
representations: it is among the corollaries which, before the
parousia, follow from the mystery of the Resurrection.

While, therefore, we should not dismiss transubstantiation too
lightly as a mere matter of vocabulary, we should be even more
careful not to rely too much upon it, as though it were by itself
the *nec plus ultra* we may say about the Lord's Supper. Correctly
understood, transubstantiation is, much more certainly, what we
might call the *nec minus infra*: the lowest point below which
we must not go if we are not to suffer a diminution of faith, just
when we seem to be obtaining an increase of it – and, moreover,

precisely because we are trying to obtain it.

We are now in a position considerably to advance our theological understanding of the mystery.

A new approach to transubstantiation

The credit for this goes to Père de Baciocchi, who in 1959 published an article in the review *Irénikon*. That article itself cannot be divorced from the writings of Franz J. Leenhardt, the gist of which should first be explained.

Returning to the biblical notion of 'word', Leenhardt suggests that we should listen to Christ speaking to us at the Last Supper as we would listen to a Hebrew speaking: not in a static, 'Greek', way, but dynamically, so that the very words effect a transformation. 'Here ontology is an eschatology. The world is a call to being.'[32] The *substance* of things is not definable apart from the 'divine intention which is realized in them'.[33] 'Things', says Leenhardt, 'are what God has made of them: they are what they realize of his active will; their reality depends on the creative will of his Word, which destines them to serve creation.'[34] Thus, 'when the believer receives from the hands of Christ this bread which he calls his body, the relation of the believer to this bread has become something quite other, since God wishes to give – and does so give – to faith, through this bread, as Jesus Christ told us, something quite different from the nutritive substance contained in the flour which has been made into the form of bread. God has introduced here a new intention. The ultimate reason for this piece of bread received from Jesus Christ in these circumstances is to be the body of Christ. At this moment faith can only believe that Jesus Christ does in fact do what he wishes to do. For faith, the substance of this bread is the body of Jesus Christ, as he himself told us when he was distributing it.'[35] And since substance is 'the being of things in relation to this particular intention of Jesus Christ, then, from the very fact that this new purpose is attached to the bread, faith will accept that it no longer has the same substance'. Leenhardt concludes: 'The word *transubstantiation* expresses this transformation without claiming to give an explanation of it' and without speaking of it, either, 'as relating to a phenomenon of the physical order.'[36] Is it true to say that Leenhardt was clothing his Protestant thought in a Catholic idiom?[37] I think not. There was a real agreement between the two, even though it was limited to the *act* of the Last Supper and perhaps *only* to the bread.[38] He opened up for Catholic thought a road which could profitably be followed. Instead of taking transubstantiation, in its effect upon *things*, only as the *starting-point* of eucharistic thought, is it not better to see it as the *consequence* of an act which, for Christ, consists in *his giving of himself*? to see in the *transubstantiation of the elements the direct consequence of the authenticity of the gift of Person*?

Père de Baciocchi also starts from the notion, as liturgical as it is scriptural, of memorial; for him, the Last Supper legitimately corresponds to what 'the first paschal meal had been in the exodus from Egypt'. 'Every Jewish family', he points out, 'which celebrated the Passover met in it, through the medium of signs, the saving act of God; it welcomed in its own present day the salvation that had entered history in days gone by. In future every Christian gathering which celebrated the Eucharist was also to bring back into its life the redemptive act by receiving the risen victim of the cross.'[39] Everything derives from that. If 'the redemptive act is indeed the *gift* which Christ makes of his body and blood *to the Father and to us*, consummating for all eternity, before heaven and earth, the hidden offering of the Incarnation', then the eucharistic memorial 'signifies and contains' both this act and this gift.[40] As Leenhardt had said, Christ's presence which determines the memorial is a *'purposive presence'*,[41] and it is by such a presence that the Church is nourished. It is true that the bread and wine which condition this presence in this place are indeed *things*, but they are things within the context of a purpose which converts them into the words and the *signs* of a gift. The fact that they are *given*, and given *by Christ*, becomes what constitutes their reality. Presented by Christ as that by which his presence is mediated to us, bread and wine are really incorporated in him for us. The act which transmits them to us transmits also the Person who gives them to us, and the love of Christ the giver is so real and so powerful that it causes the *things* through which he gives *himself* to pass into his *domain of person*. 'The bread and wine given in the celebration', says Père de Baciocchi, 'are signs and media of the presence of Christ, given body and blood to the Church.'[42]

Not only, we may say, 'does Christ's word direct these gifts to a completely different social and religious end, without altering their experiential character', but by so doing it affects their very identity. 'In future,' continues Père de Baciocchi, 'this bread and this wine will no longer serve to nourish and refresh bodies (except in a subsidiary way and to a negligible degree); they will no longer be material for a common meal. They are now signs and instruments of Christ's gift in his body and blood.'[43] Their only content is that very Person into whose service they have just passed, and who is no other than Christ in person. Leenhardt had already emphasized, in connection with the bread at least, that the incorporation of the gifts into the mystery of Christ is not a mere matter of *words* but of the attitude taken up by the whole *person*, and, as he then said, 'even in the absence of any declaration, this bread *is* his body, *because* he gives it, and what he gives is his body, his life, his person'.[44] 'The bread and wine', Père de Baciocchi adds in turn, 'then become that very thing as which they are *given* . . . Given as body and blood of Christ, they become body and blood of Christ.'[45] In brief, none of the elements involved in the *gesture* of the gift remains external to the *Person* who is giving himself.

The antiquity and modernity of this approach

The simplicity of these affirmations is perfect: it echoes that which we find in the thought of the Fathers. 'The Lord did not say,' writes one of the latter, ' "This is the symbol of my body, this is the symbol of my blood", but, "This is my body, this is my blood"; thereby teaching us that we must not consider the nature of what is offered; we must understand that by the intervention of the thanksgiving, a conversion of the body and the blood is effected.'[46] Cyril of Jerusalem, again, explains it thus: 'When he himself has said of the bread in so many words, "This is my body", who will be so rash as to doubt henceforth? And when he himself categorically states, "This is my blood", who will ever question this and say it is not his blood? Long ago, of his own free will, he changed the water into wine at Cana in Galilee, and are we to withhold our faith when he changes wine into blood? Invited to an earthly wedding, he performed this astonishing miracle, and when he now gives the bridegroom's companions the delight of his body and his blood, shall we not proclaim our belief even more willingly?'[47] And St Ambrose, the most explicit of them all on the subject of the 'operative'[48] power of Christ's words, has this to say about them: 'You may perhaps say, "This is my ordinary bread." But the bread of which you are speaking is bread before the uttering of the sacramental words: as soon as the consecration takes place, the bread is changed into the flesh of Christ. Come, let us prove it. How can something which is made of bread be the body of Christ? By what words is the consecration effected, and whose are those words? They are the words of the Lord Jesus . . . And what is this word of Christ? It is the word by which everything has been made. The Lord spoke, and the heavens were made. The Lord spoke, and the earth was made. The Lord spoke, and the seas were made. The Lord spoke, and all living creatures were born. You see, then, how powerful is Christ's word. If the word of the Lord Jesus is of such power that that which had no being came into being, how much greater is its power to make what already was in being to exist and be changed into something else?"[49]

Today, it is true, we would emphasize not so much the *power* of the Lord, which more or less may be taken for granted, as the *truth* of the *gesture* which Christ enacts. Even so, in either case, emphasis is laid on the *Person*, who alone explains what happens to the *things*. In this lies the *vindication of* the realism of faith, as opposed to the hesitancy of a false 'symbolism' which is afraid to speak of the *reality* of Christ's body in the *signs* which indicate his *presence* to us. Thereby, too, we *put out of court* an exclusively 'physicist' reaction, which, for all practical purposes, considers nothing but the *mutations of the elements themselves*. Anxiety to answer the technical questions *about the structure of things* raised by transubstantiation can lead to a neglect of the *very act of gift* which causes Christ so to give himself to us, whereas we should constantly return to this *act* as our starting-point and keep it as our guide. The Eucharist is a mystery *residing in* the Person before it is (though it does not exclude) a miracle *effected upon things* – things which, moreover, are part of his Person! The great value of Père de Baciocchi's work is that it gives clear expression to this change in the point of view, which allows us to understand that the transubstantiation of the eucharistic elements is an integral part of the authenticity of the love which gives itself.

For Père de Baciocchi – and here we shall follow him – the gift effected by Christ in the signs, because it is gift of Person, is real and is true only if the elements involved in the gift truly *become* the Person himself who declares that, by means of them, he is making a gift of himself. The reality of the presence, therefore, derives from the truth of the gift and authenticates it. A Christ who did not transform into himself the things *which he gives us as mediations of his own Person*, would be meaningless; for the gift of himself which he intends to make would have no effect on the means he selects for realizing the gift. Such a hypothesis would be absurd. Christ's *gift* is *absolute*: that means that his *offering* of himself is *carried through*. Bread and wine become his body and his blood, and his *presence* is *true*. Of this we must be quite clear in our minds. We do not start from the transubstantiated *elements* and so lay hold of the reality of his presence; we start from the *gift* itself, and so discover its full depth in the trans-formation of the elements of the world, involved by Christ in this gift. In brief, and once more, because this matter is truly central, *the transubstantiation of the elements* is the result of the *authenticity of the gift* which is expressed in them and which alone can explain the *presence*.

We have still, it is true, to show how these affirmations are specifically applicable to the mystery of Christ. This, I believe, we cannot do without a theology of the Resurrection and of the glorified *body*, which we have referred to earlier and will have to say more about later. The road is, at any rate, clear for rescuing the Eucharist from what I might call a profitless enslavement, in which its depths are explained as mere reflections of the actual being of the Lord.

Transubstantiation and the mystery of Christ in creation
'Only Christ', as Père de Baciocchi concludes by explaining, 'can act in this way; only he can "transubstantiate" things in creation, for he alone in his Man-God being is the centre of reference for all created being. No creature is itself without being also *for* him and *through* him, for "in him", St Paul tells us, "all things were created, in heaven and on earth . . . all things were created through him and for him. He is before all things, and in him all things hold together" (Col. 1:16–17).'[50] What in Leenhardt was no more than an indication primarily concerning man[51] becomes now an explicit Christology. Transubstantiation is not an isolated mystery that could be regarded as arbitrary; it is a direct consequence of the structure of a world created in Jesus Christ. Things undoubtedly have their own substantial consist-

ence, but the world is ordered around a mystery which 'resumes or brings together everything' (Eph. 1:10). The Eucharist is the *sacramental* emergence of this mystery. While in all the other sacraments, and *a fortiori* in the normal course of the world, 'the substantial being of things' is not changed and the natural order is fully respected, in the Eucharist, on the other hand, 'Christ's act consists in *giving* the bread and wine not as bread and wine but, in complete reality, as his body and his blood'. 'Such a gift, therefore, which *affects the very being* of the bread and wine',[52] and so makes it into 'the very being of Christ',[53] reveals the final destination of the world, and is organically related to the 'new heaven' and 'new earth'.[54]

TRANSFINALIZATION

Slight though the change of attitude appears to be which consists in considering in the first place the *act itself of Christ given to his Church*, in order then to understand better *the nature of his gifts*, such a change has far-reaching and unmistakably evident consequences. Questions relating to the '*how*' become subordinate to understanding the '*why*', and perhaps even more – and here we are following the line of the great patristic tradition – to consideration of the '*for whom*'.

The 'spiritual' point of view of the Fathers

'Why', asks St Ambrose, 'do you look for the order of nature in the body of Christ, when the Lord Jesus himself was born of a virgin outside the course of nature?'[55] Four centuries later, St John Damascene quotes the same example to turn aside the same unprofitable question. The Virgin, too, when the angelic messenger came to her, reacted with the 'how?' And the answer she received was a reference to the power of the Spirit. 'And you, too,' continues John Damascene, 'who presume the function to be known of the epiclesis we shall later be invoking,[56] you ask *how* the bread becomes the body of Christ, *how* the wine and the water become the blood of Christ. I answer you by saying, the Holy Spirit has intervened and he acts in ways which transcend thought and word.'[57] Released from the unreal problems that ask *how*, the Fathers can then ask *for whom* this body of Christ exists, and so explain the fact that it is present there. 'He spoke and this was done, he ordered and this was created,' says St Ambrose in the treatise we were quoting earlier.[58] And he adds, bringing together in the most impressive and infinitely suggestive way the *conversion* of the eucharistic elements and the *changing* of Christians at baptism: 'You yourself lived, but you were the old creature. You ask how far does this new creature extend? Whoever lives in Christ, he tells us, is a new creature.'[59]

If, then, explains St Ambrose, you wish to understand what *happens* to the eucharistic *elements*, consider *what happened to you yourself* at baptism: from the old man you were then, you became a new creature in Christ! So it is with the bread and the wine of your eucharists: they, too, are transformed into Christ by the same virtue that includes you in his life. The same theme constantly recurs in the catechetical sermons of Augustine, who himself had listened to St Ambrose in Milan: 'You begin to receive what you are beginning to be,'[60] he was later to say to the newly baptized of Hippo. And again: 'You hear: The body of Christ! and you answer: Amen! Be therefore a member of the Body of Christ, so that your endorsement may be true.'[61] Beneath all these forms of expression lies the same truth: *become* the *member of Christ* if you wish to understand how *the Eucharist becomes his body*. The eucharistic truth is not arrived at, in the first place, by the speculative intelligence. Make your way yourself into *Christian becoming*, and you will be able to understand *eucharistic becoming*.

Later an heir of Ambrose and Augustine[62] was to develop this baptismal analogy of the Eucharist in a way that is now familiar; even so, it sheds such light on the modern view of 'trans-finalization' that it is worth quoting at length: '*Ask yourself,*' says Faustus, '*you who are already regenerated by Christ,* is there any limit to the blessings effected by the divine virtue; *why should it seem to you out of the question and impossible that the earthly and mortal elements should be transformed into the substance of Christ?* Hitherto you have been exiled from life and a stranger to mercy, deprived within yourself of the road to salvation. Suddenly initiated into the laws and saving mysteries of Christ, you have entered into the body of the Church, not in a visible manner, but by faith: by a hidden purity you have merited[63] becoming, from child of perdition, an adopted child of God. While remaining, so far as the eye can see, within your own dimension, you have become greater than yourself.

While still remaining the same, you have become other through progress in faith: *externally nothing has been added to you, but internally you have undergone a complete change.* It is thus that man has become the son of Christ, and that Christ has been formed in man's spirit. Without any physical sensation, you have cast aside your former low estate and have suddenly taken on a new dignity; the wounds God has cured in you, the evil he has destroyed, the stain he has washed away, are apparent not to your eyes but to your mind. And so, when you approach the venerable altar, there to receive full nourishment, look upon the sacred body and blood of God with faith, wonder at them in all honour, touch them with your understanding, receive them from the hand of your heart and take them with an eagerness that remains entirely within yourself.'[64] In this admirable eucharistic passage we see how the eminently spiritual *experience* of conversion into Christ serves as a specially apt *model* by which the Eucharist can be understood. The approach is so illuminating, that we may disregard such expressions as seem to us somewhat out of date. The author has grasped the important point; this lies in the clear establishment of the correspondence between the *change* operated *in us* by Christ's grace and the *conversion* affecting the eucharistic elements *in themselves*.

The re-emphasizing of meaning

The various influences we have noted, and the effects they combine to produce, have led in our own day to a desire to present the Eucharist in a similar way, taking the *subject* as the starting-point. To believe in the Eucharist and to take part in the Lord's Supper is to believe that we take, as food and drink, bread and wine which are not merely flour ground from wheat or juice pressed from grapes. Although they are elements of this world – and have lost nothing of their physical characteristics, for they are still *real* food and *real* drink – nevertheless they have changed in *meaning*. We receive them, as Christ gives them, only subject to accepting that we see in them something quite other than what we would, left to ourselves, see in them or read into them. Thus we may say that their significance, and their final purpose too, are raised to a higher level. What Christ has said is to be done with them no longer relates to a purely natural need. The order to which their use belongs is no longer biological; it corresponds to this new identity which, in the first place, was conferred on us. Having been baptized in Christ, we must live *in* him and also *by* him; we must therefore be introduced to *his* table and nourished by *his* life. 'As the living Father sent me, and I live because of the Father, so he who eats me will live because of me' (John 6:57). If, then, it is simply our bodily or physico-cultural life that we wish to sustain, then we must turn to other refreshment; at this table, Christ tells us, the food and drink are directed to resurrection and life; that is to say the transcending, inaugurated by Christ himself, of mortality. His meal divinizes; and that is why bread and wine, table and meal, meeting and communion, everything is loaded by the Lord with a hitherto unknown weight of mystery, enriched by a *new aura and a new meaning*.

At the same time, nothing is 'de-naturalized'; rather is everything 'trans-naturalized'; everything is the same and yet everything is new. The simplest things sym-bolize and harmonize with the loftiest. Without destroying the everyday realities of the world, the Eucharist imposes upon their initial meaning, their present finality, their original function, a vast increase of significance, which corresponds to the Person whom we find in that new meaning. At Christ's table, which is one of our own tables transformed, something is offered and given which still lies at the heart of this world and yet is greater than the world itself, for it is the Lord himself who is making himself into food and drink so that we may live. Trans-finalization – which is also referred to as trans-signification[65] – denotes precisely the absolutely new *meaning* which *this* meal possesses, in virtue of the *Person*, who is served at it.

Whatever the necessary reservations, Paul VI has not discredited the idea of 'trans-finalization'.[66] When reminding us of the importance of the dogma of transubstantiation, he does not say that this is *all* that has to be said; rather does he urge us, when we say everything else, not to forget *this*. He is not, therefore, opposed to this dawning idea of trans-finalization. He even recognizes that it has a sound basis. 'Once the transubstantiation has been effected,' he writes, 'the species of bread and wine undoubtedly take on *a new significance* and a *new end*, since they are no longer ordinary bread and ordinary drink, but the sign of a sacred thing and the sign of a spiritual nourishment.'[67] Thus the encyclical does not reject the points of view that this new terminology presupposes and suggests; it simply reminds us of the mistake of oversimplified exclusiveness in language.[68] 'The species', we read, 'derive this *new significance* and *new finality* from the fact that they contain a new *reality*, which we rightly call ontological.'[69] In fact, if the bread and wine *are* not in very truth the body and blood of the Lord, the completely new *meaning* which faith analyses when it speaks of trans-finality would be a mere mental concept or simply the result of man's own reaction. Transubstantiation is the basis on which rests the truth of what we mean when we speak of trans-finalization; it tells us that the eucharistic act really operates upon the elements of the world which are offered and 'blessed' at Christ's table and so become his body and blood.[70]

EUCHARIST AND ESCHATOLOGY

When we cease to concentrate on the 'technical' and accordingly secondary character of transubstantiation, retaining of that affirmation only the essence from which faith draws its vigour, when, by emphasizing trans-finalization, we bring back into the foreground the spiritual benefit at which the mystery is directed, then our horizon is endlessly widened. The meal which gives us the presence of Christ, does so, we must remember, as yet only in signs. Its effectiveness is purely *sacramental*; but, as such, that effectiveness opens out into an end of time in which what is still held back and, we might say, inhibited by love (since the historical course of the world has to be respected) will be expressed eschatologically. When that time comes, the glory which is giving life in secret will do so openly. Until that happens our faith is still an expectation; all the 'meals' it consumes are *viatica*, provisions of hope taken for a journey, 'until he shall come' as the Apostle teaches us. At the same time this expectation is active and must bear fruit. The world, and still more the Church, must grow in faith, and grow in love. And thus the Lord's Supper is a meal which sustains the growth of faith and love and prepares us for their fulfilment. If the Eucharist, then, is truly related to the mystery of Christ and not to our own petty cares, it opens the door wide into eschatology.[71] It is for that reason that it has, as it should, a festal joyfulness. With this everyone today would agree, sometimes, indeed, vociferously. But Teilhard – the first and perhaps the only person to do so in his day with such clarity – had stressed again and again the deep-rooted relationship between 'the Mass' and the parousia, and distinguished the horizons towards which a theology of the Eucharist would have to be aimed, if it were to be truly prophetic.

'When the priest says the words *Hoc est corpus meum*, his words fall directly on the bread and directly transform it into the individual reality of Christ. But the great sacramental operation does not cease at that local and *momentary* event. Even children are taught that, throughout the life of each man and the life of the Church and the history of the world, there is only one Mass and one Communion . . . In fact, from the beginning of the Messianic preparation, up till the Parousia, passing through the historic manifestation of Jesus and the phases of growth of His Church, a single event has been developing in the world: the Incarnation, realized, in each individual, through the Eucharist.

'All the communions of a life-time are one communion.

'All the communions of all men now living are one communion.

'All the communions of all men, present, past and future, are one communion.

'Have we ever sufficiently considered the physical immensity of man, and his extraordinary relations with the universe, in order to realize in our minds the formidable implications of this elementary truth? . . . Yes, the human layer of the earth is wholly and continuously under the organizing influx of the Incarnate Christ. This we all believe, as one of the most certain points of our faith.

'. . . At every moment the Eucharistic Christ controls – from the point of view of the organization of the Pleroma (which is the only true point of view from which the world can be understood) – the whole movement of the universe: the Christ *per quem omnia, Domine, semper creas, vivificas et praestas nobis.*[72]

'. . . As our humanity assimilates the material world, and as the Host assimilates our humanity, the eucharistic transformation goes beyond and completes the transubstantiation of the bread on the altar. Step by step it irresistibly invades the universe. It is the fire that sweeps over the heath; the stroke that vibrates through the bronze. In a secondary and generalized sense . . . the sacramental Species are formed by the totality of the world, and the duration of the creation is the time needed for its consecration. *In Christo vivimus, movemur et sumus.*'[73]

Even without deeper considerations, to which we shall later have to turn, we can begin to understand how the Eucharist governs a view of the world in which the presence of Christ gradually makes its way into history and the universe. The eucharistic mystery of the Church is also the eucharistic mystery of the cosmos. By ensuring what Teilhard calls on another occasion 'Christ's happy grip upon the world'[74] it is a sacrament which prefigures and heralds the parousia. It is the anamnesis of the cross, the anamnesis of a cross whose fruit, in grace, is glory: it belongs to the order of the Resurrection. It cannot, therefore, be fully understood except in terms of the 'new heaven and new earth' it heralds and prepares. Memory that it is of a past that is ever living, it is already the first-fruits of a completely refashioned cosmic future. Many of our theologians are *saying* this, too, today:[75] but few of them can be said really to *have thought it out*. What Teilhard expressed in a language of intuition has not yet taken form in thinking and teaching that can readily be assimilated: so true is this that the encyclical *Mysterium Fidei* itself speaks of the Eucharist without even mentioning Christ's resurrection.

CONCLUSION

From Eucharist to Resurrection: the gap
Although so many important truths about the mystery of the Eucharist have been affirmed and brought to light again, it is still disappointing that so few decisive conclusions have been expressed about the relation between the Eucharist and the Resurrection; and yet that relation is obviously essential. Suppose that for a moment in our minds we withdraw the risen Christ from the Lord's Supper, what remains of the latter? The table is immediately bare; it has been cleared; no dish remains to supply our needs; there is no Presence; the table is no longer sacred, and we can leave it without regret. This is what we are told by faith: without the risen Lord himself, his supper is *nothing*. In that supper, then, it is he who is *everything*. It is not that the guests are of no importance, but their value here comes from the Person who invites them and receives them. The Eucharist is the table and the supper *of the Lord*. It is there that he himself, and he alone, illuminates us by his Word,

initiates us into his resurrection, communicates to us his Presence in the Spirit, and, loading us with his love, incorporates us in his Body. Without all these blessings, would the Eucharist – if indeed it still existed – be anything but the feast of the Lord's absence, the liturgy of an imaginary gift, the rite of men who have no kingdom, and the empty forms of disillusioned hearts?

Without dismissing too lightly the valuable teaching we have already received, we feel, therefore, that we need to work our way even further ahead until we reach the point where the springs emerge into the stream of faith. That point, as we have already seen, is the Resurrection. Why have we, or for so long have we had, so little to say about it? No doubt the time has gone when a theologian who attempted to throw light on transubstantiation not in terms of atomic theory but through the risen Christ[76] had to face the objection that that mystery was itself accidental![77] Even so, we are still a long way from demonstrating that in the Eucharist, as everywhere in the order of faith, nothing can make sense, and nothing will ever be able to make sense, if divorced from the single basic event upon which everything rests: and that is the Resurrection. Does this arise from a fear of linking too closely two mysteries which both seem under attack today? And yet one cannot hold good without the other. Between the Eucharist and the Resurrection there is perfect unity, so that we must either retain them both together, or reject them both. If, then, as we have seen, the Resurrection still *holds good*, theologians must, from their side, show how the Eucharist rests entirely upon the Resurrection or say goodbye to it for ever.

Moreover, this gap between Eucharist and Resurrection does not arise from a lack of faith. There are cultural and historical reasons, we believe, which explain it. The sort of general blindness to the body in anthropology, on which we commented earlier, is sufficient to account for the very astonishing fact that when speaking of the *Body* in the eucharistic mystery, nothing has been said about the mystery of the *body* in the Resurrection, and theologians have fallen back on the concept of *substance*! The mistake committed by a compartmentalized anthropology, so strongly characterized by an obscuring, if not a rejection, of the body, cannot have affected our culture without at the same time compromising expression of faith; and in the expression of faith itself the same mistake cannot react on the Resurrection

without a similar effect on the Eucharist. I do not say that everything has gone by the board, but many things still remain up in
the air and do not fit properly into the pattern. The eucharistic
crises which twice shook the Middle Ages in the West, Protestant
dissatisfaction with the 'doctrine' of Trent, and in our own day
the scepticism which is shaking the faith of Catholics in the
eucharistic Presence, all these are perhaps symptoms of a disorder caused by the theological break between Eucharist and
Resurrection, which itself may be explained by the lack of a true
anthropology of the body. It is this aspect that we must now
consider.

CHAPTER 2

The gap widens

There can be no doubt about our starting-point in this story of the widening of the gap: it must be St Augustine (as will be more evident at the end of this chapter), and in Augustine a certain dualism, common to the men of his day, which was to govern, for the Bishop of Hippo, a view of the risen body of Christ and its relation to the Eucharist whose importance is too often neglected.

The underlying dualism

The Neoplatonism[1] which served to educate Augustine in his journey towards Christ and the faith was, for all he learnt from it, nevertheless the object of his criticism. 'They had in view', Augustine tells us, magnifying the importance of purely verbal analogies, 'what John says: that by the Word of God all things were created; for we find this, too, in the books of the philosophers: and that God has one only Son, by whom all things were created. They saw the truth, but they saw it from a distance. They would not accept Christ's humble estate; in that ship they could have reached safely what they saw from a distance, but the cross of Christ seemed contemptible to them. There is a sea to be crossed, and you despise the wood? . . . The road is cut by the flooding waters of this world, and you can no longer make your way to the homeland unless you are willing to let the wood carry you.'[2]

While criticizing the superciliousness of his teachers, Augustine remains culturally a man of their world. He recognizes that 'there is a sea to be crossed'; and that sea is precisely the gulf which, according to the Neoplatonists, separates the universe of things from the world of Ideas. Since man is, through his body, a prisoner of the sensible and at the same time, through his mind, a citizen of the intelligible world, the absolute frontier which divides shadows from reality divides man himself too; this partly

explains the 'sea to be crossed' with the help of the wood of the
cross that the philosophers despise. Merciless in his criticism of
the Neoplatonic contempt for the faith, Augustine fails to see –
though who else in those days did see it, or even could still[3]
see it? – the formidable dualism of Neoplatonic anthropology.
'For Augustine, as for Plato, the soul is a pure spirit, which in
itself has no necessary connection with the world of bodies, and
whose spiritual activity tends to be regarded as the more pure and
intense, the more it is freed and dissociated from the body.'[4]
Since the time Augustine spent in Milan, Neoplatonism had
become for him his culture and his world. It was his general
philosophy; and in particular it provided him with a way of
getting round the insurmountable obstacles presented by the
problems of the origin of evil and the nature of God.[5] He
regarded this opposition between body and spirit as fundamental,
and Neoplatonism enabled him to see how a necessary conversion
could be initiated in men, detaching them from the sensible and
leading them to adhere unreservedly to the God who is Spirit
alone.

'Being admonished by these writings', Augustine tells us in
the seventh book of his *Confessions*, 'to return to myself, I
entered into my own inward self, with you as my guide; and
this I could do, for you *were there to help me*. I entered, and
with the eye of my soul (such as it was) I saw, above that same
eye, above my mind, the light that knows no change: not this
ordinary light that is visible to all flesh, nor as it were a greater
light of the same kind, shining as though with a many times
greater brightness and filling all space with its vastness. Not so
was this light, but something different, far different, from all
these. Nor did it lie above my mind, as oil lies upon water, or
the sky over the earth; it was above because it was it that made
me, and I was below because I was made by it. He who knows
the truth knows that light, and he who knows that light knows
eternity. Love knows it. O eternal truth, and true love, and loved
eternity!'[6]

The astonishing thing is not that Augustine should have
assimilated the speculative vigour of Neoplatonism – for that was
the cultural pole of his contemporaries – but that, after he had
been so strongly influenced by it, he was able to explain, with
the depth we have already recognized and shall be illustrating
again, the *Incarnation* of Christ and the mystery of his *Church*,

which both together initiate a sensible mediation between God and men leading to absolute communion in Spirit. The reason for this was that the appeal of revelation and the charm of Christ were stronger in Augustine than the *inertia* of the culture in which he lived, and to which he applied in fact the gravitational force of faith. Even so, on more than one point, the two were by no means easy to harmonize: not that Augustine ever rejected intellectually or emotionally what his cultural background made it difficult for him to understand; but there were elements in Christianity which, for the Neoplatonic thinker he had become, could not readily be fitted into, or fully vindicated by, the line of thought he followed as a believer. Such generalizations, however, would have little value unless they were to serve us as an introduction to a close study of one precise point in Augustine's theology which is of central importance to us: his view of the body of the risen Christ in itself, and as related to the Eucharist.

Augustine's view of the body of the risen Christ
In his analysis of the modes of Christ's presence Augustine distinguishes three: 'In his presence of *glory*', he tells us in Sermon 361 on the resurrection of the dead, 'Christ is always with the Father: in his *bodily* presence he is henceforth above the heavens, on the right-hand side of the Father; but in his presence of *faith*, he is in all Christians.'[7] In the light of what we have just been saying about the world in which Augustine lived, these distinctions are drawn as a deliberate shock to his audience. That God should be *immense*, that is to say that it is proper to his glory to be *circumscribed by nothing*, is easy enough to accept. That Christ, as God, should share the same glory as the Father may again be accepted without question. But, since every body is formed from the sensible, how can Christ, in his body, belong to this divine world which is 'at the right hand of the Father' or 'above the heavens'? And yet, this is precisely what faith tells us, that Christ, in his 'body', is integrated in the order of 'spirit', and that Christ is glorified in the world *above*, in these physical and corporeal elements which have *risen* from the universe *below*! Augustine accepts from revelation what Neoplatonism would regard as a contradiction in terms; and in revelation he believes he finds it attested *as a plain statement of fact*, in other words without implying any criticism of his own ideas on the nature of the world. However shocking this Christian

datum may be to Augustine as a thinker, he accepts it without hesitation in his capacity as believer. And his merit is the greater, the more his view of the body is reified and spatialized, and so involves him in insoluble theological problems which his successors were to inherit.

'Having risen on the third day, the day he had chosen,' Augustine explains in his short, but important for us, Sermon 272, 'he ascended into heaven; it is thither (*illuc*) that he raised his body; it is thence (*inde*) that he will come to judge the living and the dead; it is there (*ibi*) that meanwhile he sits at the right hand of the Father.'[8] So far, then, from withdrawing Christ's body from the natural conditions of spatiality, the Resurrection inexorably locks it into them. 'He has ascended into heaven', Augustine explains again in his *In Joannem*, 'and he is not here (*hic*).' And yet, if we consider not the *body* of his humanity but his immensity of God, we must forthwith affirm in spite of all we have said that 'he is *there* (*ibi*), actually at the right hand of the Father, and *here* (*hic*), for, in his *presence of majesty*, he has not left us'. 'That is why,' St Augustine continues, 'according to the *presence of majesty* we possess Christ always; as for the *presence of flesh*, he rightly said to his disciples, "You will not have me with you always." '[9] *Mortal* flesh and *risen* flesh are, in fact, identified by Augustine, and therein lies the ambiguity. While it is true that, according to his presence of flesh, Christ is subject to the conditions of the sensible universe, the fact of his resurrection removes him from the passivity of the spatio-temporal, on the basis of an entirely new relationship with our world, as we have seen.[10] This obviously presupposes that the body be apprehended as a *relation* and not as a *thing*. If the body be thought of as thing – a trap that it is not so easy to avoid – it necessarily implies determination of *context* and *place*. Glory itself will not wrench the body out of space; all it will do will be to modify its place. In this case, its glorification will be a mere translation, from below to above; it will then be in-accessible to us, but it will not itself be freed from space in the empirico-physical sense of the word. Just as localized as it was in the days of flesh, but in a different way, it will not 'emerge' from this new place, which is for it the spatial enclosure of Glory. He is *above*, says Augustine, whereas he was, and we are, *below*.

Augustine was distressed at thus having condemned the risen

Christ to captivity by unwittingly *spatializing* the world of glory and *reifying* the human body; and he sought accordingly to expand the world of the risen Christ to the dimensions of the universe. In order to do this, would it not be sufficient to attribute to the body of the glorified Christ a 'presence of immensity'? Luther was to do the same later, as the great Platonist Scotus Erigena was also to do under the Carolingians.[11] 'If we ourselves', said the intrepid Irishman, 'become "like unto angels" in our resurrection, shall we demur at accepting that Our Lord Jesus Christ, in his two natures united as one insepar-able reality, is everywhere, and that nothing in him is circum-scribed by a place or a time or any modality proper to the creature?'[12] He did not see that *this* way of wrenching Christ away from the passivities of space is also a way of annihilating his body. He did not see that the Resurrection establishes *a new relation* between Christ and *our world* in his humanity, and that it is only this *relation* which enables us to *conceive* the *body* of the risen Christ, outside every empirical concept of space. Augustine also failed to see this. Even so, he was unwilling to dilute the *body* of Christ in the very immensity of God.

When Augustine comes to deal with the question of the return of the Lord, he is therefore reduced to admitting the *empirico-physical* realness of the glorified Christ. 'He will return', he says, 'as he was seen to rise to heaven, *in the same form and the same substance of flesh*. For God did not take away the nature from him to whom he gave immortality.' And so, Augustine continues, 'we must not see Christ *spread throughout all things*, and we must beware of so emphasizing the divinity of the man that we compromise the truth of this body'. To avoid such a disaster it is better to retain the body of Christ in the spatiality of glory than to dissipate it in the divine immensity. 'God and man,' Augustine therefore concludes, in a phrase that Calvin was to adopt, 'he is in fact a single person and a single Christ . . . Present in all things inasmuch as he is God, *he is on the other hand in heaven inasmuch as he is man*.'[13]

The bearing of this doctrine on the Eucharist

There can be no doubt that St Augustine did not succeed in finding the answer to the dilemma in which he thought the risen Christ was caught; and these, in the end, are the two horns of the dilemma – *either* a glorified body locally situated in heaven, *or* a divine ubiquity. The latter being inadmissible because Christ remains for ever *incarnate*, the only possibility left is a *glorification localized in heaven*. The eucharistic consequence of this is immediately evident. Since the glorified Christ has ascended *into heaven*, he cannot *be present* in his Eucharist. His presence, the presence which scripture clearly asserts, transforms our hearts in faith. But does it truly enter into the elements themselves, or rather can we *think* that it does so? It is doubtful. It has even been suggested that Augustine pictured the relation of the eucharistic elements to the *body* of Christ on the *Platonic model of the sensible universe's participation in the world of ideas*.[14] The fact that such a view could be put forward in connection with Augustine is significant, and we need do no more than note it here. In any case one thing is certain, 'for many Augustinians the localization of the body of Christ was, for centuries to come, to be the chief obstacle to sacramentary realism'.[15] This was to be true of Ratramnus of Corbie, and also of Berengar of Tours, of whom we shall be speaking. Later again, it will be true of Calvin. Moreover, the problem does not affect Augustinians alone, and, extending beyond transubstantiation (which, to my mind, avoids rather than solves it), it is still unanswered in our own day.

To return to St Augustine himself, he has too lively a sense of the mystery of Christ to remain the prisoner of his own ideas, as some of his followers were later to do, and so show themselves untrue to the essence of their master's teaching. Although Augustine was unable to crystallize *in thought* what was later to be called the *real Presence*, he did not fail to *affirm* that Christ is truly present, since he communicates his life to us. His faithful application of the scriptural texts which clearly attest the depth of Christ's gift enabled him to extricate himself from the narrow confines of the system and even to overcome the contradictions in which he would otherwise have been caught. The heritage of such a thought, however, never separable from the faith which animated it, was to prove a difficult burden. Many were to fail to find their way out from the insoluble problems that a *spatialized* conception of glory and a *reified* conception of the body were to bequeath to the West. From this arose the tensions, the deadlocks and the crises for which there was to be no solution, as we shall be seeing, except by a change in the axis of reference. Meanwhile the fundamental problems remained unchanged, touching the reality of the risen Christ's *body* and its relation to the Eucharist. Augustine never solved these, and they are still with us, even though it seemed at one time in the West that we could forget them. It is these developments that we must now examine.

AN OUTLINE OF THE TWO EUCHARISTIC CRISES
OF THE NINTH AND ELEVENTH CENTURIES

No two lives, it would seem, could be more different than those of Ratramnus (d.875), the monk of Corbie, near Epernay,[16] and of Berengar (d.1088), the canon of Tours, who, in the middle of the eleventh century, made himself heard by the whole theological world of his day, in Rome as much as in his own diocese.[17] The former belonged to the generations which knew and, in their own way, ensured the Carolingian renaissance whose vigour was soon to be dissipated in the fighting of the tenth century. Above all, like Paschasius Radbertus himself, whose pupil he first was, he belonged to the current of 'monastic theology' which was generally more concerned with spiritual wisdom than with speculation.[18] Berengar, on the other hand, was a pupil of the school of Chartres, one of the intellectual centres where earnest attention was given to harmonizing scripture, the Fathers and the natural sciences;[19] and he already heralded the dialectical, or rather scholastic, theology for which concern with rationality was to be one of the great duties of faith. Nevertheless, the two men, so different in their period and their cultural background, have something in common.

Both, being assiduous readers and, they thought, faithful disciples of Augustine, found the utmost difficulty in accepting, one of them (Berengar) the eucharistic realism, and the other (Ratramnus) the way in which that realism was understood in the circles in which he moved.

Ratramnus' difficulty is hardly surprising. His problem was to determine how the Christ who is present *in heaven* by virtue of his resurrection could be present *also* on our altars without contradicting that resurrection. The whole mystery of the Resurrection seemed to make this impossible: since Christ escapes, through his glory, from *our* space in order to live in *his*, he could in no way be dependent upon ours; and yet, as Ratramnus saw it, eucharistic 'realism' demanded that he should be so dependent. Moreover it seemed unthinkable to Ratramnus that the risen Christ, having become incorruptible in his body, could be identified with elements which the Church uses and which are manifestly sensible and perishable. Since it is impossible, on the other hand, to accept that Christ can enter the Eucharist by any sort of local movement, we can break the deadlock, thought Ratramnus, only by distinguishing a dual body of Christ. One, the body in the strict sense of the word, the *historic*, the *true*, which is now and for ever glorified *in heaven*; and the other, the *sacramental*, body, the body of our eucharists, which the bread and wine *image* for us, and which makes it possible, *on earth*, for us to draw our spiritual nourishment from the Word in faith.[20] Mistaking, no doubt, the thought of the monk of Corbie, Berengar was to regard himself as his emulator.[21] What matters here is the way in which a Radbertus, with whom a Ratramnus disagrees, fundamentally conceived the eucharistic realism, and how he connected it with the Resurrection: for, as we saw with Augustine, the crux lies not so much in the problem as in the solutions proposed.

Paschasius Radbertus: the approach through the realism of the Incarnation

As a good Augustinian, the Abbot of Corbie took the Incarnation as the starting-point for his exposition of the whole mystery of the Eucharist.[22] But while Ratramnus begins his treatise on the body and blood of the Lord by a definition of the sacrament which distinguishes between image and reality, so ranging the sacrament with image,[23] Paschasius Radbertus sees in the sacrament 'everything that is given to us in a divine celebration as a warrant of salvation'.[24] Whereas for Ratramnus the sensible is primarily a 'veil' which makes it necessary always to keep the wholly external corporeal separate from the purely hidden spiritual,[25] the consecrated bread and wine are for Radbertus that which contains in itself the very *reality*.[26] 'The birth of Christ', he writes, 'and the whole economy of his humanity are for us a great sacrament, since in those things which man can see, God's majesty, enclosed in them for our sanctification, gave invisible reality, through God's own power, to things at which man could not even guess. That God made himself man, it has been rightly said, is a mystery or a sacrament.'[27] In consequence, what gave living richness to the faith of Augustine and of his Spanish successor, Isidore of Seville,[28] on whom the Abbot of Corbie directly depends, is not watered down into an anaemic 'symbolism' but is further enriched. 'It is the whole man,' he writes, 'made up of a double element, who is redeemed and so fed by the flesh and by the blood of Christ. It is not, as some would have it, only the soul that is nourished by this mystery, since it was not only the soul that was redeemed and saved by the death of Christ; our flesh, too, is introduced to immortality and incorruptibility by this mystery. The flesh of Christ, spiritually embowelled in ours, takes on a transforming power, so that the substance of Christ may be in our flesh just as he undoubtedly took our substance into his divinity.'[29]

Radbertus, therefore, cannot distinguish, as did Ratramnus, a double body of Christ: the historic, the only *true* body, and the sacramental, which in itself is no more than a completely figurative *shadow*! Since the Eucharist is the sacrament which nourishes our life in Christ, this life must exist in the Eucharist: otherwise the Eucharist could not communicate it to us. 'If', explains Radbertus, 'life did not exist in this mystery, then the mystery would no longer be a source of life. Moreover, no food would give eternal life to those who receive it for their salvation unless the life in that food were the life of the living, eternal God; and Jesus Christ tells us that he who does not eat this flesh and drink this blood has not life in him. It *must* then be that this sacrament which confers life, itself possesses what it gives to those who receive it rightly. If life is in this sacrament, the sacrament is the flesh of the true living being, it is the blood in which is, in very truth, to be found the life which exists for ever.'[30] The *certainty*, based on scripture, that the risen Christ nourishes us with his life more than outweighs the difficulties presented by the *representation* of such a presence. In Radbertus the Eucharist found a new Augustine, who overcame every difficulty by the vitality of the mystery which inspired him.

When Ratramnus said that it was strictly impossible for the bread and wine to *be* the body and blood of the Lord himself, because of the incorruptibility of the Resurrection, Radbertus answered that this difficulty cannot outweigh the faith that makes us profess the presence in the bread and wine of the very life of Christ, given for the salvation of the world. For Radbertus, as for Augustine, systematized *views* must be subordinate to the *life* of faith. That is why, as against propositions put forward by Ratramnus, and before long by Berengar, he can unhesitatingly assert that the Eucharist really gives one single, same, Christ, born of the Virgin, who died, was buried, and rose again; and not merely a shadow of Christ, to which the term *sacramental* is then attached.

The function of the Resurrection

Are we, however, justified in saying that Radbertus has a fully developed doctrine of the Resurrection? In fact it remains for him a purely *affirmed* reality. Snatching Christ away for ever from death, as scripture says,[31] it is the unique source of 'Im-mortality'.[32] Constantly celebrated throughout the ages, it is present in all periods, and dominates them, as he had learnt from Augustine.[33] Thus it makes possible a spiritual sacrifice which truly unites us to the vitalizing flesh of the Word.[34] Moreover, it makes of Christ the pre-eminent grain of corn who, in dying, did not remain alone but became the multitude of believers, with whom he makes but one flesh in the Resurrection. 'So now,' he explains, 'since being dead, he is risen, *he henceforth bears a rich harvest* in believers. And from this harvest one single bread is made, for we are assured that Christ and the Church form but one body.'[35] This is what the Apostle also teaches: one bread making a single body out of many (1 Cor. 10:17), but Radbertus stresses that this power of union which is specific to the Eucharist is the fruit, in the Church, of a death which is integrated in the Resurrection. That is his justification for saying that, fulfilling every image, 'the flesh of Christ has become Eucharist in virtue of the Resurrection.'[36]

We must not, however, exaggerate the importance of this feature, for all its magnificence. It is true that, as opposed to the somewhat divergent view of Ratramnus writing in the cell next door, Radbertus is convinced that the Eucharist does indeed give us the risen Christ in the flesh. What is even more, whereas Ratramnus holds that it is *because* Christ is risen that the Eucharist is only *image*, for he sees heaven as containing the whole reality of the risen *body*, for Radbertus, on the other hand, the Eucharist is truly sacrament only by giving us *also* the risen Christ. Or again, for this contrast between the two touches the heart of the problem, whereas for Ratramnus it is *because there is* Resurrection that there is no Eucharist, for Radbertus it is *in order that there may be* Eucharist that the Resurrection must form part of it. The Eucharist, in fact, is the bread of life only by giving us Christ, unique in all his various states, from conception by the Virgin to glory: *therefore* it always contains the Christ of the Resurrection. Even so, this does not mean that Radbertus has a completely thought-out view of the real Presence. It was with Radbertus in mind that a Cardinal Humbert and a Lanfranc were later to force Berengar to sign a declaration which stated that we eat the Lord *sensualiter*, that is to say as one eats a dish of food. Radbertus, however, clung with his whole soul to what Augustine taught him, that 'we live because of Christ, by eating of him, that is to say by receiving him, he who is the eternal life which we did not possess through ourselves'.[37] Thus Radbertus protects the eucharistic nourishment from the destructive effects produced by the nice distinction between Christ's two bodies, which his fellow-monk was driven to invent. Even so, he left the problem unsolved.

Limitations of Radbertus' eucharistic teaching in relation to Ratramnus

The position is this: when Radbertus asks how it is possible for the Eucharist to extend in this way to the whole of Christ, he never points out in the Resurrection the real reason and principle of the type of presence that Ratramnus contested. He points out to the latter, who, *by virtue of the Resurrection*, denies the presence of *body* as specific to the Eucharist, that the risen Christ *is present* in his body, but he never really answers the precise objection raised by Ratramnus. Ratramnus deprives the Eucharist of all its realism, *precisely in virtue* of a resurrection which must necessarily, he tells us, deprive us of Christ's *body*. Radbertus, rightly and with great profundity, defends eucharistic realism by connecting it with the life that Christ gives us; but even so he does not explain to Ratramnus that it is *the Resurrection itself*, in as much as it affects Christ's very *body*, that makes *possible the presence which Ratramnus denies*. All that Radbertus says is that the Resurrection is present *precisely where* Ratramnus rejects it. He does not really show him that it is *because* the Resurrection is the mystery of the *transfigured body* of Christ that Christ can *in very truth* give himself *thus* in the bread and wine. Even though Radbertus makes Christ the real content of the Eucharist, which thus really gives life, he does not make the body of Christ in his *Eucharist* a particular instance of the body of Christ in his *Resurrection*. This is what needed to be thought out and put into words, if Ratramnus's difficulty was to be overcome. It was, in fact, left unsolved, and two centuries after Ratramnus it was to be restated by Berengar.

What Radbertus failed to do was left undone by his successors; and the philosophical problems of *substance* were to be broached in an attempt to solve the insoluble questions raised by the mystery of the *body*.

BERENGAR AND THE TRANSITION TO CONSIDERATION OF SUBSTANCE

The reappearance in Berengar, less than two centuries after Ratramnus, of the difficulties about the trueness of Christ's body has a special importance for us: it enables us to understand how thought about the Eucharist is in future to be divorced from the mystery of the Resurrection.

In 1059, Berengar was obliged to sign in Rome a declaration in which he agreed that 'it was in a sensible way (*sensualiter*) and not only in a sacramental way' that the body of Christ 'was held in the priests' hands and chewed by the teeth of the faithful'.[38] Berengar denied all personal relation between the risen Christ and the eucharistic elements; and it was on the pretext of 'preserving' the eucharistic realism which was compromised by his line of thought that the passivity of *things* was attributed to Christ. Berengar had no difficulty in showing that since Christ's body was incorruptible, and since, as he put it, it was 'impossible to cut it',[39] the Eucharist could not lead to the 'chewing up' of the risen Christ. Everyone was gradually to agree on this point later.[40] Berengar himself, however, took a false step. In order to be in a better position to sign he opened up lines of analysis that were philosophically open to objection. Making use of the still imperfectly studied notion of 'substance',[41] he denied that the bread and wine could become the body and blood of Christ without having to undergo any change in 'appearance'. The consecration could not operate upon the nature of things, as it was maintained it did, since there was no modification of the sensible elements![42]

In self-defence, Berengar thus found himself involved in a

study of problems that was to move into the order of *metaphysics*. We cannot be sure by whom, but a road was opened along which his opponents were quick to make their way. Quickly acquiring skill in a field in which Berengar had at first shown himself to be incompetent, they gradually came to determine more exactly the relation between substance and accidents. Instead of abandoning ground that had been opened up, they moved in and were quick to build up on the spot a whole metaphysical theory, which was to be precisely that of transubstantiation. As early as the end of the eleventh century, with Guitmond of Aversa, for example, and still more with Alger of Liège, the walls of the new building were well above ground level.[43] Things happened so quickly that Berengar himself, the unfortunate discoverer of his own Waterloo, was obliged, some years before his death, to sign another statement. In this he acknowledged that 'the bread and wine laid upon the altar are changed *substantially* into the true flesh' of Christ; Christ is not in them 'only figuratively and by virtue of the sacrament, but in his own proper nature and his true *substance*'.[44]

With the introduction of such a terminology, eucharistic thought had moved into a new world, even though it was not to be until the Fourth Lateran Council (1215) that the word 'transubstantiation' was publicly adopted by the Roman *magisterium*.[45]

From body to substance: the origin and consequences of a change of orientation

The transition that had just been effected was not so much one from Platonism to Aristotelianism,[46] as from the authority of Augustine to that of Aristotle: or it would perhaps be even more true to say that in *eucharistic expression* a type of language determined by the *fact* of *body* had just been abandoned in favour of another language, which was based on the *notion* of *substance*. And with this a scheme of reference, or 'referent', that belonged to the order of *anthropology* had been abandoned, in order to consider the mystery of the body of Christ in the Eucharist in the light of a referent that belonged to the order of *metaphysics*. It is true, of course, that the word 'substance' was by no means a newcomer in Western eucharistic doctrine. Many years earlier St Ambrose had sanctioned its use to express the real solidity of God's gifts; and the word had remained current.[47] Gradually, however, 'substance' came to mean more than the *reality* of the body or of any other thing, according to its specific nature,[48] and began to be used to denote that state in which a being, *whatever it be*, is deprived of its concrete or individual properties and is reduced to what reflection on the *being as such* decides it can retain of it. In short, 'substance' was by way of becoming abstract thought's cat's-paw. The introduction into the eucharistic field of a word that had been so debased in this *metaphysical evolution* served also to express that *reflection on the body had shown that it was incapable of justifying a eucharistic realism which nevertheless eminently concerned the very body of Christ*. Thus, by a paradox that has been too little noted, in order to preserve more surely the *Corpus Christi*,[49] they abandoned the concept of *body* in favour of the concept of *substance*! The theological deadlock seemed so impossible to break that the followers of Berengar, and Berengar himself,[50] adopted the new word; thereby they unwittingly made it quite plain that if they were to reach theological agreement about the mystery of the body they should be careful not to mention the body: a strange and most embarrassing situation which derived directly from Augustine.

Strongly combating the error of those who, unable to accept Christ's teaching at Capernaum (John 6:52), conceived the Eucharist in a completely 'carnal' way, and at the same time equally governed by limitations of his culture, St Augustine had insisted emphatically on the necessity of understanding the Eucharist in a *spiritual* way.[51] Here, in his view, his Neoplatonism coincided with the Gospel. Later, and particularly under the influence of John Scotus Erigena, Augustine's *spiritualism* in the eucharistic field was without qualification identified with an *intellectualism* that derived in fact from Plotinus.[52] As a result the series, traditional in eucharistic doctrine, which linked invisible, intelligible and spiritual[53] became suspect. So Berengar, for example, by stressing the purely 'intelligible' character of Christ's body in the Eucharist, thereby compromised its 'trueness'.[54] On the other hand he was faced by men who in order better, they thought, to express the *real* character of this body, seemed to *reduce* it (as we have seen) to the *sensible* which makes it apparent to us. They sailed between Scylla and Charybdis! To avoid a *physicism* of the eucharistic body, evidently incompatible with the risen Christ, they invoked an *intelligible* body which wiped out the mystery of the body proper to this sacrament. And, a crowning misfortune, the defenders of eucharistic realism were suspicious of the adjective 'spiritual', typical though it is of the somatic realism of the Resurrection (1 Cor. 15:45): quite without warrant, they interpreted it in the sense of 'incorporeal', and so regarded it as dangerous.[55] Thus they deprived themselves of the words best adapted to expressing satisfactorily the reality of the eucharistic *body*.

No doubt the mention of the glory of Christ in the declaration forced upon Berengar[56] showed in its own way that the *identity of the historical body of Christ with the eucharistic body* passed through *the discontinuity of the Resurrection*. They would have done well to develop the full significance of that statement; for they would then have seen that *only* the Resurrection could explain such a diversity of *mysteries* in the unity of one and the same body. It is the Resurrection that obliges us to call *identical*, and yet *different*, the body which is born of the Virgin, which suffers, which dies on the cross, which rises again in glory, and which is given to us in the eucharistic meal. However, in the polemical use which Ratramnus and Berengar made of it, the Resurrection was regarded rather as an obstacle to eucharistic realism than as its foundation. Their view ultimately prevailed even among those who, in their defence of realism, failed to invoke the Resurrection, and so lost their most powerful argument. It was thus, to my mind, that the *divorce* between the two mysteries became inevitable and gradually was made absolute: *no longer would the paradox of Christ's eucharistic body be wedded to the paradox of his resurrection*.

Was there anyone, moreover, who was still sufficiently receptive of the light which sound thinking would have thrown on Christ's corporeal condition to see that the mystery which was used to *deny* the real presence was the true principle which made it possible to *affirm* it? For all Berengar's opponents, and all those who followed in their wake, the eucharistic realism which was *affirmed* in terms of *body* was to be *intellectually conceived* in terms of *substance*. Anthropological in its implications (since the point at issue was a type of presence which relates to Christ's very *body*), the Eucharist was to be *metaphysical* in its explanations. Paradoxically, consideration of the properties of *substance* was in future to be regarded as alone capable of accounting for a presence which nevertheless derives in its entirety, in Christ, from the mystery of his *body*.

Since the theologian, in order to explain what was held by faith, was obliged to enter into a new system of reference that was strange to him, he felt that he had also to justify the move and vindicate the legitimacy of the transposition. The inevitable consequence was, as has been aptly observed, that 'defending dogma took the place of understanding faith';[57] 'the mystery to be understood gave way to the miracle to be believed';[58] this entailed 'a devaluing of the symbol',[59] as a result of which 'the point of view of efficience' predominates, and 'the point of view of significance'[60] gradually fades into the background. What is more, concern with the *how*, encouraged by the resources of a metaphysics inherited from Aristotle, was more and more (apart from occasional exceptions that should be noted[61]) to oust the scriptural and patristic approach to the relation between Christ and the Church in Body and Spirit – and it is not difficult to see how that happened.

The unity of Christ and the Church rests essentially on the mystery of the *body*, as is unmistakably evident in St Paul. When, however, in order to justify eucharistic realism theological thought moves into the context of substance, it abandons, without realizing it, a field of meanings within which there had formerly been no difficulty in moving, either from Christ to the Church or from the Church to Christ, inside the unity of the mystery of the Body. Since the category of substance lacked that assistance, theologians who took it as their starting-point were, not indeed to deny, but almost unwittingly to neglect the *conjugal* unity of Christ and Church. The expression *mystical Body*, gradually transferred from the Eucharist to the Church, was to be equally unsuccessful in safeguarding the ecclesiology of the time from a social juridicism:[62] only the Eucharist, expressed in language of union, could have been such a safeguard. But such a symbiosis of Eucharist and Church is fully realizable on the plane of thought only if the living economy of the mystery is not theologically eclipsed by the technical equipment used to think it out. That condition was not fulfilled.

Preponderance of the metaphysical point of view
in the scholastic analysis of the mystery

For minds eager to discover a natural order which ensured for man the consistency that their faith also demanded the way of thinking that was slowly perfected in the Schools seemed to the Middle Ages to offer the historic solidity of a 'world'. A new way of feeling and seeing, and most of all of thinking, gradually achieved complete dominance, although no one, maybe, really wished this to happen or fully understood what was happening. However that may be, this way of thinking contributed an intellectual sense of security which has left its mark on the work of St Thomas. Looked at from the precise angle which concerns us here, eucharistic faith, after a critical period that had lasted for four centuries, seemed to have settled down peacefully again. The intellectual system, then both vigorous and popular, was giving it a calm and precious intelligibility. Considered in terms of *substance*, the real presence, which set the seal on adherence to the faith, set the seal, too, on this way of integrating the universe in a general metaphysics of being, characteristic in more than one way of medieval thought.

'Change, mutation, and transubstantiation are three different things,' wrote, towards the end of the eleventh century, a man who was enamoured of this apprehension of being in widely separated degrees, which the mind of the time was finding to its taste. 'The first', he continues, 'relates to properties, the second to forms, and the third to a transformation of the reality itself'.[63] The Eucharist, therefore, was included in the order of wonderful effects that proclaim the glory of the First Cause. Although it is indeed Christ and his word which lies at the origin of this so profound mutation of things,[64] it is *as God* that he so lies. It is only in virtue of this that he can dispose of the infinite power required for taking so astonishing a liberty with the world, and instantaneously effect a change of substance which reveals the sovereign dominance of God himself in the obedient chorus of purely natural causes. For an Aquinas, whose *vision* we are more concerned here to draw attention to rather than give a technical analysis of his *system*, what dominates the *eucharistic mystery* is the *miracle*, and the limitless resources of pure Act. Is not God, in fact, the only Agent who does not contain his own boundaries?[65] He alone, then, also has the power to effect a *conversion* of substance, which operates upon the very nature of being, and enables him to give himself supremely to men, who, through him, are regrouped in the Church.[66]

'It is only in the Church', Bossuet was later to write, faithfully echoing the teaching of the Schools, 'that God is known

as he wishes to be known. We never have full knowledge either
of his essence or his attributes, unless we attain it in all the means
through which he wished us to discover them. For example, if
we are fully to know his *omnipotence*, we must do so in the
miracles through which he manifests himself, and believe the
miracle of the *Eucharist* as readily as that of the *Incarnation*.'[67]
The relationship lies not so much between the miracles themselves as between each miracle and God's power.

The movement towards nominalism

It could, nevertheless, be urged that to explain the things of
faith in this way is to weaken the very foundation on which we
seek to build. Did not this very Omnipotence involve itself freely
and 'once and for all' in an economy of love in which the various
marvels each, in some way, call for the others? The most important thing, then, is surely not so much this Omnipotence which,
after all, may be taken for granted, as the economy of love whose
centre and heart is Christ. Yet there is no denying that a
primarily metaphysical way of envisaging the mystery of God
may well insert into the instantaneousness of pure Act something
that exists only within a plan of salvation and a history of grace.
The temptation to interpret the Christian mystery solely under
the metaphysical aspect of God's powers is so great that
St Thomas himself goes so far as to affirm the *possibility* of a
number of incarnations, on the strength of the *metaphysically*
indisputable principle that the created cannot measure the un-
created![68] And, indeed, arguing from *absolute power*, in other
words considering only the limitless ontological resources of the
supreme Being, there would be nothing against God's having
been incarnate on a number of occasions! The only obstacle, but
that an insurmountable one, is, in St Paul's words, 'the plan
[economy] of the mystery hidden for ages in God who created
all things' (Eph. 3:9). In the light of the real evidence of *faith*
and not merely of the theoretical structures of being, the
Incarnation is seen to be so strictly *unique* that it rules out any
multiplication of Christ as an inconceivable anomaly.

Nevertheless, the intoxication of a purely metaphysical thought
which relativizes what should dominate it was to become almost
the normal condition of a theology in which nominalism becomes
rife.[69] These theologians arbitrarily took God's omnipotence,
considered in the pure state, that is, outside all supernatural

economy and all created structure, and used it as ultimate argument; and in consequence, they were to indulge in all the types of hypotheses that combination of disparate elements, they thought, made possible.

With any number of theologians of this period, particularly of the Franciscan school, we may speak of 'a sort of conceptual atomism, which breaks down reality into as many independent fragments as the mind forms concepts in order to represent it to itself, and then builds them up again into countless new combinations'.[70] The only rule in this jigsaw puzzle is that you must never contradict yourself: a rule that in any case is infinitely flexible. Since the power of God vastly exceeds the limits we recognize in him, can we ever tell how the road to contradiction runs? Can we map it for God as we think we should map it for men? 'From this results a universe which, contrary to the etymology of the word, seems potentially at least dislocated, broken down to dust, the beings of which it is formed being no more than artificial constructions dependent on the whim of their Creator.'[71] To achieve this, thought, if we may still so describe it, follows a scorched-earth policy and unhesitatingly tears down anything that has been built up earlier either into affirmation or negation. There is no affirmation which is not destroyed by its own contrary. There is no earlier negation which cannot or must not in turn be changed into pure affirmation. Nothing can resist this inverting force which only, and which alone, appears to be a true definition of reason. Thus, it can no longer 'be proved that God is exempt from all magnitude and all accident', that he is or is not corruptible, nor that he is 'infinite in intensity'.[72]

On all these elementary points our only certainty will come solely from faith, which itself, moreover, is reduced to blind submission to the authority of the Church. Her decisions alone enjoy the right to stabilize an intellectual uncertainty which otherwise could be absolute. Later, science was to benefit from this anti-metaphysical positivism and this spirit of analysis;[73] but in those days, fideism had taken up its abode in theology, before a complete human scepticism was to come as a quick reply to divine whim.[74]

The whole of theology, even so, was not carried away on this tide. St Thomas's successors stood out against these excesses and to some degree countered them;[75] but they were unable to prevent them from emerging, nor could they check their duration and extension. One of the great German teachers of the end of the fifteenth century was Gabriel Biel. He taught a completely nominalist theology in Tübingen. When Biel died in 1495, Luther was over ten years old and would soon be starting his studies at Erfurt, where Biel's thought was still dominant. It was from this nominalism, to which he was still indebted, that Luther was to determine to extricate himself.[76]

Uncertainty in eucharistic theology

In such a climate of thought, earlier theological convictions concerning transubstantiation were not to remain unshaken. It was Duns Scotus, the famous 'clerke of Oxenford', the infant prodigy of the Franciscan order, who, at the beginning of the fourteenth century, set the ball rolling. Transubstantiation, he said, contradicting all the recent great teachers, is supported neither by scripture nor by reason. The Church has been teach-it, it is true, ever since the Fourth Lateran Council:[77] and we must therefore accept it, but only for the sake of conformity. In itself, it has no claim to our assent. Indeed, since the true Principle of all things is solely the divine Power, how can *con*substantiation, which allows the substance of the bread to co-exist with that of the body, be less acceptable than *tran*substantiation, which effects the conversion of the former into the latter, or than *annihilation*, which suppresses the substance of the bread;[78] balancing miracle against miracle, which do you prefer?

Many thinkers, disturbed by an uncertainty whose elements we have just been describing, did not find a satisfactory answer until the Council of Trent; and that, moreover, failed to win the assent of the recently formed Protestant world. It was in that world that problems which might have been thought to be forgotten were to come to life again. Their reappearance, which was only apparently unexpected, had a profound significance, which we must try to explain.

Luther: a symptomatic mistake

Luther's mistake, which we must now consider, was not primarily his scornful[79] rejection of transubstantiation, but the way in which he believed he could justify consubstantiation by an analogy with the hypostatic union. Just as Christ, he tells us, assumed humanity and divinity in the oneness of his person, without destroying the one by the other, so in the Eucharist he makes the substance of bread 'co-exist' with the reality of his body, without reducing the former to the identity of the latter.[80] It is an attractive point of view that some Catholics have recently[81] readopted; but it is inaccurate.

The hypostatic union ('hypostasis' means 'person') expresses in fact that the humanity of Jesus is that of the Son of God *himself*; it denotes the *personal* existence of the Son in the flesh. Since there is only one Christ, there is only one hypostatic union. Were there another, it would be a new Christ. This hypothesis, which is contrary to scripture, is completely useless here; for the Eucharist knows no new existence of Christ, but is a modality of the only existence Christ has. When Christ instituted the Eucharist he did not mean us to understand: 'Here is *another* body' or 'Here is the body of *another person*'; he simply said, 'Here is *my* body, here is the cup of *my* blood.' That is why the hypostatic union, which enables us to speak of Jesus as Son of God in his history, his cross and his resurrection, also enables us to say this of him in his eucharist, which is also part of his person. That Christ in fact appropriates elements of our world and makes them into his body and blood does not mean that he *emerges* from himself and introduces elements that are alien to him. The facts are much more simple and profound.

In virtue of the Resurrection, which enthrones Christ in 'the power which enables him even to subject all things to himself' (Phil. 3:21), the elements which Christ appropriates in our eucharists are not something alien to him. On the contrary, as we have already seen and shall be seeing again, the world, our world, forms an integral part of Christ in a way which is still hidden and potential, but at the same time perfectly real. In consequence, Christ has no need of a new hypostatic union in order to make elements of our world really to pass into the unmistakably affirmed identity of his own person ('it is *my* body, *my* blood') – to introduce them so in the course of our history too, which is what happens in every single eucharist. It is sufficient for him – but this 'sufficiency' presupposes in fact his whole mystery – to exercise his power as Lord for that to be true of this bread and this wine which he tells us is already true in relation to the sovereign and hidden profundities of his resurrection.

Luther was therefore mistaken if he thought that he could justify consubstantiation by an analogy with the hypostatic union; and to adopt the same analogy, even in defence of transubstantiation, is to share his mistake. The relation of the bread and wine to the body and blood of the Lord derives from the relation of this world to the risen Christ, and depends entirely on the mystery of his body. The Eucharist does not entail any 'other' hypostatic union, but simply reveals the unplumbed depths of the one unique hypostatic union. Nevertheless Luther had the great merit, we believe, of having thus, even mistakenly, sought to reintroduce a study of the *problems of incarnation*. In this way he made it clear that, going beyond the word 'substance', or at least in order to understand it, we must get back to the mystery of the *body*, which theologians had pushed aside. This reunion of Christology and transubstantiation was so natural that it seemed, briefly, to demand the attention of the Fathers of Trent: they felt that they could not afford to discuss it – and this we can understand.[82]

With the view that Luther put forward, in fact, many unsolved problems of earlier times were once again coming to the surface! Once again, too, the lack of anthropology that could express the *essential relation of body to person* was most painfully apparent. In his desire to restore to eucharistic theology a truly Christological centre of gravity, Luther thought it necessary to *duplicate* for the bread and wine the personal mystery of Christ, whereas an *extension* of its effects would have sufficed. Luther accordingly thought that the eucharistic elements enjoyed, *in a separated state*, a union which affects them in an *integrated state* in the unique mystery of Christ and his glorified body. The *conversion* of the elements derives in him from the fact that the universe is incorporated in the expression of his person.

CALVIN'S POINT OF VIEW

No more than Luther did Calvin accept 'this fantastic transubstantiation, for which the Papists fight today more fiercely than for all the other articles of their faith'.[83] This did not mean, however, that he accepted the consubstantiation that Luther wished to impose. In his anxiety to re-establish continuity with the real Augustine,[84] Calvin urged a dynamic concept of the real

Presence, which aimed at restoring to the Holy Spirit a place that was, indeed, essential, but which was equally dominated by the questions that the West had failed to solve.[85]

'Since we have no doubt', writes Calvin in connection with the body of the risen Christ, 'but that it has its own proper *measure*' (our italics) 'as required by the *nature* of a human body, and that it is *contained in heaven*, into which he has been received until he shall come to the judgement, so too we hold that it is wrong to *degrade* him into the corruptible elements or imagine that he is present in all things.'[86] This is precisely Augustine's *aporia* (difficulty) in connection with the body of the risen Christ. Augustine, it is true, did not envisage the hypothesis of a *presence* that would locate Christ *in* the sensible element; in his view, the glorified Christ could be present only *in heaven*, and we should not try to detach him from that area on the ground of the immensity that pertains to his divine nature.[87] Calvin is in full agreement with Augustine. He reaches his agreement, however, by starting from a problem of *real Presence* with which Augustine was not concerned, but which the Genevan broached in the same terms as the Bishop of Hippo. A eucharistic presence confined to the sensible elements alone, or a cosmic presence of immensity: such, in truth, was the question that Calvin sought to answer. Neither of these modalities, one because it was too small, and the other because it was too diffuse, could be appropriate to the person who, in virtue of his resurrection, henceforth dwells in the heavens and in the heavens alone! Relying on the authority of Augustine, whom he quotes, Calvin had no hesitation in solving this difficulty. He continues, 'Jesus Christ, being but one, is God and man in his person. Inasmuch as he is God, he is *in all things*; inasmuch as he is man, he is in *heaven*.'[88] A little later, and still faithful to St Augustine, on whom he is commenting, he adds, 'For he says that the Son of God, being also man, is present in all things – is present, indeed, in his entirety; that, inasmuch as he is God, he dwells in the Temple of God, that is to say the Church; and nevertheless that he is in heaven *as man*, because a *true body must have its own proper measure*.'[89]

The Resurrection, then, did not detach Christ from the naturality of place, since he is still *contained* in space. He cannot be *here* in his body, being now and henceforth *in heaven*, in virtue of this same body, now glorified. Indeed, how could glory remove from Christ the spatial character that defines the body?

St Augustine, whom Calvin again quotes, says quite clearly, 'God, who gave him immortality, did not remove from him his *nature*.'[90] Even if Calvin's 'main concern', which made him reject the ubiquity of Christ which Luther professed, is 'to preserve the full humanity of the glorified Christ',[91] it is nevertheless true that the view of the *body* underlying this concern is completely spatialized, and that it inevitably implies *local circumscription* of Christ's glory. Thus, there had been no real progress since Augustine; the theory of substance had proved useless; and, centuries after Ratramnus and Berengar, Calvin came up against the same obstacle as they had met. How slowly, indeed, do fundamental problems evolve in history! Nevertheless Calvin's genius lay in this, that he was to restore to the Holy Spirit a role about which, *in the eucharistic field*, the West had long been silent.

In place of a real presence, necessarily conceived in a *local way*, which is therefore unacceptable because of Christ's glorious place *in heaven*, the Spirit makes it possible to conceive a dynamic presence which does not compromise the space of Glory. The Spirit, Calvin tells us, is 'as a channel or conduit through which all that Christ is and possesses flows down to us. For if we can see with our own eyes that when the sun shines on the earth it in some way transmits its substance by its rays, and so produces, feeds and causes to grow the fruits of this earth, why should the blaze and radiance of the Spirit of Jesus Christ have less power to communicate to us his flesh and blood?'[92] The Holy Spirit, then, has been given the task of filling this *imaginary gap* between Christ and his Eucharist, opened up by the insurmountable naturality which, unwittingly, we attach to the Body of the Resurrection. This is the weak point in a doctrine whose value we shall be noting.

The Holy Spirit, in fact, is not at hand to solve a 'problem' that has no real existence. As we know, in his resurrection Christ transcends the dependence on nature, in the passively spatialized form which is still our own, without thereby losing an *essential relation to this world* which, in the life he gives to us, constitutes the glorious mystery of his body. It is true, no doubt, that it is in the infinite power of the Spirit (as we have seen[93]) that this radical inversion of direction is possible which defines, in relation to this world, the resurrection of Christ. At the same time, we should not look on the Holy Spirit as a substitute for the glorified Christ in the latter's alleged incapacities in relation to space. While it is, therefore, apt that Christ should depart in order to send us the Holy Spirit (John 16:7), it is by virtue of his own mystery and power that he will henceforth 'draw all men to himself' (John 12:32). The Holy Spirit whom he sends to us from the Father (John 15:26) is not, in relation to Christ's glory, a sign of lack but of fulfilment: he bears witness that Christ's glory is truly accomplished and that 'descended from David according to the flesh' he is truly 'designated Son of God' (Rom. 1:4). The Holy Spirit is far from being a happily chosen device that enables us to cross a spatial gulf opened up between Christ and ourselves by a deceptively representational imagery. There is, indeed, a gap between Christ and ourselves, but it does not belong to the order of space: it lies in the order of parousia and freedom. Similarly the function of the Holy Spirit in the eucharistic mystery has a depth other than that of filling a completely imaginary void. Eastern tradition will help us to analyse that function more exactly.

Calvin's real merit, at a time when the Holy Spirit was, as we have already said, theologically forgotten *in the eucharistic field*, was precisely that *he thought of mentioning him*. Luther, with his mistaken analogy of the hypostatic union, makes us look again at the completely traditional relation of Eucharist and Incarnation; similarly Calvin, by his disputable view of the function of the Spirit in the eucharistic presence, presented in terms of a *spatial* problem that does not exist, reminds us of the forgotten function of the Spirit in the eucharistic mystery. Coming up, as did Augustine, against the unsolved problem of the Body, but refusing even so to imprison himself, as did the medieval theologians, in the *sole* problem of substance, he thereby, in fact, rediscovered the irreplaceable function of the Spirit. He therefore obliges us to look at the theology of the East with a fresh eye. The East never forgot the role of the Spirit in eucharistic thinking which remained closer than ours to liturgical sources, and we must turn to it to understand how the Eucharist, which concerns the *Body* of the risen Christ, cannot be an object of theological speculation apart from the *Spirit* of the Resurrection.

CHAPTER 3

A misunderstanding corrected

The function of the Spirit in the eucharistic mystery,
and the problem of the epiclesis
The difficult problems that have arisen between East and West
in connection with the eucharistic epiclesis are less serious, I
believe, than those which the West has created for itself in
connection with the Presence. Indeed, it is commonly said, both
among Catholics[1] and among Orthodox[2], at least in the West,
that the problem of the epiclesis is not primarily eucharistic; it
relates to the Church and the Trinity, and in its exclusively
eucharistic form, it has ceased to be of importance. This I believe
to be true, but only subject to this condition, that we never
forget what is at stake in the epiclesis: and that is the irreplaceable function of the Spirit in the eucharistic mystery. The
purpose of this short chapter is to re-emphasize this, and to
serve as an introduction to a real synthesis of Eucharist and
Resurrection, which will be treated at greater length in part three.

DEFINITION OF THE EUCHARISTIC EPICLESIS

In itself, the word 'epiclesis' has no directly eucharistic connota-
tion. It is a Greek word meaning 'invocation'. It is used in the
New Testament to express the nature of salvation, and is based
on a passage in the Old Testament which foretells the outpouring
of the Spirit: 'All *who call upon* the name of [Yahweh] shall
be delivered' (Joel 2:32). In his first address St Peter announces
that this prophecy has now been fulfilled: the gift of the Holy
Spirit enables us to *call upon* Jesus as Christ and Saviour (cf.
Acts 2:21 and 1 Cor. 12:3). This invocation of Jesus in the
Spirit is therefore specific to Christians, and they may be
identified by it. St Paul reminds the faithful of Corinth that what
defines them is their being in communion with all those who
'in every place *call on* the name of Our Lord Jesus Christ' (1 Cor.
1:2). Since the supreme invocation in the Church is the Lord's

Eucharist, the name 'epiclesis' attaches to the latter. Finally, in the eucharistic prayer itself, the epiclesis comes to denote *the particular invocation which is to sanctify the offerings, that so they may become the body and blood of the Lord.*

The reform of the liturgy has given us a new familiarity with such an invocation. Either before or after the consecration, the words of the liturgy direct our hearts towards the Holy Spirit, so that we may ask him to bless both our offerings and ourselves.

> Hallow these offerings,
>   pouring over them your Spirit;
> that they may become for us
>   the body and blood
>   of Jesus Christ Our Lord.

Or again:

> That our life may be no more our own,
>   but his who died and rose again for us,
> he sent from you,
>   as the first gift made to believers,
> the Spirit which forwards his work in the world
>   and fulfils all sanctification.
> May this same Spirit
>   we pray thee, Lord,
>   sanctify these offerings:
> That so they may become
>   the body and blood of your Son
> in the celebration of this great mystery
>   which he himself bequeathed to us
>   as a sign of the eternal Covenant.

In each case, the words of Institution then follow: with the time to remember so firmly brought to our minds, we again pray that we may obtain the Spirit.

> We humbly pray you [runs the first of the three forms]
>   that participating in the body and blood of Christ
>   we may be brought together
>   by the Holy Spirit
>   into one body.

The third type of prayer contains the same request, while the second sets out still more plainly the nature of the spiritual benefits we expect.

> Look upon the sacrifice of your Church, O Lord,
>   and deign to recognize in it that of your Son
>   who restored us to your Covenant;
> when we have been nourished by his body and his blood
>   and filled by the Holy Spirit,
> grant to us to be a single body and a single spirit
>   in Christ.
> May the Holy Spirit make of us
>   an eternal offering to your glory,
> so that one day we may obtain
>   the blessed things of the world to come,
> in company with the Virgin Mary, the blessed Mother of God,
>   with the Apostles, the martyrs,
>   and all the saints
>   who never cease to intercede for us.

The intention behind this was to detach the Eucharist of the Latin Church from a certain hesitancy in relation to the Holy Spirit; it is now a very long time since it put up this barrier of reserve, for it is generally accepted that the playing down of the epiclesis dates back to the fifth century.[3] It is true, of course, that in the Latin rite the eucharistic *consecration* has never dispensed with prayer specifically addressed to the Holy Spirit, and so with epiclesis in the wide sense of the word. The offertory has always included magnificent prayers to the Spirit as sanctifier, which Jungmann suggests may be regarded as 'epiclesis-formulas'.[4] It has even been asked whether the Roman Mass does not have an epiclesis in the more characteristically Eastern sense of the word.[5] Nevertheless, it remains true that the Latin eucharistic liturgy in general, and that of consecration in particular, cannot show any considerable development of the prayer to the Holy Spirit. Here Vatican II, far from regarding this as an advantage to be retained, put an end to a factual situation which both gave offence in the East and impoverished the prayer of Western Christians.[6]

THE BURDEN OF HERESY, CONTROVERSY
AND DIVISION

Having to combat, just as did the East, two sorts of errors, one which *exalted* the Father at the expense of the Son and the Spirit,[7] and the other which *degraded* the Son to the point of denying his divinity,[8] the West preferred to emphasize what it called the *community* of action of the three Persons in their relation to the world. It thus expressed its refusal to divide the Father, the Son and the Holy Spirit – all three equally God! – but it encountered the danger of obscuring the role proper to each Person, and in particular that of the Holy Spirit, both in the sacraments in general and in the Eucharist in particular. Elsewhere other Christians, in North Africa – the Donatists, as they were called after their leader Donatus (d.355) – prided themselves on being alone in enjoying the presence of the Holy Spirit and therefore refused to recognize the validity of baptism conferred outside their community. As a result of this, there came to be more emphasis laid in theology, and particularly in the procedure that was designed to correct the Donatist error, on the *institutionally qualified* role of the minister rather than on the *mystically irreplaceable role of the Spirit.*[9] This made it all the more illogical that this same West, already in danger of giving its sacramental theology a juridical bias, should introduce the *Filioque* clause into the *Credo* – to the great scandal of the East.[10] So far as the Eucharist is concerned, one thing is at any rate certain: 'With the dawn of Scholasticism in the West, the old concept of a role proper to the Holy Spirit effecting in the communicant the work of sanctification for which the body and blood of Christ are given as nourishment began to fade into the background.'[11]

Meanwhile Orthodox Christians were evolving in a completely different spiritual world. For them, the action of the Holy Spirit remained a basic datum. In consequence, and under the converging influences of liturgical life and theological thought, a doctrine was elaborated which East and West were one day to be able to regard as a cause for a rupture that nothing could heal. Originally *implied* rather than *formally stated*, this doctrine, which concerns the role of the Holy Spirit in the Eucharist, was seen in the East as dramatically self-evident. Thus St John

Damascene (d.749) – a doctor much respected in the ancient Christian East – takes it for granted in discussing an apparently trifling problem of terminology. The liturgy known as that of St Basil (d.379) uses the word 'antitype' to express, as distinct from 'type', the relation between a shadow and the reality. In the liturgy in question, as it happens, the meaning of the two words is practically indistinguishable,[12] and both seem to denote the body of Christ within the sacrament, as distinct from his glorified state. St John Damascene, translating 'antitype' by 'figure' to contrast it with *body*, thinks that the term 'antitype' is *deliberately* restricted by the liturgy of St Basil to the moment *before* the consecration, and that it thus enables us to appreciate the real action of the Holy Spirit in the epiclesis which *follows* the consecration. Thus for St John Damascene the 'post-consecratory' epiclesis, as we would call it in the West, causes the sensible elements, which before were only *figures*, to pass into the *reality*, properly so-called, of the *body* of Christ:[13] a semantically mistaken interpretation which nevertheless brings out a *theological* axiom, relating to the role of the Spirit in the eucharistic consecration, which is unknown in the West.

Weak though this argument may appear, it was to provide an answer in the East to those who, about the same time, wished to condemn the use of images in the Church. The *iconoclasts*, as they were called, or image-breakers, held that the *only* legitimate representation of Christ was the Eucharist, which St Basil, as we have just seen, said was the *antitype* or *figure* of the body of Christ. Following St John Damascene, the defenders of images could answer these purists by saying that the Eucharist was not merely the *figure* of Christ but his very *reality*. Therefore, if St Basil indeed calls the Eucharist the 'figure' of Christ, he does so *before* the epiclesis is said, and not *after*![14] And this proves, if not that the epiclesis *is* the actual consecration, at least that it is *essential* to the consecration, since *to this extent* it modifies the eucharistic words relating to the offerings! This is where the difficulty lies. From the Western point of view, in fact, *the epiclesis to the Spirit has become completely subordinate to the words of the anamnesis, which are in themselves sufficient for the consecration of the Eucharist* (the anamnesis or recalling being here the account of the institution of the Supper).

Suggestive though the disagreement is, it is surely of little moment. In any case it went unnoticed for a long time. It was not mentioned, apparently, at the time of the schism of 1054; nor was it at the reunion Council held at Lyons in 1274. It was only with the fourteenth century that any problem arose, Latin missionaries having discovered the then centuries-old usage of the 'Greeks'. Western attacks on the Eastern view produced a stiffening of opinion on the other side. Some of the Easterners even went so far as to distort their own teaching, by denying all consecratory power to the anamnesis.[15] The whole affair seemed to be peacefully settled at the Council of Florence. On 5 July 1439, the Greeks, it would appear, solemnly accepted the consecratory value of the anamnesis: a thing they had, in fact, always done. The Council embodied this result in its *Decree to the Armenians*, where the 'form', that is the fundamental act which 'makes' the Eucharist, is identified, we are told, with the Words of Institution.[16] Byzantium, however, never accepted the validity of the Florence declarations. And the fall of the ancient city, captured by the Turks in 1453, temporarily muffled the echo of these quarrels, which we must now consider from a new point of view.

The real problem of the eucharistic epiclesis does not in fact centre upon the question, itself of secondary importance, of the moment of consecration. What matters is the role we attribute to the Holy Spirit in the effecting of that consecration. When a 'Latin' wishes to understand this, he has to get over the first shock of surprise at the existence of an *epiclesis of* consecration occurring in the Eastern liturgy *after* 'our' anamnesis.

THE SUPPOSED THREAT TO THE
PRINCIPLE OF CONSECRATION

'We offer you this spiritual and unbloody worship,' says the liturgy of St John Chrysostom, 'and we call upon you, pray you, beseech you, to send your Holy Spirit upon us and upon these gifts presented, and to make this bread the precious body of your Christ, *changing*[17] *it by your Holy Spirit*, and (to make of) what is in this cup the precious blood of your Christ, *changing it by your Holy Spirit*, so that they may be for those who partake of them, for the temperance of the soul, the remission of sins, the communication of your Holy Spirit, the fullness of the Kingdom, free access to you, and not judgement or condemnation.[218] In the liturgy of St Basil we find the same epiclesis and the same formulas asking, *after the anamnesis*, that the bread and wine be *changed* by the *Holy Spirit* into the body and blood of Christ.[19] It was this that was for long a stumbling-block to some in the West. Surely, they said, these liturgies, so venerated all over the East, assumed that the *Words of Institution did not, by themselves alone, produce the Eucharist*. The fact was, as St John Damascene, among others, explained without any difficulty, that the Holy Spirit cannot play a less decisive part here in the Eucharist than he did in the Virgin's conception, because the Eucharist, too, really gives us the body and blood of the Lord.[20] This was profound doctrine, but it seemed to remove the very *principle* of the eucharistic consecration from the anamnesis to the epiclesis.

The 'Latin' answer

Generally speaking, the Latins had two answers to this difficulty: the first was that the *epiclesis is a complementary consecratory form*, which relates to the 'sacramental *phenomenon*' without operating upon its substance;[21] the second, that since men cannot say everything at the same time, *the liturgy expresses in the later, things that were already true in the earlier*.[22] To this they added that in this way the Eucharist is more clearly included in the Trinitarian economy. If the eucharistic prayer is understood in this way, we can distinguish a prayer to the Father up to the *Sanctus*, a prayer to the Son up to the *anamnesis*, and a prayer to the Holy Spirit up to the *communion*. There is something to be said for this argument, and some present-day Orthodox accept it.[23] Even so, the Latin has still another difficulty to solve. If, *before* the consecration, we pray to the Holy Spirit to effect it, why should we ask him to do so a *second time, as though our prayer had not already been granted*? For there is no doubt about the *fact* that, *after the recital of the Words of Institution*, the East introduces a consecratory epiclesis which seems to deny all efficacy to the earlier epiclesis, which should *logically* be sufficient. Here, however, we are moving in a world far removed from the mere logic of ideas! We are in a complex movement which derives from the *affectivity of faith*.

A more 'Eastern' answer to the difficulty

The clearer our appreciation of the true grandeurs of the liturgical mystery, the more inevitably we are carried away by wonder and rapture. The Eucharist is quite plainly and literally the body and blood of the Lord, given to his Church, that she may be nourished by them and transfigured in them. This means that we must necessarily exclude from such a mystery every agent except the Holy Spirit himself. If it is truly the *body* of Christ which is thus *produced*, how could such an *artefact* derive, in the Church, from any power other than that of the Spirit: the Spirit, through whom Christ was first *conceived* in the Virgin's womb? And since to acknowledge the Spirit is to invoke him, there must be an epiclesis at this point. Even if there has *already been one epiclesis*, directed towards our participation in the spiritual *effects* we have in mind, and of which we shall have more to say later,[24] there must still be *another*: but this latter, going back from the effects obtained to the cause which produces them, will say, and repeat, that all we have here is a *pure and simple* gift from the Spirit.

Thus the epiclesis of consecration, coming after the anamnesis, will be the way in which faith expresses – in a rhythmic counterpoint of emotional urgency and redoubled emphasis – that this incomparable Eucharist which gives us Christ, must be attributed, not only in its *effects* but also in its *cause*, to the Holy Spirit alone. And since the eucharistic prayer discloses the incomparable transcendence of the cause by considering the incommensurability of the effects, the 'divine' liturgy will recognize and express the sublimity of the Cause *after* the revelation of the effects. And in fact, to put it in 'Latin' terms, the *post-consecratory* epiclesis *of consecration* which so shocked 'us', appeared liturgically only after the *post-consecratory* epiclesis of *appropriation or sanctification*, in which attention was directed to the spiritual benefit looked for in this Eucharist: and, it would appear, the former depends upon the latter.[25] There is therefore no anomaly in this 'post-consecratory' epiclesis of consecration, which says and repeats that this Eucharist of the Church can really communicate the body of the Lord only by being *entirely* the work of the Holy Spirit! In the East the only anomaly would lie in thinking that there is anything odd in the liturgy's insistence on a point so essential to faith!

*Reconciliation of the Eastern teaching on the epiclesis
with the Western teaching on the minister of the Eucharist*

If we do this, however, are we not compromising the value of the words of anamnesis and the irreplaceable role of the minister of the Eucharist? Both in the East and even the West, the answer will be that most certainly we are not. In the first place the Easterners never regard the efficacy of the minister as the exercise of a power which, even ministerially, is in itself all-powerful. The 'minister' of the sacrament acts much more as the representative of the Church and in the name of the Lord than solely as the representative of Christ.[26] Since the Church *receives* what she gives, she does nothing without *praying* that she may have the power to do it. That is why, in all the sacraments, and most of all in the Eucharist, the epiclesis occupies so important a place. In this there is nothing that denies the function the Latins attribute either to the 'priest' himself or to the consecratory efficacy of Christ's words.

No one would maintain that, in the Latin view, the minister who acts as Christ's representative does so apart from the Church and independently of the gift of the Holy Spirit. Moreover, even if Christ's words possess an absolute value from the fact that *Christ* has been given the power of the Spirit without measure (John 3:34), their value is not absolute without qualification *so far as the minister is concerned*. The latter is not *immediately* Christ: he is such only by ministry and by virtue of a *gratuitously charismatic competence*, and in consequence he is in a condition of complete dependence upon the Spirit. The East brings this to his attention in a very special way in the eucharistic mystery. When the priest has spoken the words of Christ, he is then made to *invoke the Holy Spirit immediately*, so that the words may be realized. It is not that they would not be efficacious by themselves, but that they obtain their efficacy in the *ministry* which the *priest* gives them only in virtue of the Holy Spirit who is at hand to help him. The priest therefore asks the Holy Spirit to deign to act so that the bread and wine, *through the sacerdotal ministry and in spite of his unworthiness*, may become what they became at the Last Supper *through the power of Christ himself*: body and blood of the Lord.[27] The sublime ministry which the priest exercises in the Church is therefore logically eclipsed by the irreplaceably sovereign priority of the Holy Spirit. We shall have to refer to this again, in the epilogue, when we return to a problem that requires careful handling in the West, that of the sacerdotal ministry.

When, therefore, the epiclesis is understood in this way, it contains no really insoluble problem: instead it is a magnificent and imperative invitation never to understand the Eucharist apart from the Spirit who alone, here as elsewhere, is capable of *effecting* the mystery of the Lord. The fundamentally Eastern question of the epiclesis, along a different road from that followed by the Western problem of the Real Presence, brings us back to the mystery of the Resurrection through the Person and through the role of the *Spirit*: just as the question of the real Presence brought us back to the Resurrection by way of the *body*. This conclusion in itself is sufficient justification for our rapid restatement of past disputes, and makes us feel the urgency of a new effort to construct a synthesis which will indissolubly link together Eucharist and Resurrection.

Part III

RESURRECTION OF CHRIST AND EUCHARIST

As we start this third part, I must confess to the reader that I have written the preceding chapters only because they would entitle me to write what now follows. For many years now I have been quite certain (and I am by no means the only person to feel this certainty) that if we are to discuss the real Presence and, in order to do so, are unreservedly to open our minds to the mystery of the Resurrection, we must at all costs get away from a purely metaphysical language. In each case, the Resurrection and the Eucharist, we are concerned with one and the same reality, that of the *body of Christ* arising in glory or given to us in signs. From this is derived the feeling, soon to be a certainty, that if we are to understand the Eucharist as presence and gift of Christ to the Church, we must not divide our attack: we must, in a single offensive, start from the Resurrection and use that to acquire as deep an understanding as we can of the mystery of the Body. To do this, however, in a way that would be acceptable to faith, carry weight with 'theology', and prove fruitful in the lives of Christians, called for the methodical and arduous approach on which I embarked.

A BRIEF RETROSPECT

As I explained at the beginning of this book, we found it necessary to proceed in a sym-bolic way, bringing together the content of what we examined rather than keeping it separate, and at the same time getting rid of that unhealthy fear of syntheses which very often arises from a narrow and sceptical positivism: scientific integrity, on the other hand, never shies away from an overall view when it is necessary. The Eucharist makes use of food and drink and prepares a common table in order to attack in us both death and the poverty of our love; and so it implies symbolically an anthropology which, through hunger, brings into play community, physical condition, and mortality: man's ultimate profundities. In virtue of the anthropology disclosed in the light of eucharistic symbolism, the message of the Resurrection calls, too, for a new understanding. This understanding must at all costs free itself from prejudices which *a priori*, and in a highly disputable way, reject the *likelihood* of the fact of the Resurrection as attested by the gospel texts. It must also free itself from controvertible ways of representing the Resurrection which misunderstand or dilute the absolute originality of the *event*. If these requirements are satisfied, the uniqueness of the gospel testimony, which at first seemed to weaken it, will have the contrary effect of increasing its credibility. Thus, by seeing that what gives the Resurrection its depth is the fact that it concerns the very *body* of Christ, we found in it a realism and a breadth which are immediately and irresistibly communicated to the Eucharist itself.

A second part was then necessary to see whether the unity of the two mysteries, to the discovery of which the Resurrection had led us, stood up to the examination of the dogmatic questions raised by the Eucharist. In fact, under the influence of a liturgical revival which for nearly half a century has been forcing it to get back to essentials, eucharistic theology has been stripped (we saw) of a sterile and doubtful metaphysical technicality: which, we also saw, the Council of Trent deliberately avoided. For all its good points, however, modern theological study did not, we thought, solve what seemed to us the crucial question: is it possible to reformulate in language of *body* and *resurrection*, and no longer purely of *substance* and *metaphysics*, the doctrine – fundamental in spite of being so often ill-presented – of the *real Presence*? To answer this question, we had to recall how the word 'substance' made its way into theological idiom and gradually ousted the language of *body* from explanations of the mystery. This involved a quick journey along the road from Augustine to Trent, with results that seemed to us illuminating.

What, in fact, happened was just as though theologians who wished to vindicate the presence of Christ in his body and his blood had felt it necessary to bar themselves from thinking of the mystery of the *body* in order to confine themselves within the horizon of *substance*. A fresh and vigorous metaphysics was at hand to relieve a weakening anthropology. This metaphysics was of real service; it is written into the language of dogma, and we cannot go back upon it — faith has not spoken in these terms for so many centuries simply to end by saying nothing! Nevertheless one language alone is not sufficient to say all that has to be said here. A rapid summary of the question of the epiclesis showed us exactly where the liturgy of the East, by recognizing the essential role of the Holy Spirit, meets the doctrinal requirement apparent in the West, of restoring the Eucharist, and the real Presence in particular, to the illumination of the Resurrection. It is this we must now attempt.

CHAPTER 1

Resurrection and real Presence

THE EUCHARIST WITHIN THE HORIZON
OF THE MYSTERY OF CHRIST

We have already satisfied ourselves that what the Eucharist demands first of all is that we comprehend it in the organic whole to which it belongs, and which extends from Christ's incarnation to the life of the Church itself, by way of the cross and the Resurrection. All this, of course, is concentrated in the fact that 'the Word became flesh and dwelt among us' (John 1:14). This was a point the Greek Fathers delighted in elaborating. Through the very act of the incarnation of the Word they disclosed the whole mystery of Christ and the Christian, so completely did this first phase govern the entire sequence of development and all its furthest ramifications. 'God became man', they said and repeated time and time again, with St Athanasius, 'in order that man might become God.'[1] In particular they moved, with admirable and justifiable flexibility, from the Incarnation to the Eucharist itself. In these they saw a single unique mystery of the *body* of Christ, *produced* here in an astonishing manner by the Spirit, just as he had earlier been *conceived* in the Virgin's womb by the power of that same Spirit. They found this comparison both illuminating and convincing. We remember the answer St John Damascene gives to the man who asks 'how' the Eucharist is possible. He does no more than repeat the words addressed to Mary. 'You, too,' he says, 'ask *how* the bread becomes the body, the wine and water the blood, of Christ. And I in turn answer you: the Holy Spirit "has come upon them", and these his deeds surpass word and thought.'[2]

Nevertheless, for the Greek Fathers the mystery of Christ was never reduced *solely* to Christ's virginal conception in the womb of Mary. They always had in view the historical development of the life of the Lord, from his birth to the *Resurrection* through the cross, to be continued in the Pentecostal Church of the Spirit. This was sufficient ground for their freely affirming, without always having to state it explicitly, that the body of Christ whose presence the Eucharist gives to us is indeed the *same* body of *one and the same* Christ, born of the Virgin, dying on the cross, present on our altars, just as Radbertus affirmed and Berengar in turn was obliged to confess. The Eucharist which gives us Christ in his body, does not do so for the Greek Fathers 'after the flesh' (cf. 2 Cor. 5:16), in a sense that neither Paul nor the Church after him can or will ever accept. Christ's words about his flesh and his blood having become food and drink are, for them, 'spirit and life' (John 6:63). The body, served by the Lord to those who come to his supper, is therefore indeed for them the 'spiritual body' of the Resurrection: the body the mystery of which St Paul, again, outlines for us (1 Cor. 15:44–50), the body, too, of which the Church until the end of time is the witness and the fruit.

The obscuring in the West, during the eucharistic controversies, of the importance of this 'spiritual' body has weighed heavily on the doctrine of faith: for if we are to be fully justified in asserting that the Christ of the Eucharist is the same Christ as was born of the Virgin Mary and died on the cross, we must always insist that between these two phases of a single mystery of Christ – the conception by the Virgin and the eucharistic mystery – there lies *the* supreme, irreplaceable, phase, the vital link; and that is the resurrection of the Lord. If we ever omit to mention this, we may well see the coalescence of cross and Eucharist as an *identity of states*, whereas it derives from an *identity of person* according to the different states of *one and the same body*; for if Christ is indeed given in the *memorial of his death*, the Christ who so gives himself is *the Christ of the Resurrection*.

As the Eucharist is inseparable from the risen Christ, so is it inseparable from the mystery of the *Church* herself. By an admirable reciprocity, not only does 'the Church produce the Eucharist' which appears to be the more visible effect, but the 'Eucharist produces the Church',[3] and this effect, though hidden, is also the most indispensable. 'Because there is one bread, we who are many are one body, for we all partake of the one bread,' says St Paul (1 Cor. 10:17). Built up from the very foundations by the energies of the Resurrection, which unite the countless multitudes of men in the Body of the Spirit, the Church continues to exist also only because she is continually given strength by the risen Christ. Under the temptation that we all experience of shutting ourselves up in the prison of man's resources alone, the people of God gathered into a Church is destined to be the permanent centre of a defiance as much as of a rejection; and both of those bring freedom. The Church differs from the 'world', not because she is concerned to stand out against the world, but because she is aware of her origin and of her responsibility to bear witness; and, as a community of the Resurrection, she sees that she is withdrawn, in her source, in her duties, and in her end, from everything in the world which tends blindly to throw men back upon themselves. She bears witness to, and must bear witness to, an origin, a road, and a goal, of which Christ himself, sharing this with nothing and nobody, is 'the Alpha and the Omega, the first and the last' (Rev. 22:13). But if the Church is really to hold firm in the confession of a 'mystery' which governs the fulfilment of the world in salvation, forbidding it to find its own self-sufficiency in itself and yet fulfilling its deepest hopes, then she must not only be *born* initially, once and for all, of the Spirit – that happened at Pentecost – but she must also be *fed* every day from the Body of Christ and given to drink from his Spirit: and that food and drink are the Eucharist. With scripture, the Eucharist is the twofold bread, the 'trans-cultural'[4] bread which the Lord 'who is Spirit' obtains for the Church and gives her, so that she may remain in this world as the witness of an artefact which is not of this world and yet attaches her to this world by links that nothing can snap.

What, then, is the nature of this bread which sustains this Church, of this wine which intoxicates her with a love which is not *of* the world and yet is vital *for* the world? What does it mean, that the Lord *is there* to feed his Church from the Body and Spirit of his Resurrection? To answer such a question calls for a synthesis, and presupposes a language, in which will be interwoven, so far as possible, the combined meaning of the Resurrection, of the Spirit and of the body; and thereby, too, of the Church seen in the fulfilment of her most profound mission.

MYSTERY OF CHRIST AND MYSTERY OF MAN
IN THE ONENESS OF THE BODY

The human body, we have seen,[5] is a relationship with the universe, unique, personal and historically determined. Since we are inseparable from the reality of the world, we are not truly ourselves so long as the whole world does not, in very truth, form one body with us. This assimilation, this concord – or, we may say, this sym-bolism – and communion of man with the cosmos, under the sign of a mutual incorporation of *man* with the world and of the *world* with man, define one of the essential goals of culture and history. The fact that man lives from nature means for Marx, and quite rightly, that 'nature is his *body* with which he must remain in a continuous interchange in order not to die . . . for *man*', he concludes, '*is a part of nature*'.[6] Every man, therefore, contains within himself the real and ineradicable longing for a total reconciliation with the universe, as Marx again proclaimed: but this longing cannot be satisfied in a world from which the absolute Principle of Life is *a priori* excluded. If man is to find this '*definitive* resolution of the antagonism between man and nature',[7] he must have revealed to him the *absolute neg-entropy* which the resurrection of Christ can alone provide. Jesus the Lord is, in fact, the only person in history to make nature into his own body: not, as man himself does, in a way that is purely cultural and so doomed to death, but in a way that is trans-cultural and ensures for Christ in the Resurrection absolute dominion over the universe and death.

The first and the second Adam

We must not shrink from saying this: that the fundamental identity of the world is not only that which man gives to it when, by *culture*, he makes the world into his own body, in the sense that Marx means and explains; the fundamental identity of the world is the identity which Christ gives it when he acquires in his *resurrection* the 'power which enables him even to subject all things to himself' (Phil. 3:21). 'As it is,' says scripture, 'we do not yet see everything in subjection to him' (cf. Heb. 2:8): and in this, moreover, we are fortunate, for it is this obscurity surrounding the glorified identity of Christ that makes history possible. If the world were already seen here and now in conformity with its potential truth as very body of Christ, this would mean the conflagration of the world in the glory of God, and so the parousia too. But history must endure, and man must 'become' in a world which he makes his own, by culture, as he does his body. We would, therefore, seek in vain for the least real incompatibility between the two phases of one single genesis: the *cultural phase* which makes the world man's *historical body*; and the *parousiac* fulfilment, founded upon the Resurrection, which makes from the world Christ's *glorified* body and humanity rising again in Christ.[8] Christ, as second and last Adam, in no way annihilates the first Adam. We may say more, that he is really himself only by 'seconding' the historical genesis of our humanity. He supplants our humanity, it is true, but only at the final term, when man proves that he suffers from an incurable cultural weakness, and the risen Christ, without ever having dispensed us from the duties implicit in history, reveals to us and gives us an absolute fulfilment which is drawn from the power and glory of the Spirit.

History and parousia

'We continue', writes Teilhard, 'from force of habit to think of the Parousia, whereby the Kingdom of God is to be consummated on Earth, as an event of a purely catastrophic nature – that is to say, liable to come about at any moment in history, irrespective of any definite state of Mankind.' That is one point of view. 'But why should we not assume, in accordance with the latest scientific view of Mankind in a state of anthropogenesis[9] that the parousiac spark can, of physical and organic necessity, only be kindled between Heaven and a Mankind which has biologically reached a certain critical evolutionary point of collective maturity?

'For my own part I can see no reason at all, theological or traditional, why this "revised" approach should give rise to any serious difficulty. And it seems to me certain, on the other hand, that by the very fact of making this simple readjustment in our "eschatological" vision we shall have performed an operation having incalculable consequences. For if truly, in order that the Kingdom of God may come (in order that the Pleroma may close in upon its fullness), it is necessary, as an essential physical condition,[10] that the human Earth should already have attained the natural completion of its evolutionary growth, then it must mean that the ultra-human perfection which neo-humanism envisages for Evolution will coincide in concrete terms with the crowning of the Incarnation awaited by all Christians. The two vectors, or components as they are better called, veer and draw together until they give a possible resultant. The supernaturalizing Christian Above is incorporated (not immersed) in the human Ahead! And at the same time Faith in God, in the very degree in which it assimilates and sublimates within its own spirit the spirit of Faith in the World, regains all its power to attract and convert!'[11]

Eschatology, then, does not wipe out history; it passes judgement on history and serves to crown it. If such views appear extravagant we should remember, Teilhard tells us, that 'on the cosmic scale (as all modern physics teaches us) only the fantastic has a chance of being true.'[12] In any case it is clear that if the world's finality consists in becoming, in the Resurrection, the very body of Christ – as the parousia will make it manifest at history's transmuted term – then that ultimate finality cannot in any way alter the fact that, in history, this world is, and must become, man's cultural body. The two entities are not mutually exclusive, but complementary. The world into which man is born historically is the world in which Christ is revealed eschatologically, and in which he already reigns, here and now, even though in a hidden way, growing ever greater himself and making men, too, grow greater and their world with them. Christ, therefore, is never himself without men: still less is he so in opposition to men – it is *for* men that he is himself. That is why the hidden identity of the universe as body of the Lord in virtue of the Resurrection, not only does not in any way destroy the identity of the world as man's historical body, the fruit of his culture, but passes through that second identity and includes it in itself. Christ exists at the heart of our history like a hidden furnace which will one day blaze up and illuminate the universe, with a life which will have conquered all death and so will vindicate the world's secretly invincible expectation.

'Among you', said John the Baptist, 'stands one whom you do not know' (John 1:26). He was speaking of the as yet unavowed historic presence of Jesus Christ. What the Baptist said still holds true for our world, on which lies the secret imprint of the Resurrection. The hall-mark of such a world is, in St Paul's words, 'Christ in you, the hope of glory' (Col. 1:27). The risen

Christ is indeed the world's eschatological identity, its *truth*, the Christ who is already making the cosmos into his body, silently acquiring for his humanity in the Resurrection a mastery over entropy and death that is absolute even if deferred. At this point we could say of the cosmos what St Paul says elsewhere of the faithful themselves: the identity of the universe is now hidden with Christ in God; when Christ, the Christ who is our life, is made manifest, then the true identity of the world will be made manifest with him (Col. 3:4). The parousia, therefore, will be the full emergence of the glory of a world much more fully incorporated in Christ by the Resurrection than it is incorporated in human mortality by history, or than human history is incorporated in the entropy of the universe. It will not be another world, in the sense of a 'duplicate' already there but invisible; rather will it be this world of ours in a completely different form, which nevertheless completes this one: it will be this world enthroned in the course of the ages, eternally, in a life without death, a being without any *nil*, an energy without entropy, eyes without tears, tongues without lament, hearts without sin: not a world that lies behind, but, as Teilhard says, a world which is 'ahead'. Of such a world and of its future the only herald is the risen Christ, present in a hidden manner in the folds of history, until the time comes for him there to unfold visibly his transfiguring newness.

Such points of view are so often overlooked, and even disputed, and yet are so important for understanding what the Eucharist itself is, that we must do our best to find a new way of expressing them and so make it familiar ground.

THE RELATION OF THE RISEN CHRIST
TO OUR WORLD: A RECAPITULATION

Christ, by his incarnation, makes the world a reality which is so personal to him that it is *incorporated* in his mystery of the Son, without this world being in any way withdrawn or taken from us. The relation which Christ thus gives himself with the world sets him, in fact, among us, and makes of him a true man. His body is body of finiteness and passivity; by that body Christ is so contained in this world, as we are, that in it he can suffer the passion of passions, and that it is our death, as it was our life, which becomes his in very truth. But this body of activity and passivity, and so of mortal finiteness, is transformed in Christ into a body of transfigured finiteness, in other words of a dominance over the world which is both filial and sovereign. The Resurrection, the glorious manifestation of absolute Spirit in man's mortality, means that in his *constitutive relation with the world* – that is, *his body*, Christ enjoys all the sovereignty that attaches to God himself; and thus he possesses the effective power of 'ruling over the whole universe'. That is why St Paul again, echoing what Psalm 8 says of Adam, can say of the risen Christ, that 'God has put all things in subjection under his feet' (1 Cor. 15:27). And that is why, in St John, Christ too can say (transposing his elevation on the cross into the enduring image of the glory of his resurrection), 'I, when I am lifted up from the earth, will draw all men to myself' (John 12:32). All these sayings express one and the same reality, that the manifestation of Christ's divinity is truly contained in this *constitutive relation* with the world which forms his *body* and gives us the foundation of the *new universe of the Resurrection*.

The argument against the greatness of man

The question then arises: is it a mistake to give a new reality to the mystery of Christ in a way which presupposes and demands a view of man that is so unusual? Surely God's death itself entailed 'man's' death or at least that sinking into oblivion which is the herald of his death? Has man not found out that 'he is not at the centre of creation, nor of space, nor perhaps at the peak and ultimate end of life'?[13] That is why scripture, with its teaching of the two Adams, perched, we might say, upon one another at the peak of the world, is obsolete both in its outdated geocentricism and in its unwarranted anthropocentrism. The more, indeed, we think we can or must elevate chance to the position of a new absolute, and so reduce Christian thought, or religious thought of any kind, to an antiquated animism, the more readily can we minimize man's position in the world complex. This is, in fact, an argument we hear: but can anyone really believe that problems of such width can be governed by statements of this sort, even if they are the accompaniment of a neo-stoic reaction – itself not without its own nobility – to the reaffirmation of man's nothingness? For, even though it be true that the most trustworthy science rejects a facile anthropocentrism, it is also true that evolution allows us to see that 'if man is no longer at the centre of space' nevertheless he would indeed appear to be 'at the summit of duration'.[14]

Teilhard explains this in one of his latest and most remarkable essays which, whatever may be said, is as applicable now and as up to date as when he wrote it: 'Since Galileo (as Freud remarked), in the eyes of science, man has continually lost, one after another, the privileges that had previously made him consider himself unique in the world. *Astronomically*, first of all when (like and with the earth) he was engulfed in the enormous anonymity of the stellar bodies; then *biologically*, when like every other animal he vanished in the crowd of his fellow-species; *psychologically*, last of all, when an abyss of unconsciousness opened in the centre of his *I*; by three successive steps in four centuries, man, I repeat, has seemed definitely to redissolve in the common ground of things. Now, paradoxically, this same man is in process of re-emerging from his return to the crucible, more than ever *at the head of nature*; since by his very melting back into the general current of convergent cosmogenesis, he is acquiring in our eyes the possibility and power of forming, in the heart of space and time, *a single point of universalization* for the very stuff of the world.' Speaking in such terms can only mean the acceptance, expressed in the dynamic language of evolution and genesis, of the impossibility of reducing man's value, expressed earlier in the essentially static terms of guaranteed supremacy. This involves a great change, but one that can be made without any difficulty. In fact, everything works in its favour. 'For, if the entire sphere of things', Teilhard continues a little later, 'is now found to have the essential property of gradually contracting on its centre by an increasingly reflective drawing together of its component elements, how can we help realizing that, however alarmingly we have seen it grow around us in power and size, the universe in no way tends, as we have feared, to crush our individual values but on the contrary to exalt them by its vastness.'[15]

Cosmic reintegration of the greatness of Christ

Such a restoration of man's value entails also, for the Christian, the enthronement of Christ in the new universe which science is enabling us to form an idea of and also to build up. While scripture saw the greatness of Christ in the extension of the greatness of a primitive Adam, static and to some degree fixed, it is now possible and necessary to express the mystery of Christ in the light of a wider cultural horizon: and this, not in order to alter revelation itself, but to explore it more deeply. Better than anyone, Teilhard saw that we must integrate what it was sought to break down, and re-establish the bold synthesis between Christ and the universe which would allow the ultimate meaning of the whole process of terrestrial development to reappear in the potential field opened up by the Resurrection. 'On the one hand,' he writes, 'the risen Christ of the Gospel can be maintained in the consciousness of the faithful, above a creation that he must by definition consummate, only by incorporating the evolution that some have used as an argument against him. On the other hand, this same evolution, in order to satisfy the needs of a reflective action born of its transformations, seeks anxiously in the heart of each one of us for a universal centre of thought and affection. Here a sphere calling for a centre. There a centre awaiting a sphere.'[16] The conjunction of the two produces the Christ of the Resurrection, 'the first-born of all creation', who assumes the headship of a universe made ready for this coronation. 'On the one hand (and this is too often overlooked), the Christian universal Christ would not be conceivable if the universe, which it is his function to gather to himself, did not possess (in virtue of some evolutive structure) a natural centre of convergence in which the Word could be incarnate, thence to radiate through and exert influence on the whole of the universe. On the other hand, unless some universal Christ were, positively and concretely, plain at the term of evolution, as now disclosed by human thought, that evolution would remain nebulous and uncertain, and we would not have the heart to surrender ourselves to its aspirations and demands. Evolution, we might say, preserves Christ (by making him possible), and at the same time Christ preserves evolution (by making it concrete and desirable).'[17]

Too beautiful to be true? Or is it not just the opposite, that here, as in so many other fields, beauty is the surest sign of truth? Here beauty and truth radiate from this Christ in whom 'all things were created' (Col. 1:16), and who is therefore the only key to the secrets of history.

So long, therefore, as the term towards which the whole of creation 'is groaning in labour' is not granted to it, the world is at the same time *culturally* subject to man's historic initiatives and *spiritually* open to the informing action of Christ.[18] By virtue of the power of the Spirit, made manifest in the Resurrection, Christ makes all things subject to him, and, without doing violence to any, 'gathers all things up' in himself. Because of this power of integration that Christ exercises over the whole of the world, St Paul can say of the *Christian* that, while remaining *in* the world, he is no longer subject to 'the elemental spirits of the universe' (Col. 2:8) but to Christ himself: for, deep below all, it is Christ who reigns over them and controls them. It follows from this that we must say of the *world* itself that, while it is and must continue to become, through culture and activity, man's historic body, at the same time it is, in hope and in the final (as yet withheld) form of its reality, *pledged* to becoming the actual body of the glorified Christ. With the parousia, in fact, the world will become the cosmic radiance of the mystery of the Lord and of ourselves in the Lord. We have, it is true, to allow the necessary time for growth and development, but we have to say that the ultimate finality of this world is that it must *emerge* in the form which the existence of the Lord is already promising for it: and that form is the wholly glorious body of the Lord and of humanity, transfigured in him by the Spirit of the Resurrection. In this *final* identity it will assume, the world will no more lose its trueness as world than man ceases to be man when he becomes, in the Spirit of adoption, a son in the Son. On the contrary, the world will find its trueness, that trueness at least which Christ is reserving for it historically and giving it eschatologically.

THE SPIRITUAL SACRIFICE OF MANKIND, AND THE EUCHARIST

Quite without design, we have in fact just defined the nature of *the sacrifice* that man must offer to God from his position in history, the sacrifice of which the Eucharist is the *sacrament*. 'I appeal to you therefore, brethren,' writes St Paul, 'by the mercies of God, to present your bodies as a living sacrifice, holy and acceptable to God, which is your spiritual worship. Do not

be conformed to this world but be transformed by the renewal of your mind, that you may prove what is the will of God, what is good and acceptable and perfect' (Rom. 12:1–2). The spiritual sacrifice consists, to put it briefly, in accepting that the continued transition from nature to culture, which determines the human content of 'this present world', does not, even so, represent in itself alone *the last word* of man and history: that is uttered only in the Spirit who makes possible the 'trans-cultural' Pasch, of which Christ is at the same time the beginning, the first-fruits, and the reality. In this world, man is not only the develop-ing being who is continually rising from nature, following up the cultural potentialities proper to mankind: he is also, and in-separably, the being who must, as St Paul says, 'put on' in this world the image of the second and last Adam. The latter, born from on high in the power of the Resurrection, *alone* possesses – but possesses *for us* – that divine incorruptibility which we are to attain through a 'second birth', which in an incomparable way extends beyond and puts the crown upon all the powers, the acquirements and the knowledge of man and history. The divinizing act in which men consent to 'put on' the identity of the Christ of the Resurrection – an act that is never finished and can always be beginning – is man's unbloody Pasch, and the daily content of the spiritual offering of which St Paul tells us.

This truly paschal sacrifice is offered *once and for all* by Christ on the cross, in the bloody context of a history of sin, which includes in particular the agony in the garden, the suffer-ings and indignities in the praetorium, and the death on Golgotha. This sacrifice is effected *once and for all* in him, and *every day* in us: with the Christ of the cross there rises over the horizon of time, never again to sink, the bloodied harvester of the divine fruits of the world's suffering, he of whom the prophet (Isa. 63:1) had had a glimpse; with him there rises, too, for ever now in his own person, the truth of the man of sorrows discerned by the same prophet (Isa. 53:3), advancing towards glory along the road of the sufferings and Calvaries of history. Christ's lordly sacrifice, which sums up, foretells and signifies every other sacrifice in itself, is incessantly realized in the Church by this permanent *memorial* of the eucharistic mystery. If it is true that 'the activity of recalling belongs to another order than the automatism of memory',[19] then no anamnesis will ever be more living than that which results from Christ's *act*, when he takes from men's table both their bread and their cup, to give himself as food and drink. By physical gestures he thus guarantees the otherwise faulty memory of tongue and heart. So, by redoing *in him* what he did *for us*, we *proclaim* the death which destroys our death, until the Lord, who to all appearances had ceased to be, shall return to fulfil us himself by his glory.

Even though, or rather precisely because, it is unbloody, this anamnesis can receive the world's daily offering. No doubt every day our world holds, on the sides of its cup, blood that has been shed in twenty different ways. Nevertheless, the significance of these sufferings is not the suffering itself but its underlying directive force of mutation and growth. Every day the Eucharist recalls this fundamental world economy and links men to it, far more closely than they ever realize and in spite of their apparent rejection. The presence of Christ's transforming Passion is, in fact, effected symbolically in the Eucharist, and, as Casel says, is realized for us in the 'mystery'. For the risen Christ is still at work and even in agony, as Pascal said, 'until the end of the world'. The sovereignty he acquires over the universe through his resurrection does not cut him off from our sufferings: rather does it bring him into, 'interiorize' him, in them, and it is bread that has known the mill and grape that has known the wine-press that become at his table his flesh and our flesh, the blood which allows us to consecrate our own.[20]

Thus the Eucharist is the sacrament of this Pasch which is to lead every man beyond his death and introduce him through the Spirit into the existence of the Father. If, however, this shedding of the old man is to be effected, man must accept – and this is the mystery of which the Church is servant and witness – that Christ possesses, in the Spirit, the power to make us consent to an artefact which exceeds all purely cultural power, and which determines, in faith, our *conversion* from creatures and sinners into our identity as sons.

In so describing the spiritual Pasch of mankind, we meet the best possible analogy of transubstantiation. The latter fulfils in bread and wine man's vocation and the term of the universe. In the Eucharist *whatever happens to a double element of this world must also happen to the entire world, and to man himself, when they are looked at in the light of the Resurrection*. Through the Resurrection, Christ became man's ultimate identity in the virtue of the Holy Spirit: 'It is no longer I who live, but Christ who lives in me,' St Paul tells us (Gal. 2:20). The world, on its side, is made in order to become *eschatologically* the body of a Christ who makes of the world, in his incarnation, an essential constituent of his eternal personality as Son. The reality of the world as Body of the risen Christ is *already* revealed as possible, although we *still* have to await its manifestation: and it is towards that reality that man's work and the work of the whole of creation must be directed. It is this reality of the world as the body of the risen Christ that the Eucharist gives us in signs.

EUCHARISTIC PRESENCE AND BODY
OF THE RESURRECTION

'When Christ, carrying further the process of his Incarnation, comes down into the bread in order to dwell there in its place, his action is not confined to the particle of matter that his Presence is at hand, for a moment, to etherealize. The transubstantiation is encircled by a halo of divinization – real, even though less intense – that extends to the whole universe. From the cosmic element into which he has entered, the Word is active to master and assimilate to himself all that still remains.'[21] Until the end of his life Teilhard never ceased thinking about this 'cosmic function' and these 'planetary dimensions'[22] that belong to the Eucharist. In his very last essay, *Le Christique*, he is still considering how the convergence of the cosmos and the emergence of Christ 'inexhaustibly react upon one another as they meet' – and what does he see resulting from this? What he sees is a light 'so intense that it was transfiguring (or even "transubstantiating") for me the very ultimate depths of the world'. For Teilhard, in fact, 'it is the eucharistic mystery itself which is prolonged to infinity in a veritable universal "transubstantiation" in which the words of consecration fall not upon the sacrificial bread and wine alone, but, in very truth, upon the convergence of the world'.[23]

Too often, it must be admitted, we have been enslaved to a view of the eucharistic presence that is unwarrantably limited, in its effects, to the *sacrament* alone. Teilhard showed us that the 'transubstantiation' which confines faith to the 'species' should, on the contrary, expand it. He thus opened the world to eucharistic 'extensions'[24] and helped us to understand that if we are to grasp the true mystery of the Presence, we must start from the Resurrection: and this is precisely the point we are making now. Teilhard moved on from the sacrament itself to its universal extensions: and these, though he did not always say so in so many words, are in fact extensions of the *Body* of the Resurrection. It is from these that we must try to start if we are to understand how it is that, in virtue of the body of the risen Christ, the Eucharist is itself pre-eminently the sacrament of the *Presence*.

The mediation of the body as the foundation of the Presence
A remark of St Gregory of Nyssa, from his *Catechetical Oration*, is important at this point. That great theologian, when explaining how Christ was able to say as he held up the bread, 'This is my body,' says that we too can use the same words. All that is needed is that we shall fully appreciate how closely our own body depends upon the bread we eat. 'When we look at these elements, we are looking at what is potentially our physical volume: once they enter into me, these elements become my blood and my body, because of the faculty of assimilation which causes nourishment, taken from here or there, to assume the form of a body.' Therefore, 'when we see bread, in a sense we see the human body, for as the bread enters into the body it becomes the body itself'.[25] It is perfectly logical, then, that Christ should have been able himself to offer the bread and wine of the Eucharist as being his body and his blood. The great Cappadocian was content with the analogy as it stood; we now know that we can carry it further in a way that fits in with the mystery of the Christ of the Resurrection.

When Christ takes the bread and takes the wine, and tells us to follow him in so doing, what he takes, and what we, in obedience to him, also take, is a double element of man's cultural and cosmic body. In addition to the fact that bread and wine give us the food and drink necessary to our lives, one of them represents basic subsistence, while the other expresses the delight of living. By taking both, Christ symbolically[26] accepts both the seriousness of life which always needs to be sustained and the happiness of living which makes us enjoy it. In his own way, through the bread and wine which he takes from his table, the Christ of the Last Supper gives his personal endorsement to man's history. He endorses our cosmic and cultural reality, as he does the boundless project of making the whole universe our own, which obsesses the whole of mankind. But this endorsement is not simply one more 'symbolic' approval. If, through the medium of these two allied elements, Christ, in his turn, takes possession of man's cultural body, it is because he knows its distress and wishes to transcend it. He knows that this bread and this wine are still no more than the food and drink of mortality. What he wishes to give is a bread that will be the supreme bread: not a bread baked by men or a wine merely from the vineyard; not just a stop-gap bread, like the manna of Exodus, manna that did, it is true, save our forefathers from the inhospitable desert, but did not snatch them away from death. And yet, if Christ is indeed what he says of himself, 'the Resurrection and the Life', then he must be able to give his own a bread which is pure life, a wine that is a pure draught of im-mortality.

How can he do this, except through the medium of his body and blood, that is to say of his own fullness of truth, inasmuch as, by the transfiguring mystery of his resurrection, he inaugurates a relation to this world which annihilates death? This transformed relation of Christ to the world in the Body of his Resurrection cannot as yet be seen by us in its full trueness; at the same time, in virtue of this universe already incorporated with man, we cannot be entirely deprived of it. For, just as the bread and wine are truly man's authentic body, so this same bread and this same wine, when subjected to Christ's power and drawn by him into the domain of his person, can surely themselves also become some part of him? Of course they can, provided that Christ himself indeed wishes to integrate into the *Body of his resurrection* these elements which, for us, form part of the *body of mortality*. He therefore takes the elements of the world which *historically* sym-bolize with us in time as our culture works upon them, and makes it possible for them to sym-bolize *eschatologically* with him through the truth of his resurrection. He gives this double world-element the power to become and *to be* for us, here and now, what the whole world will become and *will be*, in virtue of glory, at the time of the *parousia*.

This, in truth, is what the Eucharist is: the sacramental anticipation in history of the world's fundamental identity in the order of the Resurrection. The Eucharist makes manifest for faith, in signs, what still remains hidden from human experience in history; in a symbolic, and so fragmentary and hidden way, it realizes the ultimate content of the Resurrection: which is that the world is so made as itself to become really the Body of Christ. Veiled in our eucharists, the world becomes here and now what it will become with radiance, too, when Christ openly integrates it into himself as the pure cosmic expression of his glory and makes of it, for ever, his living body, as he frees it from all subjection to death.

Until that time everything takes place, and must necessarily take place with us, only *in* faith, and is without content except *for* faith. It is not that the Eucharist, as some maintain in the case of the Resurrection, has content only *through* faith and is itself empty: yet even so it is true that *faith alone can apprehend its content*. Who would want to discover what Christ alone does and alone can do, if he did not adhere to Christ? On the other hand, if the Christ of the Eucharist is indeed the Christ of the Resurrection, is there anything for faith to wonder at in his *wishing* to give himself to us in order that we may live? or, if he gives himself, at his doing so through the medium of his *body*, which is the expression of his self? and at his transfiguring the *elements of the world* in order to give us his body, when we consider that the power he has of transforming the world into himself is an integral part of the mystery of his Christ-risen body?

Presence of Christ in symbolic form

We see, then, that in giving us his body through the medium of the elements of the world Christ does not step outside his own domain. He does the exact opposite; he penetrates his domain, or rather he makes its nature plain to faith in signs. Christ *anticipates* for the Church, in a limited but nonetheless real way, the transfiguring effect of the Resurrection, before that power bursts into the world in a blaze of glory. In a veiled and partial manner he transforms the world of history into what that world will become in eschatology. Christ gives us our bread and wine as *things that have become in advance*, at the level of sign, what the whole world will become in the blaze of glory – the deathless life of the Body of his resurrection. This he does symbolically, and therefore in a way that is still limited to signs and relative to our own time. And this explains the *sacramental* separation, so strange in relation to the risen Christ (for whom it does not exist) of the body of Christ *and* his blood. Such a distinction, it is evident, can exist only in the signs and in relation to ourselves. It does not evoke a physical structure of the risen Christ, but reminds us of the fact that his resurrection truly possesses the plenitude of life which is expressed for us by body and blood, and is given to us unreservedly, even though still in signs. Thus the sacramental symbolism signifies precisely the *totality of Christ*, giving himself, and the *totality of the gift* of himself he thus presents to us. The glorified Christ gives himself completely in the Eucharist of history. Completely: *body and blood*, just as we say of a ship that it is lost with all hands. It is thus that Christ gives himself in his entirety, as he makes a fragment of the world into an expression of his person.

This incorporation is so real that although the Eucharist is *still* fragmentary it nevertheless *already* announces the end of all time. The Eucharist is eschatological, for, invisibly and only in its action upon a double element, it anticipates what the parousia will make of the whole world when it transfigures it by the annihilation of death. It is, as has been said, a sacramental parousia: *parousia*, since it involves the Body of the Resurrection, but *sacramental* parousia, since its effects remain related to signs. In view of the fact that this world in which our humanity grows in stature must be a continuing world, Christ's glory cannot appear in it except by way of symbol. 'Elements of the first creation become', as the Windsor declaration puts it, 'pledges and first fruits of the new heaven and the new earth.'[27] Thus, without putting a stop to history, the risen Christ prefigures for us its term. He also enables us to have a foretaste of that term, so that when we proclaim it, as we must do, what we have to say about it will contain something of the savour of things still to be fulfilled and as yet deferred. This eucharistic mystery, however, which, in the form of symbol and the 'shorthand' of sign, realizes the development of the world into the body of Jesus Christ, thereby ensures the *real* presence of the Lord.

The real presence of the risen Christ

When Christ says that this bread and this wine *are* his body and blood, and so already does in a fragmentary way what he will be doing in the parousia in a way that extends to the whole, he is giving *himself in person* to the Church. The power he exercises of transforming elements of the world into the reality of his

M

Body – the body which destroys death – is not a power that lies outside him; that power is *Christ himself in person*, making the truth of his resurrection valid for us. The whole Lord, therefore, is really present there as the life-giving master of this world. He subjects the world to himself, that so he may give himself to us in the still veiled act of his lordship. In giving us this *world*, clothed in the sovereign identity that *he alone* will ever be able to confer upon it, it is *his own self* that Christ gives us. It is in his aspect of the Lord who dominates death that he seeks to reach us *in person*. Similarly we should not try to envisage a Christ who is contained *beneath* the species, when he gives himself to us only in virtue of a sovereignty that he exercises *over* them in the foretelling, veiled but real, of his still awaited glory. Just as the risen Christ is much less contained in the world than the world is contained in him, so we may say that Christ is much less *in* the bread and wine than the bread and wine are *in him*, 'converted' and changed in the newness of his life.

The mystery is still complete: nevertheless we can see *of what nature* it is. It is a mystery that entirely relates to the Body of the Resurrection; and the Presence that Body guarantees is illuminated by the contrast of the Presence it guaranteed in Christ's appearances. In those the presence of the risen Christ is a visible and personal presence. Masked for a moment by the banal excuses of the gardener, the passer-by on the road to Emmaus, the dweller by the shore of the Lake of Tiberias, even so this presence calls forth an eager acknowledgement which is usually followed by direct personal encounter or an embrace. In the Eucharist, on the other hand, the encounter takes place within an apparent absence. The Christ whom we affirm and whose presence we confess remains faceless, or rather his face is that of things which normally *are not* Christ: food and drink. He is present, therefore, under the stigmata of absence and the kenosis of his glory; the communion of life takes place only in faith. The earthly appearances, too, presuppose this faith, but the *fact* was there – the fact of Christ's visible and personal manifestation in the management of voice, of bearing, of body and of face. In the Eucharist faith travels alone on the road of Christ's presence: it is presented with *things* which it calls *signs*, only because of the *words* of Christ, which give these signs their vitalizing identity by virtue of the *Body* of the Resurrection: but in himself, Christ is still invisible. 'Blessed are those', said Christ to Thomas, 'who believe without seeing.' Here we have the blessedness of the Lord's Supper, in the simplicity of the dressed table, but also in the austerity of the absence for the senses. And at the same time Christ is so profoundly absent only in order to be more really consumed as the supreme living being for man and the world.

The Church, accordingly, is now attending her wedding-feast, fed by her Bridegroom, and his deputy in his absence. While she waits for his return, she combats the oblivion that would swallow up her Lord if it were not for the memorial which he instituted. 'In signs,' she tells those who can understand her, 'I proclaim the new identity of man and of the world. Here the Gospel becomes bread that we eat, a cup from which we drink. I am receiving, in symbol, the universe of grace which will finally burst forth in glory. Christ is given to me in the things of the world which, in an invisible and yet certain way, he transforms into the body of his resurrection. In the full flood of history, I am already reaching the goal, so that I may the better guide men to it. Far from feeling hampered at still existing among signs, I am already savouring the Presence which makes possible the duty of hoping, and I am gathering together in love those who are ready to live in faith for as long as the genesis of the world and the total fulfilment of the Lord shall continue hand in hand.' And here the Church speaks with truth : the world is no longer merely the place where men feel their way in the flesh; it can be the place where every day Christ comes close in the Spirit, and where, accordingly, there takes place a transformation which, in very truth, cannot but pass from the heart of Christians into this world.

CHAPTER 2

The Eucharist and the genesis of man

And so we reach the last stage of our task: the shortest, it is true, but one that calls for great nicety.

More than one reader who has followed the argument up to this point may have been inclined to say, 'This is all very well, but what in fact do we make of it?' Others, on the contrary, will have thought, 'That is not the real problem! The Eucharist is nothing *in itself*, if its mystery does not first make itself apparent *in us*!' This is not true: the value of the Eucharist comes from the risen Christ who continues to give us his life. And yet this mystery, which is to transfigure the world, remains a dead letter unless we live by it and really bring out its meaning. If, then, it is not our quality as Christians which *defines* the Lord's Supper (and that is very far from being true), it is that quality, nevertheless, which must *express* its value.

We have two roads open to us: we may start from the riches that are proper to the Eucharist and see how they should be revealed by us; or we can observe the weakness of the effects of the Eucharist discoverable in our lives, and consider how we may try to check such a waste by allowing the mystery which we are frittering away to bear fruit. Moreover, these two roads cross one another, since they both connect the mystery and life. The second, however, makes more obvious the danger in which we involve the mystery through our lack of realism as Christians. This, accordingly, is the road we shall choose. In the light of the failings which obscure it and of the conversion it calls for, we shall be able to see the Eucharist as man's source of life and his real constructive power.

THE EUCHARISTIC COMMUNITY
AND THE WORLD'S DEMANDS

The Fathers of the Church have always commented on the incomplete character of our Eucharist: for them the Eucharist was – as it is for us too – a shadow in comparison with the ultimate reality it prefigures in signs.[1] They regarded its incompleteness as belonging to the order of *mystery*: an area in which man was helpless. The incompleteness we have in mind here is that which derives essentially from our *worthlessness*. We betray the Eucharist. The lack of completeness concerns not so much the actual form of the Lord's Supper as the poor quality of us who share it.

We may say that the Eucharist is brotherhood, cure, divinization, building up of the Church, thanksgiving and resurrection;[2] we may emphasize more the service, the sharing, the emancipation, the celebration, or even, again, the prophetic character;[3] but everyone is agreed in saying that the eucharistic mystery must embrace the whole of life. 'We frequently hear it said today that Christian truth, handed on from generation to generation, is not something abstract, but a way of thinking that is also a way of acting. The practical proof found in Christian experience is here most illuminating, and orthodoxy asserts its authenticity in the orthopraxis recognized by all.'[4] Ortho*praxis*, as rightness in *acting*, is the true sign of ortho*doxy*, as rightness in *judging*.' This relation of truth to life holds good with special force for the Eucharist itself, for in the Eucharist we have the endorsement of a gift which, normally, transfigures us. The ancient rule of the *arcanum*, that is of the *secret*, which in the very first days of the Church protected the Christian mystery against sacrilegious violations, will always be operative because it means that the Eucharist is not the result of negotiations conducted by man when and how he pleases; only *faith can truly attain the mystery of faith*.[5] However, this rule never dispensed Christians from confessing Christ in the imperial praetoria, and still less from bearing witness to him in their daily behaviour. Thus our faith has to be made manifest in its practical effects. If Christ himself suffered 'outside the camp' (Heb. 13:13) it was in order to show that the offering he made of himself was directed to the profane and commonplace life of men even outside places that were regarded as sacred.[6] What is more, bread and wine are far from meaning that the Eucharist cannot be called to account for its human repercussions: on the contrary, they impose this obligation even more stringently, for they, the bread and the wine used in the Eucharist, are unmistakable signs of the human. We are therefore accountable for not despising in everyday life what we venerate so deeply in the liturgy. The character which Christianity stamps upon the Eucharist is determined by these premisses, from which endless conclusions can be drawn: some of which, in our own time, have been expressed with considerable sharpness.

'What sort of community is this', some ask, 'which is said to be formed in the Church from men who fight among themselves, with real savagery, in economic, social or political life? What sort of community is it which claims to be at the service of the poor and the most deprived, but in fact is made up of men of property, a community in which the poor cannot possibly feel at home?'[7] Did not St James, too, condemn a Christian gathering in which the rich could be respected because of their riches and the poor correspondingly humiliated?[8] We hear violent denunciations, again, of these eucharists at which the money-barrier makes a mockery of a unity which those eucharists presuppose but fail to produce.[9] Those who use such language believe that faith, their own faith and that of others too, must be or become a 'totalizing fact' by adherence to 'the Word which is embodied'.[10] Accepting that 'the Church is indeed the place where enemies can speak to one another',[11] they propound the truth in their own way and even in their exaggerations (for the eucharistic table takes us from where we *are* and not simply from where we *ought to be*) that the Eucharist must not be a living falsehood in our lives.

Faced with these or with even further demands, the Eucharist cannot be understood without the 'moment of repentance',[12] when our communities recognize before him who invites them to his table the meanness that closes us against others. There is, however, a new aspect to this: that we cannot stop short at the mere *moral* admission and must move on to *living acts*. The demand can become unhealthy if, in order to be 'concrete', we lay the blame only on others, just as it can remain merely formal if, out of exaggerated regard for complex situations, we continually refuse to judge and act. There was no such fear in the early days of the Church. 'To be true,' explains a commentator on the Acts of the Apostles, 'the "communion" of all with the risen Christ demanded, if there were real urgency, even the sale of land or houses. Can those who have more than enough happily retain what they do not need so long as a member of Christ, individual or collective, is destitute, without thereby breaking up the "communion"? This practical awareness of others is an exact measure of our belonging to the risen Christ.[13] It was from this, from a standpoint that coincides with the views quoted earlier from François Perroux,[14] that the social importance of the Resurrection and the Eucharist was derived; for the fact of eating and drinking with the risen Christ inaugurates a new art of living in the world. 'The faith of the early generations was realistic and concrete. Those who, when they became Christians, had not given all they had to the Lord brought at least something of their possessions to the eucharistic gathering in order to express their gratitude to God by serving the community. The offertory expressed this readiness to share with God, but also their concern to unite in one and the same act of worship the service of God and the service of the poor, and so fit their actions into the rhythm of the divine economy. Whatever the forms of its incorporation in the liturgy, the exercise of charity and the will to serve must "bear fruit" in proportion to the grace received. From him to whom all has been given, all is asked. Generosity passes judgement on faith and measures charity.'[15]

Who could ever, then, determine the social, economic and political limits of such eucharistic realism? 'If faith', we are told, 'is not realized in a charity that transforms the world, then it is without meaning.'[16] The true revolution must emerge from the Lord's Suppers, and no one should be able to check the transforming consequences that this mystery imposes on the historic structure of the world. When we speak of 'political theology', it is this that we have first of all to recognize. The self-criticism of Christians derives originally, in any case, from this evident fact that they take as symbols of their Eucharist elements that are indispensable to human life. So to involve human food and drink *symbolically* in a meal of love implies at the very least that *in real life* we have done nothing to deprive others of them; and, even further, that we are doing or have done – though will this task ever be finished? – everything that is humanly and Christianly necessary and possible to ensure that these elementary supplies are *produced* in sufficient *quantity* and *shared* equitably. If this were not done, to take the bread and wine and offer them to the Lord would become intolerably false, since we would be seeking to give God with one hand what we were unjustly withholding from men with the other.

Does this mean that in future political and social action must take the place among thinking Christians of the eucharistic offering? Such a secularization of the mystery would be *spiritually* as serious (even though *socially* less shocking) as its profanation by injustice or lack of care for the deprived of this world. To leave Christ in the belief of finding man, to leave the Eucharist in order to find a better solution to the world's hunger – this would again be to misunderstand the humanity we seek to serve in others and which, itself too, cannot do without the Bread of Life for which no bread can be a substitute. At the same time it is true that our participation in the Eucharist must entail in our lives an action which truly transforms the inhuman conditions that are to be found in the world. 'In her very early days,' Vatican II reminds us, 'the holy Church added the "agape" to the Eucharistic Supper and thus showed herself to be wholly united around Christ by the bond of charity . . . At the present time, when the means of communication have grown more rapid, the distances between men have been overcome in a sense, and the inhabitants of the whole world have become like members of a single family, these actions and works have grown much more urgent and extensive. These charitable enterprises can and should reach out to absolutely every person and every need. Wherever there are people in need of food and drink, clothing, housing, medicine, employment, education; wherever men lack the facilities necessary for living a truly human life or are tormented by hardships or poor health, or suffer exile or imprisonment, there Christian charity should seek them out and find them, console them with eager care and relieve them with the gift of help. This obligation is imposed above all upon every prosperous person and nation.'[17] For the Christian, *this presence which he must ensure himself among his fellow-men conditions the Presence which he relies upon receiving from the Lord,* and the former presence is the *measure* of the latter.

PRESENCE AND HOLINESS

St Augustine is still the essential guide to understanding the relation between Christ's Presence and the holiness that is required of Christians. Against the at once pretentious and ingenuous Donatists, who claimed to constitute the true Church of the saints, he followed Ambrose in successfully asserting the mystery of a Church 'herself pure, her human material impure'.[18] The true Church is for St Augustine the more modest reality of which Jacob, blessed and wounded, is the ancient image. 'Look at this man,' he tells us; 'on one side he was "touched" by the angel with whom he wrestled, and that side shrank and was dried up; but on the other side he was blessed. It is the same man, one part of him shrunk and limping, and the other blessed and strong . . . The shrunken part of Jacob signifies the evil Christians, for in the same Jacob there is both blessing and limp. The Church of today still limps. One foot treads firmly, but the other drags. Look at the pagans, my brothers. From time to time they meet good Christians, who serve God. When they do, they are filled with admiration, they are attracted, and they believe. At other times, they see evil-living Christians, and they say, "There, that is what Christians are like." But these evil-living Christians belong to the top of Jacob's thigh, which shrank after the angel had touched it. The Lord's touch is the hand of the Lord, straightening and giving life. And that is why one side of Jacob is blessed, and the other shrunken.'[19] This, again, is what the Council, under the direct guidance of Augustine, means when it says of such a Christian that 'he remains indeed in the bosom of the Church, but, as it were, only in a "bodily" manner and not "in his heart".'[20]

If we receive the Eucharist without being really 'in our *hearts*' members of the Church, then we, too, are receiving a sacrament which has lost for us its *reality* and *life*. Our communion tends to become aimless, or rather, as happens when a love is betrayed, the *presence of the other* becomes for the betrayer the presence of *denial*: a frightening possibility against which the Eucharist, from the time of its oldest epiclesis, seeks to guard us.

'Lord Holy Spirit,' runs the prayer in a Syrian liturgy of the fourth or fifth century, 'obtain for us this food of your holiness, so that it may not turn to our judgement, nor to our shame or our condemnation, but to the healing and the consolation of our own spirit.'[21] A liturgy of Antioch, known as 'The Liturgy of the Twelve Apostles', which probably dates from the fifth century, asks the Father 'to send your Spirit upon the offerings which are presented and to manifest to us that this bread is the holy body of our Lord Jesus Christ, this cup the blood of this same Jesus Christ, our Lord, so that all who taste of it may obtain life and resurrection, the forgiveness of sins, healing of soul and body, the illumination of the Spirit and assurance before the awesome tribunal of your Christ'.[22] We find the same prayer in a fourth-century Roman liturgy, which prays that the Father will 'send down upon this sacrifice thy Holy Spirit, the witness of the sufferings of the Lord Jesus, that he may declare this bread the Body of thy Christ, and this cup the Blood of thy Christ, that they who partake thereof may be strengthened in godliness'.[23]

We must not expect to find in these ancient prayers an explicit awareness of the social responsibilities of all sorts which are today incumbent upon Christians who wish to show that they are worthy of the Body which nourishes them. In their own way they make one thing quite plain to us: that we shall not find the proper forms in which our loyalty as Christians must be shown unless the Spirit effects in us the manifestation of a love with which the Eucharist nourishes us and of which it makes us witnesses. That is why these ancient prayers to the Spirit are still important to us: they tell us that we must pray, *stripped of every other need but that of receiving the Spirit* without whom we can no more continue to *bear witness* to Christ in the world than the Church, by herself, can *produce* him in the Eucharist. 'And we beseech you', says a third-century Roman liturgy, 'to send your Holy Spirit upon the oblation of Holy Church. And in bringing [them] together, grant to all those who partake of your holy [mysteries] [to partake of them] in order that they may be filled with the Holy Spirit, and for the strengthening of [their faith] in truth; that we may praise you and glorify you through your Child Jesus Christ, through whom be to you glory and honour with the Holy Spirit in the Holy Church, now and for ever. Amen.'[24]

It is a long and arduous road that leads our eucharists to their glorious consummation, and often it runs through deserts or skirts volcanoes. In this we share the experience of those who lived at the same time as the great crises of the past, and so, perhaps even more than other Christian generations, we are discovering that with the greatness of the world there comes its burden and the insistent demands of necessary action. Destitution, in particular, seems implacably to cry out for a world-wide justice which will be not merely planned but realized. To shirk would be a betrayal. If we have truly been fed at this table, we must make up our minds to play our part in life. If we say that we have drunk from the fountain which effects absolute terrestrial transmutations, then we too must change something on the face of the earth. Participation in the Body of Christ presupposes acceptance of the daily effort for justice in love. Otherwise our 'love' is a snare and a delusion, our professions of faith are empty words, and our sacramental entry into the Resurrection is no more than a derisory gesture. Such a task calls for unremitting vigilance, and as Christians we will surely be found lacking if we are not sustained by the transforming energies of the Resurrection. Eating the bread of life as a defence against the forces of death is a necessity that belongs to the order of biology. To fight against forces whose roots are embedded in the hardest core of selfishness requires that Christ shall first break down the structural barriers within us which shut us off from the new economy that should be changing us.

The more we discover the extent of the programme implied by the appreciation of such a mystery, the more we find also that what is called for relates to a progressive transformation of personality. Moreover, the Eucharist, which so authoritatively mobilizes our active powers so that they may manifest the transforming presence of Christ in our lives, asks nothing from us which it does not first offer in itself. Since the Eucharist is, in the Spirit, the gift of Christ of the Resurrection, it surpasses all merit and every good work; nor will it make those who understand it into real men, capable of introducing real change into the world, except by first making them into children who are receiving a kingdom as a gift. To take the Eucharist to oneself is to *receive*, as a gift, the person who, in his life, far exceeds all our active powers, and who, without destroying a single one, increasingly purifies them all.

THE SACRAMENT OF IMMORTALITY

Irenaeus of Lyons was the first to introduce the West to views that we must certainly rediscover if we are to rediscover the incomparable savour of the Resurrection and the Eucharist. Arguing against the Gnostics, who belittle the flesh and dissociate it from Spirit, Irenaeus asks, 'How can they say that the flesh passes into corruption, and does not partake of eternal life, if that flesh has been fed on the Body and Blood of the Lord? Let them either change their doctrine or cease to make their offerings. But our doctrine is in perfect harmony with the Eucharist, and the Eucharist confirms our doctrine. For we offer to God His own, and we consistently set forth the union and fellowship of flesh and spirit, and confess our belief in the resurrection of both flesh and spirit. For as the bread from the earth, receiving the Invocation of God, is no longer common bread, but is a Eucharist consisting of two parts, an earthly, and a heavenly, even so our bodies receiving the Eucharist are no longer mortal, seeing that they possess the hope of the resurrection to eternal life.'[25]

The Lord's Supper, therefore, is indeed a feast at which we eat the bread of absolute life and, by favour of the Spirit, drink from the well of glory. The Eucharist realizes *in us*, through the bread and wine, what the Incarnation effected *in Christ*; or, to put it even more precisely, through the Eucharist Christ introduces us into that for which he destines us by his incarnation. In our eucharists is realized, according to the *mode of sacramental symbolism*, the mystery which Christ reveals and fulfils in his incarnation, according to the *mode of historical manifestation*. Without the Eucharist, which makes available to us the fruits of the Incarnation itself, the mystery of the Lord would remain '*self-contained*', if I may put it so – something to which we could relate ourselves as though from a distance – but it would not be fully something *for us*, something which love can take to itself in a flesh, the flesh of Christ, transfigured by the free communication of the Spirit. It is this that produces the quality of joy and hope which should characterize all eucharists, as it necessarily did the meals that long ago were shared with the risen Christ.[26] Such joy flows directly from the fact that the Church's epiclesis is heard by God, and that in the Eucharist the Spirit, who was promised by Christ to those who asked him of the Father in his name (John 16:26-7), gives food and drink to the Church from the bread and drink of the Resurrection, and so fulfils in the Church the benefaction of Christ's incarnation. 'We cannot, in fact,' explains Irenaeus, 'receive "incorruptibility" and "immortality" without a close union with immortality and incorruptibility; and how would we be able to achieve this union, if this incorruptibility and this immortality had not first made themselves what we are, so that the corruptible

element might be absorbed by incorruptibility and the mortal
element by immortality . . . and that so we should receive the
adoption of children.'[27]

As the divine nurse of man in his genesis, the Eucharist is
thus included in the mystery of growth which gives us our own
position between the two Adams. It is thanks to the Eucharist
that the first Adam, who is 'living breath' in us, is nourished by
the second, to whom we adhere as 'life-giving Spirit'. Just as
we constantly receive the image of the first, through culture and
continual participation in the life of this world into which we
were introduced at our birth, so we receive the image of the
second by being reborn 'of water and the Spirit' (John 3:5).
Imperfectly modelled though we are on the face of the Lord, we
can even so, thanks to the Eucharist, surrender ourselves to the
secretly transfiguring reality of his body. In an interlaced pattern
of symbols which expresses the fullness of the mystery that
gathers them together, the Lord's Supper, because it recreates
our mortality by Christ's own immortality, is the condition – at
once biological and of the order of the holy – which enables us
to meet our obligation of 'putting on Christ' (Rom. 13:14).
Christ, in fact, is never a *model* outside us, to which we have
to relate ourselves by a *moral* effort, in the pejorative sense the
word can bear. He is the Figure of Figures, the sovereign Form,
in whose image we are created and re-created, and whose features
we must learn to know so that they are part of our lives: a
knowledge that we acquire in the first place by our communion
with the condensation into the Eucharist of his resurrection.
Inseparable from the Gospel, which illuminates the disarming
simplicity of Jesus' being in a veritable rainbow of values, the
Eucharist uses its vitalizing power to govern our spiritual transformation into the image of Christ. We have to be nourished by
the transfiguring flesh of the risen Christ if we are gradually
to come into the domain of the Spirit, who slowly moulds and
remoulds our humanity in accordance with the Truth and Life
of his own.

We find statements of the same sort as those of Irenaeus, but
less exuberant, in the East during the fourth and fifth centuries:
in Gregory of Nyssa, for example, or Cyril of Alexandria. The
former, obviously influenced by the physical science of his time,
explains that flesh needs the watery element which is included
in the blood and, under the action of wine, is transformed into

heat! The importance of his remark lies not in that detail, but in the humble nature of the roads that Christ follows in order to divinize us. For 'the glorious flesh inhabited by God', explains Gregory of Nyssa, 'accepted this element too for his subsistence, and the God who revealed himself, mixed himself with perishable nature in order to deify mankind with himself, admitting him to a share in godhead. That is why (following the plan of grace) he distributes himself like a seed among all who believe through the medium of this flesh made of bread and wine; and mingles himself with the body of the believers, so that this union with the immortal body may allow man, too, to share in incorruptibility.'[28] 'Eat the bread which renews your nature', writes Cyril of Alexandria, putting the words into the mouth of Christ, 'and drink the wine whose savour is immortality. Eat the bread which brings freedom from primeval bitterness, and drink the wine which soothes bodily pains. Here is the place where our nature is healed, here we parry the murderer's stroke. For your sake I have become as you are; and I have not changed my nature, so that, through me, you may become sharers in my divinity. Be transformed, therefore, by this magnificent change which so happily turns you from earth to God, from flesh to the Spirit.'[29]

The East delighted in seeing in the eucharistic communion this admirable exchange of properties whose beauty both enchanted and provided material for its liturgical thought and its epiclesis. The West was no less sensitive to what one might call, echoing Urs von Balthasar, the *aesthetics of the Incarnation in the eucharistic meal*; but it retained an anxious interest in the *ethical* repercussions of the mystery on man's *personal subjectivity*. We find in the West a didactic and almost punctilious concern to ensure that human life shall effectively conform to the splendours glimpsed in faith. And this concern was to extend to the eucharistic prayer itself.

THE EUCHARIST AND
MAN'S SUBJECTIVE CONSISTENCY

The concern to harmonize mystery and life is so evident in the eucharistic prayer of the Latin Church that almost any random quotation will serve to demonstrate it. Thus: 'As these paschal

festivities come to an end, grant to us, Almighty God, that, by
your grace, we may retain their *reality in our behaviour and our
lives*.'[30] And again: 'May the feast of St John the Baptist, Lord,
enable us to revere in the sacraments we have received the
wonders of which they are the *sign*, and even more to rejoice in
the mark they leave upon us'[31] – '*Conferat nobis, Domine,
sancti Joannis Baptistae solemnitas: ut et magnifica sacramenta,
quae sumpsimus, significata veneremur, et in nobis potius edita
gaudeamus.*' Here the Latin plays upon the difference between
the *signified* (*significata*) which defines the sacrament and the
mark (*edita*) which is its effect in our own lives. The sacramental
symbolism will bring us what it has in store for us only if it is
expressed in the living of our daily existence. Thus the Christian's existential transfiguration is an immediate effect of the
Eucharist he receives. We find this again in another prayer, a
post-communion: '*Supplices te rogamus, omnipotens Deus: ut
quos tuis reficis sacramentis, tibi etiam placitis moribus dignanter
deservire concedas*' – 'Humbly we beseech thy gracious goodness,
Almighty God, to grant that we whom thou renewest with thy
sacrament may lead acceptable lives in thy service.'[32] Life is here
moral behaviour (*placitis moribus*) or practical conduct, an *ethics*
that governs all one's living; and the eucharistic sacrament is an
assertion of the importance of holiness for this life of ours.

Another prayer shows the same attitude, this time one of the
prayers for Easter Friday: '*Omnipotens sempiterne Deus, qui
paschale sacramentum in reconciliationis humanae foedere con-
tulisti: da mentibus nostris ut quod professione celebramus,
imitemur effectu*' – 'Almighty ever-living God, who through the
Easter mysteries restored man to your covenant, grant to us that
we may *express* in our whole lives the faith that our ritual
celebrations *proclaim*.'[33] Here there is a contrast between the as
yet purely liturgical *profession* of faith and the *effective imitation*
of what we say that we believe. In the Secret for Whit Wednes-
day we pray: 'Accept, Lord, the sacrifice we offer you, and let
your mercy work upon us, so that as we carry out these sacramental rites we may be able to *live* their mystery'[34] – '*Accipe,
quaesumus, Domine, munus oblatum: et dignanter operare; ut,
quod mysteriis agimus, piis effectibus celebremus.*' In every case
the point that is made is the gap between the *fulfilment of the
mysteries* (*quod mysteriis agimus*) and the *life* we should lead.
This gap has to be bridged by a *celebration* which is no longer

only of the *liturgical* order (essential though that is, of course)
but also that of living and life. Such a process, which transforms
existence itself into a *practical celebration of the mystery*, works
at such a depth, and is also so difficult, that it must belong to the
efficacy which defines the mystery itself. What we are praying for
is, indeed, a veritable existential transubstantiation. The post-
communion for the twentieth Sunday of the year[35] runs: *'Mentes
nostras et corpora possideat, Domine, doni caelestis operatio:
ut non noster sensus in nobis, sed jugiter ejus praeveniat effectus'*
– 'We pray you, Lord, that the effective working of the heavenly
gift may take hold *both* of our minds *and* of our bodies, so that
it will be not *our way of feeling* that predominates but the
permanence of its effect.' The direct reference to 'our way of
feeling', that is to say our affectivity, is a clear indication of the
depth to which the Eucharist claims to transform us; and we
shall do well to consider that operation for a moment.

Affectivity, being intimately connected with the mystery of the
body, is in many respects the inmost centre of our personality.
It is a power specific to man of being affected by 'pleasure or
pain',[36] and for this reason it expresses in a special way the
uniqueness of man. If 'my own body', as has been said, 'is not a
thing, but an access to things',[37] it also represents my own
personal way of being handed over to the world and of leaving
my mark upon it. In this indissoluble mixture of activity and
passivity, of initiative and conditioning, which defines the human
state, I am this being which experiences, in pleasure or pain, the
way in which I affect the world and other men, and the way in
which, correspondingly, I am affected by them. It is here, in
this place that is completely occupied by a source or a centre,
that personality is born, accepted, moulded or changed. It is here
that men are born or wither away, normally with no witnesses
but themselves. That is why, so long as education, or love or
friendship have not made their way down into those depths, a
being retains the feeling of never having been apprehended by or
presented to another, or even, in a sense, of having yet been really
engendered.

It is undoubtedly one of the marvels of the Church's liturgy
that it has instinctively perceived the existence of this centre,
which is so often left unexpressed in man. The liturgy has done
this in the restrained chiaroscuro of the eucharistic prayers in
which, under the inspiration of a mystery which is 'spirit and

life', liturgical prayer opens up the most hidden and decisively influential depths of our personality, and dedicates them to Christ's transforming scrutiny. The idiom it uses, difficult to translate, of *penetralia, viscera*, and *affectus*, which symbolically feels its way into the secret network of man's subjective roots, seems to us full of boldness and evocative power. 'May the divine libation of your sacrament, Lord, penetrate to *our inmost hearts (penetralia nostri cordis)* and make us by its power partakers of its reality.'[38] Formerly, during the ablutions, the priest offered the same prayer, 'May your body which I have eaten, and your blood which I have drunk, cleave to my *entrails (viscera)* and grant that there may remain in me no stain of sin, now that I have been made anew by these pure and holy sacraments.'[39] *Viscera* denotes here what is the most biological, and therefore the most infra-conscious, in our personalities: the ground upon which they rest and at the same time the prison in which they are locked; the whole of this organic and concrete foundation, the whole non-rational element which my reason integrates, and which, still more, dominates my reason; *viscera* means, in brief, all that constitutes my affectivity, or in other words my fundamental way of existing in the world, of feeling my self in it, of feeling others in it, to my happiness or to my pain, and to theirs also – and my own way, too, of encountering God.

In this idiom, which accordingly denotes those dispositions which are radical to being, the liturgy defines the Christian attitude as a '*sincerum christianae pietatis* affectum'. To translate this as a 'sincere attachment' or 'affection' is misleading, unless it is made plain that we are concerned with our very *affectivity*, which has been won over by a Christian sentiment's invasion of our whole being. It is this affectivity again – the source from which, deep down, we are drawn, and can also trickle away completely – which the Secret for the first Saturday in Lent has in mind when it makes us say: 'Receive, Lord, the sacrifice whose offering you have accepted in reconciliation: grant that purified by its power *our hearts may be able to offer you a love which will be truly pleasing to you (beneplacitum tibi nostrae mentis afferamus* affectum).'[40] What is more, when the Eucharist penetrates into our depths in the hope of transfiguring us, it is not lost in those depths. Working in the deepest abyss of man's being, it makes him ready to open himself to the immensity of the kingdom of the Resurrection. As a further help to understanding how we have, spiritually, to make our own these two infinites, each the sacrament of the other, the Eucharist and the Resurrection, we cannot do better than follow the movement of Teilhard's 'The Mass on the World'[41] and adopt its language – even though there are other guides who may express the same thing in different terms.

'THE MASS ON THE WORLD'

Teilhard is explaining the true nature of the *offertory*: 'Once upon a time,' he writes, 'men took into your temple the first fruits of their harvests, the flower of their flocks. But the offering you really want, the offering you mysteriously need every day to appease your hunger, to slake your thirst is nothing less than the growth of the world borne ever onwards in the stream of universal becoming. Receive, O Lord, this all-embracing host which your whole creation, moved by your magnetism, offers you at this dawn of a new day. This bread, our toil, is of itself, I know, but an immense fragmentation; this wine, our pain, is no more, I know, than a draught that dissolves. Yet in the very depths of this formless mass you have implanted – and this I am sure of, for I sense it – a desire, irresistible, hallowing, which makes us cry out, believer and unbeliever alike: "Lord, make us *one*." ' What we are asking for, therefore, when we make this offering is not simply that the crown be set upon our own being; rather is it a transformation and a transcendence of that being: absolute gratuitousness! 'Far from light emerging gradually out of the womb of our darkness,' Teilhard continues later, 'it is the Light, existing before all else was made which, patiently, surely, eliminates our darkness!' – and the Light does this by sinking into our world, to dissipate the night just as the sun does every time it dawns.

'Without earthquake, or thunderclap,' Teilhard writes of the universal effect of *consecration*, 'the flame has lit up the whole world from within. All things individually and collectively are penetrated and flooded by it, from the inmost core of the tiniest atom to the mighty sweep of the most universal laws of being: so naturally has it flooded every element, every energy, every connecting link in the unity of our cosmos, that one might suppose the cosmos to have burst spontaneously into flame. In the new

humanity which is begotten today the Word prolongs the un-
ending act of his own birth; and by virtue of his immersion in
the world's womb the great waters of the kingdom of matter
have, without even a ripple, been endued with life. No visible
tremor marks this inexpressible transformation; and yet, mysteriously and in very truth, at the touch of the supersubstantial
Word the immense host which is the universe is made flesh.
Through your own incarnation, my God, all matter is henceforth
incarnate.' 'If I firmly believe', he continues, 'that everything
around me is the body and blood of the Word, then for me (and
in one sense for me alone) is brought about that marvellous
"diaphany" which causes the luminous warmth of a single life
to be objectively discernible in and to shine forth from the
depths of every event, every element: whereas if, unhappily, my
faith should flag, at once the light is quenched and everything
becomes darkened, everything disintegrates.' Only faith, in fact,
can bring us face to face with what the Eucharist, through the
power of the Resurrection, effects in secret in this world *for us*.

For, by thus revealing to us the true and ultimate identity of
the world, faith also leads us into another unity in which flow
together in us, ultimately to be brought into harmony, 'the
excitement of action and the delight of passivity: the joy of
possessing and the thrill of reaching out beyond what one
possesses; the pride in growing and the happiness of being lost
in what is greater than oneself.' 'And, lost in the mystery of the
flesh of God,' Teilhard adds, thus anticipating the transforming
effects of the Lord's parousia, 'I cannot tell which is the more
radiant bliss: to have found the Word and so be able to achieve
the mastery of matter, or to have mastered matter and so be able
to attain and submit to the light of God.' The completely
prophetic character of this outburst need not disturb us! Of this
we can be certain; that activity and passivity, the whole formidable complex which makes the physical man to be a reaching
out to the universe, because he is fundamentally a limitless yearning for God, that, for us, all this can, through the 'Sacrament
of the World' find full satisfaction in a love of *communion* which
everything fosters and nothing can hold in check. 'For all things
are yours,' says St Paul, '. . . the world or life or death or the
present or the future, all are yours; and you are Christ's; and
Christ is God's' (1 Cor. 3:21–3). That is why, as Teilhard says,
'the man who is filled with an impassioned love of Jesus hidden

in the forces which bring increase to the earth, him the earth
will lift up, like a mother, in the immensity of her arms, and
will enable him to contemplate the face of God'. Such is the
communion with the Lord *in the forces of life* with which the
universe enchants us, but which brings with it a similar and
deeper *communion* through *the subjected forces of death*: and so
Teilhard adds, 'The man who is filled with an impassioned love
of Jesus hidden in the forces which bring death to the earth, him
the earth will clasp in the immensity of her arms as her strength
fails, and with her he will awaken in the bosom of God.'

In consequence, just as the Apostle St Thomas found in the
wounded body of Jesus the identity of the risen Christ, so the
man who thus takes to himself the world in the light of the
mystery of Christ, sacramentally signified in the Eucharist, will
be able, himself also, to proclaim the glory of the Lord eschatologically revealed in his resurrection. 'Glorious Lord Christ: the
divine influence secretly diffused and active in the depths of
matter, and the dazzling centre where all the innumerable fibres
of the manifold meet; power as implacable as the world and as
warm as life; you whose forehead is of the whiteness of snow,
whose eyes are of fire, and whose feet are brighter than molten
gold; you whose hands imprison the stars; you who are the first
and the last, the living and the dead and the risen again; you
who gather into your exuberant unity every beauty, every affinity,
every energy, every mode of existence; it is you to whom my
being cried out with a desire as vast as the universe, "In truth
you are my Lord and my God." '

By way of epilogue

In his first letter to the Corinthians St Paul is speaking of precisely this question, the apostolic ministry; and he says of it, 'No other foundation can any one lay than that which is laid, which is Jesus Christ' (1 Cor. 3:11). To say that we agree with this, and that in fact it goes without saying, will involve us in more consequences than we might at first anticipate: for, as soon as we come to 'priesthood' there is a danger that we may be too hasty in speaking of Christ *in his capacity* of Sovereign Priest. In so doing, we fail to see that a verbal analogy, which, moreover, is not scriptural, conceals a serious ambiguity. We are not priests, as Christ is a priest in a strictly unique and individual way. We are priests in his service, in the spiritual communication of his mystery of Priest which he effects for all who are baptized, teaching them to offer themselves just as he offers himself. Here we meet again what is so often found, the priesthood of one man in the first place, later to be followed by that of all men, and finally by that of some men in the service of all. We shall not dwell on this, for there is another ambiguity which we can now expose without much difficulty. This consists in overlooking in Christ an even more fundamental aspect of the mystery than the priesthood itself, and one which links the 'priestly' ministry to the *apostolic* ministry of the Resurrection.

Christ is, of course, in very truth *priest* and even *Sovereign Priest*: of this there can be no possibility of doubt, and the Epistle to the Hebrews makes this unmistakably plain. Nevertheless, when St Paul speaks of Christ as the *foundation* of all apostolic service to be provided in the Church, his intention is not to speak of Christ in the first place as priest. Supremely important though Christ's priesthood may be, it is still, in fact, only an *aspect* of the mystery of Christ; it is not *the* mystery *itself*, apprehended at its source, made manifest in the power of the Spirit, so that to overlook it would be to overlook Christ

himself. *The mystery, the removal of which means the annihilation of Christ himself, is the Resurrection.* St Paul's words are
categorical and hardly bear repetition, they have been quoted so
often: 'If Christ has not been raised, then our preaching is in
vain and your faith is in vain (1 Cor. 15:14). And again: 'If you
confess with your lips that Jesus is Lord and believe in your
heart that God raised him from the dead, you will be saved'
(Rom. 10:9). This, too, is the kernel of the infant Church's
kerygma at Pentecost. Taking his stand on the Resurrection,
St Peter proclaims, 'Let all the house of Israel therefore know
assuredly that God has made him both Lord and Christ, this
Jesus whom you crucified' (Acts 2:36). This Christ, thus con-
fessed in the Spirit and in the Spirit alone (1 Cor. 12:3) is
Priest and High Priest and even *sole* Priest (1 Tim. 2:5) since
his glory is the glory of the Son annihilated in the offering of
the servant; but he is above all *Lord.* It is as such that he is
revealed to us 'in the form of God' (Phil. 2:6) and 'designated
Son of God in power according to the Spirit of holiness by his
resurrection' (Rom. 1:4). It is therefore this Christ, made Lord
in the Spirit of the Resurrection, who must always be our
starting-point, if we wish to have any understanding at all of the
mystery, and in particular of the 'priestly' ministry within the
mystery. This latter cannot be anything but a *ministry of this
resurrection, without which everything in faith is in vain.*

The Resurrection cannot in itself derive from any human
resource, power or knowledge. Everything in it belongs to the
Person, to the work and the mystery of this Second Adam who
comes from 'heaven', that is to say from the Spirit, and who
gives to the First Adam the incorruptibility of the Kingdom.
This mystery, this message, and this life of the risen Christ
appear, therefore, in our history in the only form in which they
can so appear, the indefeasible form of a *gift.* We can be receptive of the Lord who exceeds all human power and wisdom (cf.
1 Cor. 2:9) only as a result of the attraction of the Spirit, who,
moreover, is at work everywhere and at all times, but is never
supplanted. 'I, when I am lifted up from the earth, will draw all
men to myself,' says Jesus in John (12:32). Christ, conceived of
the Holy Spirit, raised from the dead by his power, is thereby
again the unique revealer of the work of the Spirit, who has
been exalting all mankind ever since its origins and who, since
Pentecost, is visibly gathering together the Church in the con-

fession that 'Jesus is Lord'.

As the Council has strongly emphasized, it is the Church as people of God which is the first chosen in the divine plan. In her is developed, and by her is given, the essential witness which is to awaken all men and the whole man to the existence and mystery of Christ, dead and risen again. The Church, however, cannot render this service unless she is constantly begotten to Christ of the Spirit through a ministry which itself comes from the Spirit. The Holy Spirit, as invisible witness of Christ, is the initiator in this world of the very visible witness constituted by the Church of the Resurrection. For, 'how are men to call upon him in whom they have not believed? And how are they to believe in him of whom they have never heard? And how are they to hear without a preacher? And how can men preach unless they are sent?', as St Paul asks (Rom. 10:14–15). Indeed, the Spirit is as necessary for making men alive to the life of faith through the ministry of the Church, as he was for engendering Christ on the truth of the flesh, in the Nativity and the mystery of Easter; and it is to this Church, instituted by Jesus Christ until the time of his return, that the Holy Spirit has attached both his love and his power. The Church, therefore, exists in the world only as the sacrament of the Holy Spirit, who by confessing that Jesus is Lord reveals Christ in history and engenders men in order that they may thus attain their eternal truth (Eph. 1:4). Entrusted, not because of her innate competence but in virtue of the gift of grace, to spread abroad the indissoluble communion with the Person, the Thought, the Work – in short, with the mystery of the Christ of the Resurrection – the Church, gathered together apostolically, is the visible body of those who believe in Jesus Christ and who do everything in their power to proclaim him.

If, then, there is an apostolic ministry of which one can say that it is necessary to the Church's own loyalty to the Spirit of the Lord, then this ministry is necessarily derived in its entirety from the single unparalleled fact of the Resurrection; it derives, in its turn, from the uniqueness of the works of the Spirit, who divinizes mankind in the mystery of Christ just as he incorporates Christ with us. And so, too, the Apostles in the first place (in a very special way) and their successors after them and in close continuity with them, are, in the Spirit, the servants and guardians of the uniqueness of a Church which reveals in this world the form of the Spirit's infinite works. The 'priestly' ministry is, again, and in the same sense, an 'apostolic' ministry. It follows in the footsteps of the episcopal ministry. Like the latter, it involves an extra charismatic competence, and is therefore directly assimilated to the service which the Apostles rendered and are still rendering to the spiritual generation of the world, so that Christ may be loved by it as the Form, the Church, the Servant and the Spirit, the First Principle. Such a ministry no more comes from men than does the Person whom it serves. It comes entirely from Christ and the Spirit, in its source, its means and its true end. It cannot look upon itself as a property, flowing from the Church and its initiatives, just as the Church herself cannot reduce herself to the world she is made to serve without ever being absorbed in it. Since the Church is not the originator, but the servant and the first beneficiary of the gift that Jesus Christ makes to her of his resurrection, for her to communicate it to the world, she wholly accepts her own dependence on the Lord, receiving from him, in herself, a ministry of which she is not the source. The group of *Apostles*, the whole *episcopal order* which implies, in a sacramentally integrated mode, the whole body of *priests*, constitutes, in and for the Church, what one may call the *charismatic body of the apostolic ministry of the Resurrection*. The Spirit does not exhaust his gifts in that body, but he thereby guarantees its permanent and life-giving identity. 'Jesus Christ', says scripture, 'is the same yesterday and today and for ever' (Heb. 13:8), and the Holy Spirit ensures the permanence of a ministry whose first function is to proclaim the truth of Christ preached by the Apostles and teach men how to live by it.

Since the Eucharist is pre-eminently the act in which the Church is united in *body* to the life of her head, it will also be pre-eminently the place where she will recognize her dependence on a ministry which, in the function it performs, reveals the dearly treasured emergence of the Lord. The Church, in fact, becomes herself only within the conjugal union which the Bridegroom effects with her in the impregnable oneness of the body of the Resurrection, fully incorporated into the power of the Spirit. This oneness runs so deep that the Lord holds back nothing of himself, and thus the Church can have no doubt but that she is the true Bride to whom the Bridegroom is completely given. 'All that is mine is yours and all that is yours is mine' (cf.

Luke 15:31): this is not only what the Father says to the Son, but also what Christ says to his Church in the unity of a single flesh and a single Spirit. And since this union is truly conjugal, it unites without loss of identity. Even this is not putting it strongly enough: since it is a *true* love, as it personalizes it differentiates. And that is why this communication of the Lord to the Church, in which nothing is held back, and which *makes* the Church in her being as Bride, does not *unmake* Christ in his mystery of Bridegroom. The Christ who gives himself so fully remains, in the gift, still Lord: not in order to hold himself back, but in order to preserve the identity of the Person who gives himself and not to be annihilated in a false offering which would remove him.

Since it is the more indefeasible the more wholly it gives itself, the Person of the Lord is so constitutive of the mystery of the Church that it must constantly be signified in the very structure of the Body, in which his Spirit is given to us. And this is precisely the function of the priestly ministry, in the most generic sense of the word, including inseparably bishops and priests: to represent in the Church the fact that she possesses nothing of Christ but what she receives, and to signify this in the very Body of the union. The priestly ministry is the sign that the Church who receives as Bride the most complete gift of her Bridegroom does not annihilate, in her embrace, the person whose love fulfils her. What holds good in the most intense phase of the spiritual union of Christ and the Church which defines the Eucharist holds good too in every other domain in which Christ *signifies* and *accomplishes* his gifts. We see again why the existence of the Church is so deeply governed by an *apostolic* service which, even so, never contains, nor can ever contain, exclusively within itself the Holy Spirit and all his other gifts.

Understood in this way, the apostolic ministry constitutes, with scripture and the gratuitousness of charisms, a 'service' which is never 'paramount'. In its own irreplaceable way it manifests and guarantees, for the well-being of men and to assist what is most authentically their genesis, the emergence, the function, and the irresistible magnetism of Jesus Christ, Lord, in the Holy Spirit of the Resurrection.

Could any man hope, with the words of which he disposes, to

solve all the problems we have to face? On the other hand, how can we hope to solve them unless, in this field as in every other, we look without hesitation towards the Resurrection? This modest epilogue to so vast a subject may, perhaps, help to widen the impact of a book which can for the moment be content with having signposted some few theological roads in a truly Christian reshaping of our thought.

Notes

INTRODUCTION

1. See pp. 83–4 for the *absolute metabolism* of Christ's resurrection and the consequent mutation or transfiguration.

PART I

1. THE MEANING OF SYMBOL

1. H. G. Liddell and R. Scott, *A Greek-English Lexicon*, 9th ed. (Clarendon Press, Oxford, 1925–40), s.v. *symbolon*.
2. ibid.
3. *The Works of Aurelius Augustine*, ed. Marcus Dods, vol. IX, *On Christian Doctrine* (T. & T. Clark, Edinburgh, 1873), book II, ch. I, p. 34.
4. 'Symbolism', say Laplanche and Pontalis, 'covers all forms of indirect representation, without distinguishing more precisely the various forms of mechanism: transference, condensation, super-determination, figuration. As soon, in fact, as we can recognize in a behaviour, for example, at least two meanings, one of which is substituted for the other, simultaneously obscuring and expressing it, then we may qualify their relationship as symbolic' (*Vocabulaire de la psychanalyse* (P.U.F., Paris, 1963)). Paul Ricoeur writes to the same effect in *Le conflit des interprétations* (Le Seuil, Paris, 1969), p. 16.
5. Gérard de Champeaux and Dom Sébastien Sterckx, *Introduction au monde des Symboles* (Zodiaque, Saint-Léger-Vauban, 1966), pp. 7–9; cf. A. M. Farrer, *A Rebirth of Images* (Dacre Press, London, 1949, and P. Smith, Gloucester, Mass., 1970); E. L. Mascall, *Words and Images* (Longmans, Green, London, 1957); H. Musurillo, *Symbolism and the Christian Imagination* (Helicon, Dublin, 1962).
6. A. N. Whitehead, *Symbolism: Its Meaning and Effect* (Cambridge University Press, Cambridge, 1928), pp. 67–8.
7. cf. Jacques Arsac, 'Les ordinateurs', in *La science informatique* (Dunod, Paris, 1970), ch. 3, pp. 60–87.
8. Henri de Lubac, *La foi chrétienne: Essai sur la structure du Symbole des Apôtres* (Aubier, Paris, 1970), pp. 19–53.
9. The modern idea of a plurality of 'Symbols' as an expression of unity is accordingly surprising, to say the least.
10. For more details, see Dom Cabrol, 'Catéchuménat', in *Dictionnaire d'archéologie chrétienne et de liturgie*, col. 2592–4. It is regrettable that this stage is not more clearly marked than it generally is in the modern liturgy for the baptism of adults.
11. 'The Saussurian sign is the combination of a concept (the signified) with an acoustic image (the signifier)' (*La linguistique, Guide alpha-*

bétique, sous la direction d'André Martinet (Gonthier, Paris, 1969), p. 347). The signifier often expresses the sign-system taken as a whole.

12. Noam Chomsky, *Language and Mind* (Harcourt, Brace & World, New York, 1968, and London, 1972). The astonishing originality of language is rightly emphasized, again, when reference is made to the 'infinite potentiality of meaning contained in the linguistic code' (J. L. Houdebine, writing in *Critique,* 297 (1971) p. 330, about Julia Kristeva's *Recherches pour une sémanalyse* (Le Seuil, Paris, 1969)).

13. We may recall the three points of the programme put forward by Michel Foucault in his inaugural lecture at the Collège de France, 2 December 1970: 'To re-examine our will for truth; to restore to speech its character as event; finally, to emphasize the primacy of the signifier' (Edition du Collège de France, Chaire d'histoire des systèmes de pensée, no. 53, p. 25). 'The discussion is shifting from the message to the medium, in other words to language in its structure, its norms, its power to signify' (Lapassade, *Le livre fou* (L'Epi, Paris, 1970), p. 90).

14. We may remember that great phrase of St Augustine's, which defies translation: '*Deus intimior intimo meo et superior summo meo*' (*Confessions,* 3.6.11).

15. H. Trilles, *Les Pygmées de la Forêt Equatoriale* (Bloud et Gay, Paris and Liège, 1931). 'Khmvoum' is the pygmies' name for God.

16. Raymond Didier, 'L'Eucharistie et le temps des hommes', in *Lumière et Vie,* 94 (1969), p. 30; François Xavier Durrwell, 'Eucharistie et Parousie', in *Lumen Vitae,* 26 (1971), p. 122. Christ, says the latter, 'makes use of the sacramental elements, not because he would be incapable of total presence in the Church and of the total gift of self, but because he wishes to effect these within sensible realities to which he no longer belongs'. In consequence, 'he comes in his capacity of one who is absent from this world'. But he *does come,* and through the Eucharist (in a special way which we shall have to explain) he is *truly always present in the world.* The modern one-sided emphasis on the *lack,* on the *elsewhere,* on the *other* – itself a reaction against an equally one-sided logical emphasis on *identity* (a point admirably treated by Lévinas in his *Totalité et Infini* (La Haye, 1961)) – is apt to obscure, in analysing the sym-bol, the function of conjunction and union. This leads to speaking of Christianity as though it were only an adjustment to absence, and almost entirely neglecting the element, in Christ and the Spirit, of conjunction, presence and communion. So, for example, Michel de Certeau who, in 'La Rupture instauratrice, Réflexion sur le christianisme dans la culture contemporaine', in *Esprit,* June 1971, does not even mention the Eucharist.

2. EUCHARISTIC SYMBOLISM AND MAN'S CONDITION

1. Jewish blessing at table, in L. Bouyer, *Eucharist: Theology and Spirituality of the Eucharistic Prayer,* translated by C. U. Quinn, (University of Notre Dame Press, Notre Dame and London, 1968), p. 80.

2. *The Didache,* or *The Doctrine of the Twelve Apostles* (first quarter of the second century), translated by Charles Bigg, rev. A. J. Maclean (SPCK, London, 1922), IX.4, pp. 27–8.

3. *Letters*, LXIII, XIII, 4.

4. Though Irenaeus, it is true, mentions human skills, *Adversus Haereses*, V, 2, 3 (*The Treatise of Irenaeus of Lugdunum against the Heresies*, vol. II (SPCK, London, 1916), p. 94).

5. Edmond Barbotin, *Humanité de l'homme, Etude de philosophie concrète* (Aubier, Paris, 1970), pp. 297–9.

6. Claude Lévi-Strauss, *Structural Anthropology* (Basic Books, New York and London, 1963), p. 353. 'The incest prohibition', he says elsewhere, 'expresses the transition from the natural fact of consanguinity to the cultural fact of alliance' (*The Elementary Structures of Kinship*, ed. R. Needham, rev. ed. (Eyre & Spottiswoode, London, 1968, and Beacon Press, Boston, 1969), p. 30).

7. Pierre Grassé, *Toi, ce petit Dieu: Essai sur l'histoire naturelle de l'homme* (Albin Michel, Paris, 1971), p. 12. Ch. 4, in particular, is a well-balanced summary.

8. Pierre Teilhard de Chardin, *The Phenomenon of Man* (Collins, London, and Harper & Brothers, New York, 1959), pp. 164–6. See his earlier essay, 'The Phenomenon of Man' (1930), in *The Vision of the Past* (Collins, London, and Harper & Row, New York, 1966), p. 161. He speaks also of mankind as a 'sort of peak'. This idea is constantly to be found in Teilhard, and is characteristic of what he himself calls a 'neo-anthropocentrism of movement', in 'The Singularities of the Human Species', in *The Appearance of Man* (Collins, London, and Harper & Row, New York, 1965), p. 209.

9. Paul Ricoeur, *Freud and Philosophy: An Essay on Interpretation* (Yale University Press, New Haven and London, 1970). The phrase 'libidinal deflection' (*'la déviance libidinale'*) comes from Georges Lapassade, in his *L'Arpenteur, une intervention sociologique* (L'Epi, Paris, 1971), p. 126.

10. Noam Chomsky, *Language and Mind*, p. 59. The common analogy is that of bees, for a factual account of which see Karl von Frisch, *The Dancing Bees* (Methuen, London, 1954, and Harcourt, Brace and World, New York, 1966). For the originality of human speech as compared with signals recorded in the animal world, cf. Emile Benvéniste, *Problèmes de linguistique générale* (Gallimard, Paris, 1966), pp. 57f.; and Georges Mounin, 'Communication linguistique humaine et communication non linguistique animale', in *Introduction à la séméiologie* (Editions de Minuit, Paris, 1970), pp. 41–57.

11. E. Benvéniste, op. cit., p. 44.

12. 'The Singularities of the Human Species', in *The Appearance of Man*, pp. 243–4.

13. André Leroi-Gourhan, *Le geste et la parole; Technique et langage* (Albin Michel, Paris, 1964), pp. 232–6. For the successive stages of culture, food-gathering, hunting, animal husbandry, plant cultivation, large-scale growing of cereals, see Joseph Goetz, in F. M. Bergounioux and J. Goetz, *Prehistoric and Primitive Religions* (Hawthorn Books, New York, 1965, and Burns & Oates, London, 1966), pp. 63–8.

14. See *La Maison-Dieu*, 1949, and, better still, R. Guardini, *Besinnung der Feier der Heiligen Messe* (Mainz, 1939), pp. 263–74.

15. E. Barbotin, 'Humanité de Dieu, Approche anthropologique du mystère chrétien', in *Theologie*, 78, 1970, pp. 326–8. From an exegetical point

of view, M. Kehl, 'Eucharistie und Auferstehung', in *Geist und Leben,* 1970, pp. 90–125.

16. E. Barbotin, op. cit., pp. 332–4; H. Urs von Balthasar, *Sponsa Verbi,* vol. II, *Schauen, Glauben, Essen,* (Johannes Verlag, Einsiedeln, 1960), pp. 502–13.

17. 'The table', says E. Barbotin, 'is *pre-eminently the furniture of society,* and in the first place the furniture of meeting' (*Humanité de l'homme,* p. 294). In 'Humanité de Dieu', p. 330, he says, 'Pre-eminently the furniture of society, the table is for the Church the assembly-point.' Cf. T. Corbishley, *One Body, One Spirit* (Faith Press, London, 1973), p. 15.

18. Leroi-Gourhan, *Le geste et la parole,* p. 210.

19. Leroi-Gourhan, ibid. We know the part this hypothesis of the primitive horde emerging from the murder of the father plays in Freud's explanation of the origins of religion. The chief passages in which he relies on this myth for an 'explanation' of 'religion' are: *Totem and Taboo,* 1913 (Routledge, London, 1919), pp. 235–43; *The Future of an Illusion,* 1927 (Hogarth Press, London, 1928), pp. 39–42; 'Malaise dans la civilisation', in *Revue française de psychanalyse,* 1934, pp. 756–65 (reissued P.U.F., Paris, 1971); *Moses and Monotheism,* 1939 (Hogarth Press, London, 1939), pp. 130–5.

20. Leroi-Gourhan, op. cit., p. 216.

21. Walter Dirks, in the *Frankfurter Hefte,* September 1948, published in French translation in 'Le pain quotidien', in *La Maison-Dieu,* 18, pp. 107–8.

22. Edgar Haulotte, 'Trois signes de crise dans le monde' (Acts 11:27–12:25), in *Vie chrétienne,* 134 (1971), pp. 8–12; and, similarly related to the text of Acts, 'Modèles économiques?', in *Vie chrétienne,* 127 (1970), pp. 9–14.

23. Paul VI to UNO, in *Documentation catholique,* 1965, col. 1736.

24. *Géo-politique de la faim* (Editions Ouvrières, Paris, 1970). He demonstrates, too, the existence of destitution in the midst of plenty, as in the USA for example.

25. Georges Friedmann, *Le Monde,* 3 December 1968.

26. *Documentation catholique,* 1965, col. 15. Paul VI repeated this appeal two years later in *Populorum Progressio.* After speaking of the need for co-ordinated plans for the relief of impoverished countries, he added, 'We must go further. In Bombay we pleaded for the setting up of a great *world fund,* financed by a portion of expenditure on armaments, to assist those whose poverty was greatest. What applies to the immediate fight against destitution applies also to the relative scale of development. Only really world-wide collaboration, of which a common fund would be both the symbol and the instrument, would make it possible to overcome barren rivalries and stimulate a fruitful and peaceful dialogue between all nations' (*Populorum Progressio,* 51, in *Documentation catholique,* 1967, col. 692).

27. François Perroux, *A Challenge to the Church* (Westminster Press, Philadelphia, 1965), p. 92, quoted in *Informations Catholiques Internationales,* 218 (1964). There must be an examination of conscience about the system of providing help for underdeveloped countries, for it introduces problems which Christians cannot refuse to face.

H. Perroy, in *L'Europe devant le Tiers Monde* (Aubier, Paris, 1971), pp. 186–9, analyses the phenomenon of 'siphoning', which brings back into the country which provides help the wealth of the country which is receiving help. In less technical terms, Mgr H. Camara is continually denouncing the 'injustice and absurdity of international trade'; see 'Catholicisme 1970', in *La Nef*, 41, p. 123 in particular. Is there really no cure for all this?

28. cf. below, pp. 180–4.

29. Karl Marx, 'Critique of Hegel's Dialectic', in *Early Writings*, trans. and ed. T. B. Bottomore (C. A. Watts, London, 1963), p. 207.

30. We find this in the North-west American Indians' 'potlatch' or lavish distribution of gifts of food and drink; cf. Marcel Mauss, 'Essai sur le don', in *Société et anthropologie* (P.U.F., Paris, 1960), pp. 195–210. Similarly, in Melanesian societies, M. Leenhardt, *Do Kamo: La personne et le mythe dans le monde mélanésien* (Gallimard, Paris, 1947), p. 172.

31. *Gaudium et Spes*, 27.3, in *The Documents of Vatican II*, ed. W. Abbott (Geoffrey Chapman, London, and America Press, New York, 1966), pp. 226–7.

32. ibid., 26.2, p. 225.

33. *La création de l'homme*, in *Sources chrétiennes*, 6, (Le Cerf, Paris, 1943), p. 106.

34. Paul Wintrebert, *L'existence délivrée de l'existentialisme* (Masson, Paris, 1965), p. 126.

35. *Le Milieu Divin* (Collins, London, 1960), pp. 31–2; *The Divine Milieu* (Harper & Brothers, New York, 1960), pp. 28–9. We know, too, how strongly the young Marx emphasized the importance for man of his cultural appropriation of the sensible world. 'It is not only the five senses, but also the so-called spiritual senses, the practical senses (desiring, loving, etc.), in brief, human sensibility and the human character of the senses, which can only come into being through the existence of its object, through *humanized* nature. The cultivation of the five senses is the work of all previous history' ('Private Property and Communism', in *Early Writings*, p. 161).

36. 'A Note on Progress' (1920), in *The Future of Man* (Collins, London, and Harper & Row, New York, 1964), p. 17.

37. 'What Exactly is the Human Body?' (1919), in *Science and Christ* (Collins, London, and Harper & Row, New York, 1968), p. 13.

38. Jean-Paul Charrier, 'Relire Freud, La sexualité fonction ou conduite', in *Christus*, 66 (1970), p. 202. Here the author refers to Jacques Lacan, *Ecrits* (Le Seuil, Paris, 1966), pp. 237–322, whose distinctive stamp can be seen in the phrase which concludes the passage quoted: 'The non-significant, the sense-less, then become the signifier coded with a latent signification.'

39. Gisela Pankow, 'Du corps perdu au corps retrouvé, une introduction à la psychothérapie analytique des psychoses', in *Tijdschrift voor Filosofie*, 30 (Louvain, 1968), pp. 223–47.

40. Maurice Merleau-Ponty distinguishes the *own* body from the *habitual* body, referred to above as the 'generic', in order to emphasize that, in ourselves, it derives from the *genus* of man as such (*Phenomenology of Perception* (Routledge & Kegan Paul, London, and Humanities Press, New York, 1962), pp. 98ff., 174ff.

41. H. Urs von Balthasar, *Phénoménologie de la Vérité* (Beauchesne, Paris, 1952), p. 49.

42. Karl Rahner, 'The Theology of the Symbol', in *Theological Investigations*, vol. IV (Darton, Longman & Todd, London, and Helicon Press, Baltimore, 1966), p. 245. Jean Guitton mentions, in connection with 'the functions of the body', 'that of *resemblance* to the mind', which he calls also a functioning as *symbol*, and as *'insertion* in life and the cosmos', thus bringing together two aspects that are often kept separate (*The Problem of Jesus* (Burns & Oates, London, 1955), p. 138).

43. Claude Bruaire, *Philosophie du corps* (Le Seuil, Paris, 1968), pp. 219–27.

44. Marcel Jousse, *L'anthropologie du geste* (Resma, 1969). Jousse, we may recall, was passionately interested in 'situating living thought in the *whole* body' (p. 87).

45. *Origen on First Principles*, IV, II, 7 (SPCK, London, 1936, and Harper & Row, New York, 1966), p. 282.

46. *Alcibiades*, 129b–130c. For the history of the notion of body as instrument, see Witmar Metzger, *Der Organongedanke in der Christologie der Griechischen Kirchenväter* (Vier-Türme, Münsterschwarzach, 1968), upon which the whole of this passage is based.

47. 'There is no other name under heaven given among men by which we must be saved' (Acts 4:12). 'There is one God,' says St Paul, 'and there is one mediator between God and men, the man Christ Jesus' (1 Tim. 2:5).

48. *Dogme et critique* (Bloud et Cie, Paris, 1907), pp. 240–1.

49. *Metaphysical Journal* (Rockliff, London, 1952, and H. Regnery, Chicago, 1967), p. 242.

50. L. Van Bogaert, O. Petre-Quadens, G. A. Ribière, 'Neurologie développementale et sciences de base, comme méthodes d'approche dans l'arriération mentale', in *Médecine et Hygiène*, 25 (Geneva, 1967), pp. 1–11; G. A. Ribière, 'Contribution à la recherche méthodologique pour l'étude du comportement humain', in *Revue de médecine fonctionnelle, Supplément*, 1967, pp. 61–95; *Fédération mondiale de neurologie, Groûpe de travail de neurologie développementale*, Cahier no. 1, 'Contribution à l'étude du langage', by A. Grisoni-Coli, F. Breschi, R. Beccari and G. A. Ribière (Paris-Milan, 1968).

51. The phenomenon is well known. 'Possessing hands as well as intelligence, and being able, in consequence, to devise "artificial" instruments and multiply them indefinitely, without becoming somatically involved, [man] has succeeded, while increasing and boundlessly extending his mechanical efficiency, in preserving intact his freedom of choice and power of reason' (Teilhard de Chardin, 'The Formation of the Noosphere', in *The Future of Man*, p. 164).

52. So to translate Aristotle's well-known *thurathen* (*De Generatione Animalium*, 736b, 27–9,II,3), often used later in Western philosophy to express the transcendence of spirit, so providing a foundation for a *dualism* that has seldom been intellectually overcome.

53. Rahner, op. cit., has got down to the anthropological root of the body as symbol, but along the lines of scholastic philosophy.

54. On the soul's transcendental relationship with the world, see K. Rahner, op. cit., vol. 3, pp. 263–76. Among the books which I have found most illuminating, either directly or by the contrast they provide, and besides

those mentioned in notes 35–50, I should mention also John A. T. Robinson, *The Body: A Study in Pauline Theology* (SCM Press, London, and Allenson, Naperville, Ill., 1952); Gustave Siewerth, *L'homme et son corps* (Plon, Paris, 1957); Michel Henry, *Philosophie et Phénoménologie du Corps, Essai sur L'Ontologie biranienne* (P.U.F., Paris, 1965).

55. *L'eau et les rêves: Essai sur l'imagination de la matière* (Corti, Paris, 1942), and the whole body of his 'symbolic' work.

56. 'The Spiritual Power of Matter', in *Hymn of the Universe* (Collins, London, and Harper & Brothers, New York, 1965), pp. 63–4.

57. *Philosophie du corps*, p. 153: a key idea in the book.

58. For example, Maine de Biran, on whom, see Philip Hallie, *Maine de Biran, Reformer of Empiricism* (Harvard University Press, Cambridge, Mass., 1959).

59. *Beyond the Pleasure Principle* (Hogarth Press, London, 1950, and Liveright, New York, 1970).

60. In 1892 the German biologist August Weismann (d.1914) had proposed to distinguish within the cell the reproductive *germen* from the alimental *soma*. This celebrated distinction has governed all later writing on genetics and has, in particular, supplied the basis for the science of heredity. We meet it in Monod's views on what he calls the 'replicative mechanism' of DNA, the 'telenomic coherence' of organisms, and the 'irreversibility of evolution' (*Chance and Necessity* (Collins, London, 1972), pp. 106–130).

61. *Beyond the Pleasure Principle*, p. 50. It is only the second proposition, it will be noted, which is an elementary observation of fact; the first, on the other hand, in its reference to 'goal', is a judgement not of fact but of value. Without adducing sufficient reason, it rules out the possibility that there may be in the condition of mortality something which forbids us to accept this *factual* observation as the last word when we come to consider *ends*. This criticism of Freud applies *a fortiori* to Monod, who, perhaps unconsciously, is led into adopting identical views.

62. op. cit., p. 51.

63. *Ananke* means 'necessity' in the strict sense of 'fate', and as Freud uses it of the 'remorseless law' (ibid., p. 59).

64. ibid., p. 86.

65. ibid., p. 51.

66. ibid., p. 72.

67. ibid., p. 82.

68. ibid., p. 83.

69. ibid., p. 27.

70. ibid., p. 37.

71. The phrase is Freud's (ibid., p. 76).

72. *Le Cœur de la matière* (unpublished); so again in 'Cosmic Life', in *Writings in Time of War* (Collins, London, and Harper & Row, New York, 1968), p. 31: 'And thus it was that in one flash the bewitching voice that was drawing me far from the cities into the untrodden, silent spaces, came through to me. One day I understood the meaning of the words it spoke to me; they stirred the little-known depths of my being, holding out the promise of some great bliss-giving repose; and I knew what it meant when it whispered "Take the easier road." '

This is precisely release of tension and the principle of economy built up into a life-system.

73. To be exact, from spring 1919 to spring 1920: Ernest Jones, *The Life and Work of Sigmund Freud*, vol. III (Chatto & Windus, London, 1957), p. 43. Teilhard's 'The Spiritual Power of Matter', in *Hymn of the Universe*, pp. 59–71, in which his lyrical language expresses views that completely contradict those of Freud, dates from August 1919.

74. 'Science and Christ or Analysis and Synthesis', in *Science and Christ*, pp. 21–36. Père François Russo criticizes Jacques Monod on the same lines, in 'La vie et le hasard', in *Etudes*, April 1971, pp. 205–9.

75. Looking back in 1950, Teilhard came to the conclusion that, as he puts it, 'I might well find myself up against Freud's unconscious . . . My position was then determined irrevocably, for I had seen once and for all that if the world is left to itself it is in the direction not of obscurity but of light that, with all its vastness and all its weight, it heaves itself forward into equilibrium' (*Le Cœur de la matière*, p. 17).

76. 'Man, no longer the centre, but an arrow shot towards the centre of the universe in process of concentration' ('The Singularities of the Human Species', in *The Appearance of Man*, pp. 209–10).

77. To take one example from among any number: 'Man's Place in the Universe', in *The Vision of the Past*, p. 217: 'Perhaps I shall risk an "ultra-physical" excursus. But look for no metaphysics here.' For Teilhard 'ultra-physics' means deepening our knowledge of the world from a starting-point in total man, regarded as a phenomenon in which the significance of the world is disclosed.

78. C. Cuénot, *Nouveau Lexique Teilhard de Chardin* (Le Seuil, Paris, 1968), s.v. 'Physique', p. 169.

79. *The Phenomenon of Man*, p. 36.

80. On this, see E. Borne, *De Pascal à Teilhard de Chardin* (Bussac, Clermont-Ferrand, 1963), in which, however, there is more of Pascal than of Teilhard.

81. 'The Planetization of Mankind', in *The Future of Man*, p. 130.

82. The 'quanta' represent the elementary unit of calculable energy of which, speaking in terms of energy, matter is made up.

83. Thus Einstein gets rid of the Newtonian idea of an absolute standard of reference, the 'ether', as a function of which every movement would have to be described. Jacques Merleau-Ponty and Bruno Morendo, *Les trois étapes de la cosmologie* (Laffont, Paris, 1971), pp. 190–204.

84. *Man's Place in Nature* (Collins, London, and Harper & Row, New York, 1966), pp. 23, 36.

85. 'The Phenomenon of Man', in *The Vision of the Past*, p. 170n. By 'irreversibility' Teilhard means the definitive character of spirit in the evolutive universe which serves as its cradle. This idea contrasts with that of total death to which we shall be referring later. The idea of the 'enfolding' of the world or of 'centricity' gives a better picture than does that of *irreversibility*; the latter, on the other hand, is a better expression of the 'nature' of spirit.

86. ibid., p. 170.

87. *Creative Evolution* dates from 1907. On the relationship between Teilhard and Bergson, see M. Barthélemy-Madaule, *Bergson et Teilhard de Chardin* (Le Seuil, Paris, 1963), where it is studied more from the philosophical than from the scientific point of view. In *Creative*

Evolution (Macmillan, London, 1911), Bergson speaks of life as 'an ascending wave opposed by the descending movement of matter' (p. 284).

88. 'Universalization and Union', in *Activation of Energy* (Collins, London, 1970), p. 88. There is the same metaphor of dotting the i in 'Some Reflections on Progress', in *The Future of Man*, p. 66.

89. 'Entropy', writes Jacques Monod in *Chance and Necessity*, 'is the thermodynamic quantity which *measures* the extent to which a system's energy is . . . degraded . . .' 'The "degradation of energy",' he continues, 'or the increase of entropy is a statistically predictable consequence of the random movements and collisions of molecules. Take for example two enclosed spaces at different temperatures put into communication with each other. The "hot" (i.e., fast) molecules and the "cold" (slow) molecules will, in the course of their movements, pass from one space into the other, thus eventually and inevitably nullifying the temperature difference between the two enclosures. From this example one sees that the increase of entropy in such a system is linked to an increase of *disorder* [or statistically undifferentiated mixture of molecules]. Once statistical equilibrium is achieved within the system, no further macroscopic phenomenon can occur there.' On the other hand, 'an increase of order corresponds to a diminution of entropy or, as it is sometimes phrased, a heightening of negative entropy (or "neg-entropy")' (pp. 185–7). See also François Jacob, *La logique du vivant, une histoire de l'hérédité* (Gallimard, Paris, 1970), pp. 210–20.

90. Erwin Schrödinger, *What is Life? The Physical Aspect of the Living Cell* (Cambridge University Press, London, 1944), pp. 68–76, where we find 'negative entropy'.

91. *Le second principe de la science du temps* (Le Seuil, Paris, 1963), pp. 85, 135, 141.

92. *L'ordre biologique* (Laffont, Paris, 1969), p. 170.

93. 'L'Evolution et le Temps', in *Etudes Teilhardiennes* (Brussels, 1969), p. 94. Following the same line of thought as O. Costa de Beauregard (though he does not quote him), de Rosnay speaks of life in terms of 'structural neg-entropy', and, associating neg-entropy with *chromosomic* information, he arrives at the irreversibly significant value of man for the universe. F. Jacob, too (op. cit., pp. 270–3), connects the ideas of information and entropy, and gives an admirable account of the processes of chromosomic information.

94. 'The Atomism of Spirit', in *Activation of Energy*, p. 28.

95. 'The Human Rebound of Evolution', in *The Future of Man*, p. 206.

96. 'Critique of Hegel's Dialectic', in *Early Writings*, p. 207.

97. 'Private Property and Communism', ibid., p. 159.

98. Alexandre Kojève, *Introduction à la lecture de Hegel* (Gallimard, Paris, 1947), p. 573.

99. On this, and with the same point already in mind, see G. Martelet, *Victoire sur la mort, Eléments d'anthropologie chrétienne* (Chronique sociale, Lyons, 1962), ch. 2, 'Le marxisme devant le fait de la mort', pp. 43–84.

100. Thus Claude Bruaire himself, at the end of his *Philosophie du corps*. Unlike Bruaire, Claude Tresmontant, *Le problème de l'âme* (Le Seuil, Paris, 1970) most convincingly exposes the falsity of the principle that

'everything which disappears from the field of experience is annihilated' (p. 191). Similarly, he accepts the Platonic and Thomist proofs of the immortality of the soul (pp. 193–6), which Bruaire rejects. Nevertheless, in his conclusion, Tresmontant is unwilling to affirm the *certainty* of nullity's being transcended in death, because he does not wish to compromise the Christian doctrine of the creation, which involves man's receiving himself from God (pp. 196–201). Here, though the agreement is somewhat forced, he falls into line with Protestant thought: see Henri Bouillard, *Karl Barth*, vol. 3 (Aubier, Paris, 1957), pp. 264ff.; and Oscar Cullman, *Immortality of the Soul or Resurrection of the Dead?* (Epworth Press, London, 1958). Equally unexpectedly, Tresmontant argues against the body itself being really involved in resurrection (pp. 212–15). Bruaire, on the other hand, is in complete agreement with tradition on this point, and accepts the complete philosophic plausibility of resurrection, in view of the basic significance of the body for man and of God's creative mystery. To my mind, Bruaire's philosophy of the body should enable us to express the question of human emergence, as related to death, in a *completely* new way. One thing, at any rate, is evident: the uncertainty that prevails among thinkers about a question of such cardinal importance.

101. *Letters to Two Friends (1926–1952)* (The New American Library, New York, 1968, and Fontana, London, 1972), p. 42. We find the same argument used in 1931, to reject total death, in 'The Spirit of the Earth', *Human Energy* (Collins, London, 1969, and Harcourt, Brace, Jovanovich, New York, 1971), pp. 38–43. This is the road to Omega. Teilhard's most important passages dealing with this point are conveniently brought together by J.-P. Demoulin in *Let Me Explain* (Collins, London, and Harper & Row, New York, 1970), pp. 79–108. Cf. L. Boros, *The Moment of Truth* (Burns & Oates, London, 1965), published in the USA as *The Mystery of Death* (Seabury Press, New York).

102. 'Anthropology' is a word which a number of readers may find distasteful. They are inclined to think that it is a recent introduction, and that its use, acceptable in a scientific context, is unwarranted here. Nothing could be more mistaken. Although it was unknown in classical Greece, we meet it as an adjective in Philo. The noun appears at the end of the sixteenth century, in the sense of 'discussion of man', and is so used by Malebranche, Kant and Feuerbach. See Liddell and Scott, *Lexikon für Theologie und Kirche*, and Lalande, *Vocabulaire de la Philosophie*, s.v. Thus the word is not misused or distorted, but legitimately applied.

3. THE ANTHROPOLOGY OF THE RESURRECTION

1. *Lettre aux Ephésiens*, 20, *Sources chrétiennes*, 10 (Le Cerf, Paris, 1951), p. 91; *The Apostolic Fathers*, trans. J. B. Lightfoot (Macmillan, London and New York, 1891), p. 142. In a note, Père Camelot, OP, refers to the *Adversus Haereses* of St Irenaeus, who also says, 'Our bodies receiving the Eucharist are no longer mortal, seeing that they possess the hope of the resurrection to eternal life' (IV.18.5).

2. The second volume of Emile Poulat's *Histoire, dogme et critique dans la crise moderniste* (of which the first was published in 1962) will deal

with Le Roy's period. The best critical study of his ideas on the Resurrection is that by Lucien Laberthonnière in the *Annales de philosophie chrétienne* (1907–8), vols. 154 and 155, entitled *Dogme et théologie*. There are also two important letters from Blondel to Le Roy in *Lettres philosophiques de Maurice Blondel* (Aubier, Paris, 1961), pp. 251–66, 272–3. On Le Roy's scientific thought, see Gaston Bachelard, *L'engagement rationnaliste* (P.U.F., Paris, 1972), pp. 155–69.

3. 'Hermeneutics' comes from a Greek verb meaning 'to interpret'. The subject is studied retrospectively in René Marlé, *Introduction to Hermeneutics* (Burns & Oates, London, and Herder & Herder, New York, 1967), pp. 11–24, and for the nineteenth century in Paul Ricœur, *Le conflit des interprétations, Essais d'herméneutique*, pp. 7–28. Henri de Lubac has also studied the hermeneutics of the Fathers and of the Middle Ages in *Histoire et esprit, L'intelligence de l'Ecriture d'après Origène*, in the series *Théologie*, no. 16 (Aubier, Paris, 1950), and *Exégèse médiévale, Les quatre sens de l'Ecriture*, in the series *Théologie*, nos. 41, 42, 59 (1959, 1961, 1964).

4. Peter Szondi, 'L'herméneutique de Schleiermacher', in *Poétique*, 1970, p. 141.

5. 'And so the attachment of the signifying products to the constituent London, 1960). Cf. also his *Existence and Faith*, and *Jesus and the* its own subtlety.

6. Dogmatic Constitution on Divine Revelation, 12, 2, in *The Documents of Vatican, II*, p. 120.

7. Edgar Haulotte, *Symbolique du Vêtement selon la Bible*, in the series *Théologie*, no. 65 (1966), pp. 237f.

8. The title of an article written in 1957, translated in *Existence and Faith* (Meridian Books, Cleveland, 1960, and Hodder & Stoughton, London, 1961), pp. 342–51.

9. *The Problem of Jesus*, p. 141. It will be noted that the problem Bultmann raises here is by no means the same as that debated with Barth about 'pre-comprehension', which is concerned less with the relation between historical method and exegesis than with the relation between antecedent philosophy and exegesis. On this, see Marlé, op. cit., pp. 58–66.

10. *Existence and Faith*, p. 345.

11. On this question of the 'miracle', see Bultmann, *Jesus Christ and Mythology* (Charles Scribner's Sons, New York, 1958, and SCM Press, London, 1960). Cf. also his *Existence and Faith*, and *Jesus and the Word* (Charles Scribner's Sons, New York, 1958, and Fontana, London, 1962).

12. *Existence and Faith*, p. 345.

13. Reimarus (d.1768), the father of nineteenth-century 'liberal' Protestant exegesis, whose writings were published by Lessing (d.1781) in 1774 and 1778, laid down the principle, in the very title of a third group of fragments brought out by Lessing in 1777, of 'the impossibility of a revelation to which all men can give a well-founded credence'. On the influence of Lessing himself in introducing into nineteenth-century German thought Spinoza's notion of a religion which is all the more true for rejecting the idea of 'miracle', see Ernst Cassirer, *The Philosophy of the Enlightenment* (Princeton University Press, Princeton

and London, 1951), pp. 190–6.

14. As, for example, Louis Evely in his *Gospel without Myth* (Doubleday, New York, 1971).

15. 'In the natural sciences, the temptation to dismiss a newly discovered event as "apocryphal" (either from mere reluctance, or from fear of *the refashioning of the entire structure of a science which this one event can sometimes make intellectually imperative*) is continually rejected, because it is impossible for the scientist to dismiss as non-existent a new factor which cannot be fitted into our equationally expressed summaries' (Manuel de Dieguez, 'Une passion transtombale', in the *Nouvelle Revue Française*, 1970, p. 695).

16. In the light of God's work 'for us' in Christ (e.g. Rom. 5:8 and 8:37–9) it is strictly impossible to present *a priori* God's intervention in history as a work of 'supernatural powers' or of *any* 'forces outside this world', as Bultmann does. In the Gospel Christ distinctly rejects the 'signs from heaven' which his unbelieving opponents demand (Matt. 16:1–4). Christ's miracles *re-establish* man in his correct position; they do not disorganize either nature or history; they restore man (Matt. 11:4–7). To overlook this aspect of the gospel miracles and to reduce it to some vague, magical, undifferentiated 'supernatural', is to leave the subject completely untouched. 'The historian's agnosticism,' Père Le Guillou aptly remarks, 'backed by a philosophic and theological agnosticism, has invaded the thought of many of our contemporaries far more deeply than is generally believed.' And he even goes on to say, 'And there is still no Catholic exegete, with sufficient theological knowledge, who has had the courage fully to examine the philosophical presuppositions which colour and sometimes govern all contemporary historical criticism and exegesis' (*Celui qui vient d'ailleurs, L'innocent* (Le Cerf, Paris, 1971), p. 301).

17. An example of the handling of these questions will be found in Jean Delorme, 'Résurrection et Tombeau de Jésus: Marc 16, 1–8 dans la tradition évangélique', in *La Résurrection du Christ et l'exégèse moderne, Lectio divina*, 50 (Le Cerf, Paris, 1969), pp. 105–153. It may be that a 'structuralist' exegetical method (if the word is not too pompous) as advocated and practised by Edgar Haulotte and Louis Marin (in particular in *Recherches de science religieuse*, January, 1970) can contribute to the objectivity of exegete A, if it is not a victim of its own subtlety.

18. Edmond Barbotin, *Humanité de l'homme*, p. 37.

19. *Dogme et critique*, p. 18. Bracketed figures in the text refer to pages of *Dogme et critique*.

20. *Summa Theologica*, 3a, q.55, a.5, ad 2um, quoted by Le Roy, p. 180.

21. *Dei Verbum*, 19, shows how we can understand the origin of the gospels if we get rid of a similar attitude.

22. *Dogme et critique*, pp. 216–17. Le Roy prefaces this with a long critical exegesis of the Matthew tradition, which, he maintains, did not originally include the story of finding the tomb empty. The reason he gives for this is that it was Galilee and not Jerusalem which mattered to those who were responsible for this tradition (pp. 201–15).

23. A. Pelletier, 'Les apparitions du Ressuscité en termes de la LXX', in *Biblica*, 51 (1970), pp. 76–9, has shown that this is the meaning of the verb *ophthe* used of the appearance of the risen Christ, notably in

1 Corinthians 15:5, and also in the gospels.

24. A point elaborated by Loisy in *Autour d'un petit livre* (Picard, Paris, 1903), p. 120; *Dogme et critique*, p. 225.

25. We may note the analogy between Le Roy's view of the Resurrection and Willi Marxsen's contemporary definition: '*Die Sache Jesu geht weiter!*' ('The resurrection of Jesus is today a matter of dispute'), in *The Resurrection of Jesus of Nazareth* (SCM Press, London, 1970, p. 24.

26. *Dogme et théologie, Annales de philosophie chrétienne*, vol. 154 (1907), p. 580 (our italics). Would he express a different opinion about much more recent views?

27. This purely interpretative conception of what we can say about the Resurrection, which has value only as being a series of efforts, again coincides with or anticipates, in a most remarkable way, the theory put forward by Willi Marxsen in our own day. Marxsen sees in the resurrection of Christ no more than a pure *Interpretament* – itself not the only possible one – designed to account for the 'shock' of vision (*Widerfahrnis des Sehens*) which the experience of the Resurrection represents for him (*The Resurrection of Jesus of Nazareth*, pp. 16, 22, 34). C. Lehmann, *Auferweckt am dritten Tag nach der Schrift* (Freiburg, 1968), pp. 340–3, points out that the calm and peace which emerge from the accounts of Christ's appearances have nothing in common with the 'shock' and 'counter-shock' of which Marxsen speaks, as did Le Roy, following Loisy.

28. For Bultmann, too, the event of the Resurrection is not the risen Christ as such, but his disciples' faith in his resurrection ('New Testament and Mythology. The Task of Demythologizing the New Testament Proclamation', in *Kerygma and Myth* (SPCK, London, 1972), p. 42). 'If the event of Easter Day is in any sense an historical event,' says Bultmann, 'it is nothing else than the rise of faith in the risen Lord, since it was this faith which led to the apostolic preaching.'

29. This is the very same problem as that raised by Karl Rahner, too, who solves it most satisfactorily on lines very different from those followed by Le Roy. See in particular *Theological Investigations*, vol. 1 (1961), pp. 149–200; vol. 3 (1967), pp. 35–46.

30. *Dogme et théologie, Annales de philosophie chrétienne*, vol. 155, pp. 15–17.

31. Henri Pinard de la Boulaye, *Jésus Messie* (Lenten sermons, Notre Dame, Spes, Paris, 1930), pp. 244–5.

32. Gregory of Nyssa (d.394), First sermon on the Resurrection, *Patrologia Graeca*, 46, col. 615–28.

33. At least in French. German distinguishes between the resurrection of Christ (*Auferstehung*) and the awakening (English 'raising') of Lazarus (*Erweckung*). French uses the same word for both events; and this can cause ambiguity, since Christ's resurrection alone implies non-return to the system of life-involved-in-death which, historically speaking, is our own. 'It is only the exaltation', it has been well said, 'which gives the resurrection of Jesus its full meaning' (Xavier Léon-Dufour, *Resurrection of Jesus and the Message of Easter* (Geoffrey Chapman, London, 1974, p. 45). Cf. F. X. Durrwell, *The Resurrection* (Sheed & Ward, London and New York, 1960).

34. *But that I can't believe!* (Fontana, London, 1967), p. 39. Cf. Pannen-

berg, *Jesus: God and Man* (SCM Press, London, 1968).

35. *Les Evangiles synoptiques*, vol. II (Ceffonds, 1908), p. 201.

36. A theory revived recently by an English writer, according to *The Expository Times,* 81 (1970), pp. 307–11, in spite of some glaring improbabilities. His friends could not have stolen the body: if they believed, then they left everything to God; if they did not believe, they were too frightened – in any case they would obtain but a feeble reinforcement of their shattered faith by the handling, no doubt by night, of a corpse. As for Christ's enemies, if they were responsible for the theft, they would have used their action as an argument against the preaching of the Resurrection. However, we find no trace of such an argument in the Jewish polemic. This has been pointed out on countless occasions, apparently in vain: for example, in the modernist period by Eugène Mangenot, *La Résurrection de Jésus* (Beauchesne, Paris, 1910), pp. 223–40, and again in our own day by Wolfhart Pannenberg, *Grundzüge der Christologie* (Gütersloh, 1964), pp. 97–8.

37. 'The resurrection of Ieschoua', writes Tresmontant in *Le problème de l'âme*, p. 213, 'means that he is personally and actually, here and now, living, and that he proved this by showing himself to trustworthy witnesses. *Even if the skeleton* (that is to say, the matter he had last informed) *were found in his tomb, this would make no difference to the fact of the resurrection.* In other words, the question of the empty tomb, and the exegetical problems it raises, are radically different from the question of the resurrection' (Our italics).

38. Jean Delorme, art. cit., in *La Résurrection du Christ et l'exégèse moderne*, p. 147.

39. Xavier Léon-Dufour, *Résurrection de Jésus et message pascal* (Le Seuil, Paris, 1971) p. 304 (the English translation is of the later revised version). He believes that 'Le Roy might well have accepted this hypothesis', which he himself proceeds apparently to dismiss. In fact, (1) it contradicts the prophecy quoted in Acts 2:27 and referred to by Léon-Dufour: 'Thou wilt not . . . let thy Holy One see corruption', since it would be God himself who would be subjecting Christ to this so-called 'accelerated corruption'; (2) further, it destroys all *somatic continuity* between the burial and the resurrection, in spite of the explicitly stated desire to retain it; or rather it reduces this continuity in Christ to our own, in a way that, as we shall be showing later (note 53), cannot be accepted. The chief mistake here consists in saying that 'the gospel accounts offer nothing by way of solution' to the problem of what happens to Christ's remains. In fact, all the accounts presuppose that the transition from death to the life which excludes all death operated at the level, if I may so put it, *of Christ's strictly unique relation with the world*, that is at the 'level' of his body, which, in virtue of that transition, becomes *Christ's ever life-giving relation with the world*. And yet this has nothing to do with a reanimation of corpse, as we have already started to make clear from the Gospel itself.

40. *Cratylus*, 400c. Here Plato gives what he regards as the three possible meanings for *soma*: 'prison', 'sign', 'gaol'. See other references in *Les Belles Lettres* (1931), v. 2, p. 76.

41. X. Léon-Dufour, 'Présence de Jésus Réssuscité', in *Etudes*, April 1970, p. 601.

42. 'We refuse to use this kind of expression,' says X. Léon-Dufour,

Resurrection of Jesus, p. 322 again, 'because it contradicts the *meaning* of the New Testament. It moves to an improper extent from the question of *terminology* (the statement that the body was absent) to that of *fact* (what happened to the body)' (our italics). To accept that one could find Christ's skeleton and still 'believe' in the Resurrection is in complete opposition not only to the *meaning* expressed in the New Testament but also to the *facts* it records. Similarly, establishing 'that the body was absent' is not a matter of *terminology* but of *fact* – unless, of course, a fact, by being *witnessed*, becomes simply a way of expressing it. As for 'what happened to the body' being really a *fact*, this must remain metempirical; at the same time, it is implied in the *terminology used* for the Resurrection, as its necessary condition. All four gospels testify to this.

43. X. Léon-Dufour, *Resurrection of Jesus*, p. 190, calls the empty tomb a 'negative, but significant' sign, a happy phrase which, I believe, vastly reduces the effect of a distinction, to which at times he seems to attach great importance, between the 'empty' tomb and the 'open' tomb (p. 231). The two are inseparable. Here it is indeed a matter of 'words', for the 'fact' which opens out into the Resurrection is exactly the same in each case.

44. *Dogme et critique*, p. 235. See also p. 247.

45. ibid., p. 170.

46. 1 Cor. 15:12. St Paul undoubtedly seems to rely upon a certainty which relates to resurrection *in general*. Nevertheless, he constantly maintains the distinction between that certainty and his faith in, and the fact of, Christ's own resurrection: just as Christ insists in John 11:24–5. Paul uses it more as an argument *ad hominem* and as a starting-point in his apologetic. Maurice Carrez, *De la souffrance à la gloire. De la doxa dans la pensée paulinienne* (Delachaux et Niestlé, Neuchâtel, 1964), pp. 145–65.

47. Bruaire, *Philosophie du corps*, on the same lines as Merleau-Ponty and Maine de Biran, pp. 151ff., 236ff.

48. Cf. above, pp. 41–2.

49. *Dogme et critique*, pp. 238–9.

50. Karl Rahner develops the same idea in *Theological Investigations*, vol. 3, pp. 74–82.

51. *Dogme et critique*, pp. 240–1.

52. For example, 1 Cor. 15:20–9, echoing Ps. 8:7; 1 Cor. 15:54–8, echoing Hos. 14:14; Phil. 3:8–12, 20–1; Rom. 6:1–12; 8:18–26; Eph. 1:18–23; Rev. 1:17–18; 21:1–6, echoing Isa. 66:17; 8:8 and 25:8.

53. X. Léon-Dufour develops precisely the same ideas. 'If we accept', he says, 'that the first expressions of Christ's historic body were dissolved in the universe as a result of the Resurrection, why should the same not be true about what is its final terrestrial manifestation? Looked at in this way, *the corpse calls for no special treatment* [our italics] in order to maintain Christ's bodily resurrection; it is integrated in the universe of historical relationships which constituted Christ's body and his personal bearing' (*Résurrection de Jésus*, p. 303). This is precisely Le Roy's position, and criticism that holds good for the one writer therefore holds good for the other.

54. For this vast problem of exegesis, see a bibliography in Delorme, op. cit., pp. 149–51. For my part, I am satisfied with the position

restated by Max Brandle, *Die synoptischen Grabeserzählungen, Orientierung,* 1967, pp. 179–84, who maintains the primitive character of Mark 14:1–6. L. Schenke, *Le tombeau vide et l'annonce de la Résurrection, Lectio divina,* 59 (Le Cerf, Paris, 1970). We should note the very decided line taken on this matter by Pannenberg, op. cit. (cf. note 36 above), and before him by Karl Barth; the latter connects the gospel testimony to the empty tomb with that relating to the Virgin's conceiving (*Church Dogmatics* (T. & T. Clark, Edinburgh, and Charles Scribner's Sons, New York, 1936–62), vol. I, 2, p. 182; vol. IV, 1, p. 207) and to the Ascension (ibid., vol. III, 2, p. 452; vol. IV, 1, p. 318). More convenient for reference, and no less definite, are A. M. Ramsey, *God, Christ and the World* (SCM Press, London, 1969), pp. 79–80; and W. Trilling, *Fragen zur Geschichtlichkeit Jesu* (Patmos-Verlag, Düsseldorf, 1967).

55. Above, pp. 56–8. The liturgy of the dead speaks also of 'resting' in the earth; our physical dissolution in the earth is a way of belonging to it, and of once again becoming 'one body' with it.

56. Borrowing a phrase from Karl Marx, *Early Writings,* p. 155.

57. The words quoted are from Laberthonnière, who adds, perceptively, 'Faith in the risen Christ is then seen to be produced in a world in which Christ, whatever may be his realness otherwise, has never existed or acted as a risen person' (*Dogme et théologie, Annales,* vol. 155, pp. 54–5).

58. 1 Cor. 15:6, and this apart from the appearance to Cephas and the twelve, and to Paul himself, 'born', as he says, referring to the sudden shock of realization, *'tamquam abortivus'*, like a premature infant. The first letter to Corinthians was written about twenty-five years after the events that occurred in Jerusalem (about 55-6), but the *tradition* which concerns us here is that which had been entrusted to Paul from the moment of his conversion, in 33, only three years after Christ's death. Thus the testimony we have could hardly be earlier. On this, see G. Siegwalt, 'La résurrection du Christ et notre propre résurrection', in the *Revue d'histoire de Philosophie Religieuse* (Hamburg, 1970), pp. 221–233–246.

59. Adolf Harnack, *What is Christianity?* (Williams & Norgate, London, and G. P. Putnam's Sons, New York, 1904), p. 165

60. Among the reasons given by Schenke (*Le tombeau vide et l'annonce de la Résurrection,* pp. 111–16) to explain the absence of any mention of the empty tomb does not include its *uselessness for purposes of the kerygma*: an important consideration, particularly when we compare it with the more *phenomenological* style of the gospel testimony, in which it necessarily plays a central part. X. Léon-Dufour, op. cit., pp. 207–12, similarly fails to mention this.

61. Has sufficient emphasis been laid on the fact that in the synoptics it is women and not *Apostles* who are the first witnesses of the Resurrection in its negative form? Would a legend originating in a community built up around the 'teaching of the Apostles' (Acts 2:42) have attributed this priority to *women* rather than to *Apostles* at so decisive a moment of Christ's manifestation?

62. Cf. above, pp. 55–6.

63. Clement of Alexandria (d.215) in the *Paedagogus,* 'the second leaf of a triptych which describes the working of the divine Word in the life

of the Christian' (*Sources chrétiennes*, 70, p. 71), speaks of the Logos who '*prunes* these unruly shoots, and makes the forces of eager growth bear fruit and not branch out in appetite' (op. cit., I, VIII, 66, p. 231). We believe that this role of Christ, which Clement presents in its spiritual and moral aspect, assumes in the Resurrection a *cosmic* influence which it is important to emphasize.

64. It is apparent that Protestant theology is now returning, with Moltmann in particular (*Theology of Hope* (SCM Press, London, and Harper & Row, New York, 1967)), to cosmic viewpoints from which Bultmann had for many years, most unfortunately, diverted it. On this, see Heinz Zahrnt, *The Question of God: Protestant Theology in the Twentieth Century* (Collins, London, and Harcourt, Brace & World, New York, 1969), pp. 295–337. It is to be hoped that this return to the cosmic point of view contained in faith may be permanent, and not (by that compensating swing normal in Protestant theology) be the prelude to a reaction which will become more radical as emphasis on this cosmic aspect is more justified. From the Catholic point of view the importance of Teilhard cannot be exaggerated.

65. Cf. above, p. 53.

66. Teilhard uses these categories of activity and passivity with great spiritual depth in *Le Milieu Divin*. I need not enlarge on a matter I have treated more fully in 'Teilhard et le mystère de Dieu', Cahier 7 of the *Fondation et association Teilhard de Chardin* (Le Seuil, Paris, 1971), pp. 77–102.

67. Although in its beginnings life is like 'an explosive flash, it is Carnot's principle – i.e. the law which expresses the drift of the whole of cosmic energy towards the more homogeneous – which has the last word, however brilliant the dialogue of *information* and *neg-entropy* may have been meanwhile' (O. Costa de Beauregard, *Le second principe de la science du temps*, p. 136).

68. 'Metabolism', according to *Longmans English Larousse* (Longmans, Green, London, 1968), is 'the sum total of the chemical processes of living organisms, which result in growth, the production of energy and the maintenance of the vital functions, and in which the waste products of these processes are rendered harmless'. Since Christ's resurrection assured for man's body, as a relationship to the world, a state of *total* incorruptibility (1 Cor. 15:50, 25–9), it may rightly be called the absolute metabolism. It is, in truth, the *transformation of trans-formations*, for it effects in man and the universe life's unclouded victory, which excludes all death.

69. These last two sentences are pieced together from the words of St Paul, in particular 2 Cor. 5:17; Rom. 8:38–9; Eph. 4:13; Col. 1:17–19; Phil. 2:9–11.

70. Reference to Heribert Mühlen, *Una mystica Persona* (Schöning, 1964), translated into French as *L'Esprit dans l'Eglise* (Le Cerf, Paris, 1969), will suffice. His comments on 1 Cor. 15:45 (Christ having become in his resurrection 'a life-giving Spirit') are of the utmost value. They explain how the risen Christ is 'one Person in multiple persons' (vol. 1, pp. 151, 214–18, 230, 234), and how his resurrection can thus become ours. Cf. F. X. Durrwell, op. cit., pp. 215ff.

71. Jacques Derrida, *De la Grammatologie* (Ed. de Minuit, Paris, 1967) p. 71.

72. Jacques Derrida, 'La "différence"', in *Bulletin de la Société française de Philosophie*, 27 January 1968, p. 97.

73. ibid., p. 95.

74. Paul Tillich, *La dimension oubliée* (D.D.B., Paris, 1969), p. 119. There is no need to enlarge upon the theological writing which lies behind such a situation. If the undeniable God is so denied in our cultural world, it is also because his true countenance is misread, even more, we may be sure, than it is rejected. It must once again be proclaimed in terms that express the full depth of the *agape*. See O. Clément, 'Dionysos et le Ressuscité, Essai de réponse chrétienne à l'athéisme contemporain', in J. M. Le Guillou, O. Clément, J. Bosc, *Evangile et Révolution au cœur de notre crise spirituelle* (Centurion, Paris, 1968), pp. 65–123. Another, rather more old-fashioned work on the same lines is S. Breton, *La croix du Christ et les philosophies, Studi Testi passionisti*, 2 (Terano, 1954).

75. C. Bruaire, 'Connaître Dieu', in *Dieu aujourd'hui, Semaine des intellectuels catholiques*, 1965, *Recherches et Débats*, 52 (D.D.B., Paris, 1965), p. 159.

76. In scripture the two *words* – the two *realities* denoted by these two words – are one and the same thing. See X. Léon-Dufour, etc., *Dictionary of Biblical Theology* (Geoffrey Chapman, London, and Desclée, New York, 1967), under 'Spirit' and 'Power'. This dynamic and active concept of spirit – not primarily substantive or static – is essential for understanding all that we have already said about man himself and are now saying about Christ's resurrection.

77. Thus 'according to Hegel (and this is made perfectly clear) the life of the spirit is therefore a life which is identical with death – or rather a life which is attained only at the end of a movement which involves a death to all fixture (that of sensible reality which is only intuited, and that also of "determined and soldified systems of thought" – in other words fully constituted scientific and philosophical systems), death to all immediacy', what the writer calls on the next page 'the death which the concept inflicts upon itself, or, again, that "passing beyond" self which is specific to the real as concept' (Pierre-Jean Labarrière, 'Le concept hégélien, identité de la mort et de la vie', in *Archives de Philosophie*, 33 (1970), pp. 580–1). It is thus apparent that this *speculative* way of treating the question of death and of integrating it is *entirely interior to mortality* and is in no way therefore an *effective transcendence* of death itself – which is what we have in the *Resurrection* and the mystery of the *Holy Spirit*.

78. We see that to doubt the transcendent identity of the Holy Spirit presupposes and entails a corresponding doubt of the absolute significance of Christ's *figure* in history. Here 'figure' means, in the sense defined by Hans Urs von Balthasar in *Herrlichkeit* (Johannes Verlag, Einsiedeln), the form the Infinite assumes for us *in truth* in the humanity of Jesus.

79. See below, pp. 166–79.

80. P. Schoonenberg, 'Ereignis und Geschehen, Einfache hermeneutische Uberlegungen zu einigen gegenwärtig diskutierten Fragen', in *Zeitschrift für katholische Theologie*, 1968, pp. 1–21; G. Greshake, *Historie wird Geschichte, Bedeutung und Sinn der Unterscheidung von Historie und Geschichte in der Theologie Rudolf Bultmanns*

(Essen, 1963), pp. 36–42.

81. A point overlooked by so-called traditional apologetics (cf. above, pp. 73–4), which has often produced a reaction that fails to allow sufficiently for counter-reactions. A. Dulles, *Apologetics and the Biblical Christ* (Burns & Oates, London, 1964), is typical of this still purely critical awareness, which has difficulty in achieving a true *historicity*. Generally speaking, in Catholic thought the over-long predominance of the academic concentration on the *supposed crude fact*, independent of the *meaning* (or in terms of an assumedly self-evident meaning), has produced, as a reaction, concern for the *meaning*, independently of the *fact* (to which no real importance is attached). In Bultmann's idiom, only the *geschichtlich* (which relates to the *existential decision*) is of importance for faith; the *historisch*, i.e. the historically determinable fact, has no importance, and moreover, in the case of faith, is completely inaccessible. Accepting the Christological profession of faith in 'both' – 'and' (true God *and* true man) we have in reality to combine the *geschichtlich* 'and' the *historisch*, fact *and* meaning. A whole Christology of hermeneutics needs to be constructed or reconstructed.

82. Matthew's account (28:2–5), which comes closest to describing the act of the Resurrection, is at pains not to show us Christ himself. We are told about the Lord's angel, the sign of theophany; but Christ has gone. See X. Léon-Dufour, *Resurrection of Jesus*, pp. 143–5.

83. P. Grelot, in *Lectio divina*, 50, p. 50, who goes on to emphasize the necessity of well-balanced exegesis, based on hard theological thinking – where we are in full agreement with him.

84. Such, it will be remembered, is the opinion of Le Roy, of Bultmann and of Marxsen (see above, pp. 68–70). In his justified concern not to subordinate the meaning of faith in the Resurrection to the 'bare' fact, X. Léon-Dufour follows the same line: after an exegetical enquiry conducted as 'historian' (*Resurrection of Jesus*, p. 211), he comes to the conclusion that 'the material is scanty'. Nevertheless, he continues, 'the decisive event with which he [the believer] comes face to face, and which is always an open question for him until he responds to it through his faith, *is not the Resurrection itself, but the apostolic faith in God who has raised Jesus from the dead*' (ibid., p. 215, our italics). Nothing, it is true, is more certain than the Apostles' faith in the risen Jesus Christ; and we would have no knowledge of the Resurrection, we may even say, without that faith. Thus they are to us more than 'interpreters' (ibid., p. 197); they are, in a real sense, 'witnesses' (Acts 2:32). At the same time they would never have believed in the Resurrection without the objective *signs* of its reality which they received and handed on to us. It is such *signs*, though not to the exclusion of others, which still govern our faith and make us, too, adhere *to the Resurrection itself*, as we shall be seeing.

85. 'Such a resurrection', writes Karl Rahner in the article 'Resurrection of Christ', in *Sacramentum Mundi*, vol. 5 (Burns & Oates, London, and Herder & Herder, New York, 1970), p. 324, 'into a human existence finalized and bringing history to fulfilment, is essentially an object of knowledge of an absolutely unique kind. It is essentially other than the return of a dead man to his previous biological life, to space and time, which form the dimensions of history unfulfilled. Hence it is not

in any way an ordinary object of experience, which could be subsumed under the common conditions and possibilities of experience. It is an "experience" *sui generis* which, if possible at all, grasps in fact the definite transformation of the historically knowable.' Thus the historically incomparable originality of the Resurrection attaches to it not from the fact that it lacks historicity but from the fact that its own historicity concerns, in the risen Christ, the whole of human existence and gives that existence a completely new meaning.

86. *Dogme et critique*, p. 226. See above, pp. 68–70.

87. 'To say that after the death of Jesus Christ the Apostles met with something extraordinary, that they were caught up in an explosive force, that they lived through an amazing experience, and that they expressed this by saying that Jesus Christ had risen from the dead; and that they then developed this purely interior conviction in coloured and detailed accounts of events which never took place as such – to speak in this way is precisely to make them into perjurers . . . Paul analyses his experiences with great nicety, and he is far from confusing his own interior experiences with the events that overtook him. And when the disciples refer to what they are describing as facts, and bear witness to them, we have absolutely no right to behave as though they were saying something different . . .' (Jacques Ellul, 'Témoignage et société technicienne', in *Le Témoignage, Actes du Colloque de Rome, organisé par Enrico Castelli*, 5–11 January 1972 (Aubier, Paris, 1972), pp. 453–4).

88. Jean-Claude Barreau, *L'aujourd'hui des évangiles* (Le Seuil, Paris, 1970), p. 299. He would have us see the Resurrection as a theological fact; and we may well agree with him, so long as the qualification he makes does not affect the historicity – a completely unique historicity – of this 'fact'.

89. It is in this sense that what is said in the Constitution *Dei Verbum*, 19 (cf. *The Documents of Vatican II*), about the historicity of the gospels does not mean that exegesis will have to return to an outmoded conception of history – to do that would make us lose sight of its 'comprehensive' significance. The *historicity* the Council has in mind does not conflict with, but rather encourages (cf. *Dei Verbum* 21–6), understanding the meaning contained in the fact; but the Council rightly rejects the idea that such understanding can ever include a questioning of the *strictly historical* character of the actual *fact* of Christ. In the light of what has just been said, see X. Léon-Dufour in *La révélation divine, Unam Sanctam*, 70b (Le Cerf, Paris, 1968), vol. II, pp. 422–30, which deals with the historicity of the gospels according to *Dei Verbum*.

90. Michel de Dieguez, *Science et Nescience, Phénoménologie de la Résurrection* (Gallimard, Paris, 1970), pp. 516–32: a penetrating analysis of the meaning of the story of Emmaus, which the author describes as, in turn, 'a transcendental phenomenology' (p. 524), 'a divine phenomenology' (p. 525), or a 'divine pedagogy' (p. 526).

91. X. Léon-Dufour, in *Recherches de Science religieuse*, 1969, art. cit., p. 621.

92. Luke 24:5–6. It is this impossibility of separating resurrection and exaltation that makes us understand that the separation in time of the

different phases of the Lord's glorification, culminating in the Ascension, is a way of presenting things which is necessary *quoad nos*, but that, *quoad Christum*, Resurrection and Ascension are one. See P. Benoit, *Exégèse et Théologie* (Le Cerf, Paris, 1961), pp. 402–4.

93. 'Spiritual body means body wholly under the dominion of the Spirit of God, as opposed to fleshly body, or body under the dominion of the flesh of sin or flesh of corruption,' as C. Geffré puts it so well in 'La Résurrection ou la victoire de l'Esprit', in *Vie spirituelle*, 493 (1963), p. 386.

94. J. A. T. Robinson, op. cit., p. 77. On the Ascension, see P. Benoit, *Exégèse et Théologie*, as quoted above, pp. 363–411.

PART II

1. Willi Marxsen, *Anfangsprobleme der Christologie* (G-Mohn, 1960), pp. 43–9.

2. Hans Conzelmann, *An Outline of the Theology of the New Testament* (SCM Press, London, 1969): 'The present texts are clearly sacramental. Their meaning is bound up with the death and resurrection of Christ. But that means that the Eucharist was founded by him in the same way as the Church' (p. 59). Xavier Léon-Dufour, article 'Passion', in *Supplément au Dictionnaire de la Bible*, vol. 6 (Letouzey, 1960), col. 1457: 'Through the four recensions (Matthew, Mark, Luke, 1 Corinthians) we can confidently envisage Christ's words, without however saying that we are in a position to reconstruct from them a primitive text' – which must fairly soon have been given a liturgical form.

3. The epiclesis is the invocation to the Holy Spirit during the eucharistic action.

1. THE PRESENT THEOLOGICAL POSITION

1. *Vom Sinn der Kirche, Fünf Vorträge* (Mainz, 1923), p. 1.

2. R. Guardini, *The Spirit of the Liturgy* (Sheed & Ward, London, 1930).

3. The *Jahrbuch für Liturgiewissenschaft*.

4. On this aspect of Guardini's personal influence, see Henri Engelmann and Francis Ferrier, *Romano Guardini, Le Dieu Vivant et l'existence chrétienne*, in the series *Théologiens et spirituels contemporains* (Fleurus, Paris, 1966); Hans Urs von Balthasar, *Romano Guardini, Reform aus dem Ursprung* (Kösel-Verlag, Munich, 1970).

5. *The Spirit of the Liturgy*, p. 37.

6. ibid., p. 105.

7. *Missarum solemnia, Explication génétique de la messe romaine*, in the series *Théologie*, nos. 19, 20, 21 (1951), vol. I, p. 25.

8. *Von heiligen Zeichen* (1927), introduction; an abridged English version appears in *Sacred Signs* (Sheed & Ward, London, 1930), pp. ix–xiv.

9. ibid. (this passage does not appear in the English translation).

10. *The Mystery of Christian Worship* (Darton, Longman & Todd, London, and Newman Press, Westminster, Maryland, 1962), p. 99. See the chapter entitled 'The Meaning of the Mystery'.

11. ibid, p. 15. As St Ambrose says, 'It is in our mysteries that I find you', *Patrologia Latina*, 14, col. 918. Similarly the whole of the chapter,

'Le retour au mystère'.

12. 'Actio in liturgische Verwendung', in *Jahrbuch für Liturgiewissenschaft,* 1921, pp. 34–9.

13. *Le mystère de l'Eglise, Textes tirés des écrits et conférences de Dom Odo Casel* (Mame, Paris, 1965), p. 85.

14. ibid., p. 89.

15. *The Mystery of Christian Worship,* pp. 22–3.

16. Theodoret of Cyrus (d.458), *Patrologia Graeca,* 82, col. 736, quoted in Casel, *Faites ceci en mémoire de moi, Lex Orandi,* 34 (Le Cerf, Paris, 1962; German original 1926), p. 86. This is made up entirely of extracts from patristic texts, and shows that the concept of mystery as sacramental re-actualizing of the work of salvation is traditional teaching.

17. ibid., p. 41.

18. *Das Gedächtnis des Herrn in der altchristlichen Liturgie* (1919). On the fundamental and original oneness of the sacrifice and the meal, essential to this whole line of thought, see Louis Bouyer, *Le rite et l'homme, Lex Orandi,* 32 (1962), pp. 116–21.

19. On the whole complex of problems and critical comments produced by this way of thinking, which do not, however, bear upon the very general point of view from which we are examining it here, see Theodor Filthaut, *Die Kontroverse über die Mysterienlehre* (1947). A summary of Casel's thought and a guide to reading him will be found in André Gozier, OSB, *Dom Casel,* in the series *Theologiens et spirituels contemporains* (Fleurus, Paris, 1968).

20. For Casel's influence on the encyclical *Mediator Dei* and the Council's Constitution on the Liturgy, see Gozier, op. cit., pp. 121–33.

21. Constitution *Sacrosanctum Concilium,* 7; *The Documents of Vatican II,* pp. 140–1.

22. H. de Lubac, *Corpus mysticum* (Aubier, Paris, 1949), p. 60. Casel, it will be remembered, saw *the mystery as the symbolic actualization in the Church, and for the Church, of the saving reality of Christ.*

23. In G. Dumeige, *La Foi catholique* (L'Orante, Paris, 1961), no. 746. 'The Church', said John XXIII in his opening address to the Council, 'has never ceased to combat errors. She has often condemned them, and with great severity. Today, however, the bride of Christ prefers to have recourse to the remedy of mercy rather than wield the weapons of severity. She believes that, *instead of condemning, she can meet the needs of our day better by emphasizing the richness of her teaching'* (*Documentation catholique,* 1962, col. 1383).

24. So G. Ghysens, 'Présence eucharistique et transubstantiation', in *Irénikon,* 32 (1959), pp. 423–4; E. Schillebeeckx, in *Tijdschrift voor Theologie,* 1965, pp. 136ff., analysed in *Herder Korrespondenz,* 19 (Herder & Herder, Freiburg, 1965), pp. 518–19; and again in *Die eucharistische Gegenwart* (2nd ed., Dusseldorf, 1968), pp. 28–9; E. Gutwenger, 'Das Geheimnis der Gegenwart Christi in der Eucharistie', in *Zeitschrift für katholische Theologie,* 88 (1966), p. 189; W. Beinert, 'Die Enzyklika "Mysterium Fidei" und neuere Auffassungen über die Eucharistie', in *Theologisches Jahrbuch,* 12, ed. A. Dänhardt (Leipzig, 1969), p. 275.

25. R. Johanny, *L'Eucharistie Centre de l'histoire du salut chez saint Ambroise de Milan* (Beauchesne, Paris, 1968), p. 109.

26. James F. McCue, 'The Doctrine of Transubstantiation from Berenger

through Trent: the Point at Issue', in *Harvard Theological Review*, 1968, p. 425. Schillebeeckx, on the other hand, thinks that for the Fathers of Trent the Aristotelian doctrine of substance and accidents was 'the only possible way of formulating the eucharistic presence in a Catholic sense, at least so far as "the permanence of the species" is concerned' (*Die eucharistische Gegenwart*).

27. The analogy between 'consubstantial' and '*transubstantiation*' was drawn as early as the twelfth century by Baldwin of Canterbury, *Patrologia Latina*, 204, col. 662; J. de Ghellinck, 'L'eucharistie au XIIe siècle en Occident, in *Dictionnaire de théologie catholique* (Letouzey, 1924), V, 2, 1301. The *word* occurs very early in the twelfth century, cf. below, p. 138. It was used extensively in the second half of the century.

28. Ghysens, in *Irénikon*, 32 (1959), p. 425.

29. For example, the single word *conversio*, with which some would have preferred the Council to be satisfied (J. F. McCue, art. cit., p. 425). The Greek and Latin Fathers do not recognize the word 'transubstantiation' or its Greek equivalent in *ousia*. The Greek Fathers, however, had eight words for expressing the eucharistic change. Six of them carry the prefix *meta*, which implies 'change': J. Betz, *Die Eucharistie in der Zeit der griechischen Väter*, I, 1 (Herder & Herder, Freiburg, 1955), pp. 300–18. We have inherited *meta-ballein* (which gives 'meta-bolism', 'conversion' or 'change'); *meta-stoicheioun* (from which comes the Latin noun *trans-elementatio*, used in the encyclical *Mysterium Fidei*, in *Documentation catholique*, 1965, col. 1645); *meta-ruthmizein*, according to E. Benvéniste in *Problèmes de linguistique générale*, has more the meaning of 'changing the *course* of things'.

30. Max Thurian, *The Eucharistic Memorial*, vol. 2 (Lutterworth Press), London, 1960), p. 109.

31. Karl Rahner, 'Die Gegenwart Christi im Sakrament des Herrenmahles', in *Schriften zur Theologie*, IV (1960), p. 375, holds that the dogma of transubstantiation says nothing more than do Christ's words over the bread and wine. Its value is 'logical' in the full sense of the word: it vindicates the import of Christ's words, considered intellectually; it is not 'ontic' and provides no real explanation of the 'how'. The dogma states *the fact that* something is done, not *how* it is done. Remarkably similar views are expressed in another language, by Père J. Lebreton, 'Catholicisme, Réponse à M. Tyrrell', in *Revue Pratique d'Apologétique*, April–September 1907, pp. 528–9, 533. Modern Orthodox theologians point out that the patristic use of *metabole* is completely uncommittal about the *how*: B. Bobrinskoy, 'Présence réelle et communion eucharistique', in *Revue des sciences philosophiques et théologiques*, 1969, p. 402; and P. L'Huillier, 'Théologie de l'épiclèse', in *Verbum caro*, 53 (1960), pp. 317–18. 'The general intention of the dogma', writes F. J. Leenhardt, again, 'is basically unconcerned with a particular philosophical interpretation, and this certainly entitles us to view with suspicion any extension of the philosophical expressions used in formulating it' (*Parole, Ecriture, Sacrements, Etudes de théologie et d'exégèse* (Delachaux et Niestlé, Neuchâtel, 1968), p. 198). We may note, however, several examples that show that this terminology of substance is not obsolete for everyone. Benvéniste does not hesitate to speak of the *consubstantiality* of signifier and signified to define the properties of language (*Problèmes*

de linguistique générale, p. 52). So H. Marcuse, *Eros and Civilization* (Beacon Press, Boston, 1966), refers to the *transubstantiation* of pleasure (p. 13), of the Messiah (p. 70), and even (p. 70) of the *transubstantiated* Son. Similar instances are noted by Schillebeeckx, *Die eucharistische Gegenwart*, p. 88, in Goethe himself. Cf. *Thinking about the Eucharist* (SCM Press, London, 1972), pp. 99ff.

32. *Ceci est mon corps, Explication de ces paroles de Jésus Christ* (Delachaux et Niestlé, Neuchâtel, 1955), p. 28.

33. ibid., p. 31.

34. ibid.

35. ibid., p. 53.

36. ibid.

37. *Etudes théologiques et religieuses* (1956), pp. 36–45, after *Revue des sciences philosophiques et théologiques*, 1956, p. 788.

38. *Ceci est mon corps*, pp. 37–8.

39. J. de Baciocchi, 'Présence eucharistique et transsubstantiation', in *Irénikon*, 1959, p. 139.

40. ibid., p. 140.

41. 'La présence eucharistique', in *Parole, Ecriture, Sacrements*, p. 195.

42. *Irénikon*, 1959, p. 144.

43. ibid., p. 150.

44. *Ceci est mon corps*, p. 39. Similar remarks, and carried even further, in H. Schürmann, 'Les paroles de Jésus lors de la dernière Cène envisagées à la lumière de ses gestes', in *Concilium*, 40 (1968), pp. 103-4.

45. This teaching is echoed in the doctrinal agreement arrived at by the ecumenical group of Les Dombes. 'Christ's act', we read there, 'being the gift of his body and blood, that is to say of himself, the reality given in the signs of the bread and wine is his body and his blood. It is by virtue of Christ's creative word and by the power of the Holy Spirit that the bread and wine are made a sacrament and hence "a sharing of the body and blood of Christ" (1 Cor. 10:16). They are henceforth, in their ultimate truth, beneath the outward sign, the given reality, and so they remain, since their purpose is to be consumed. What is given as the body and blood of Christ remains given as his body and blood and requires to be treated as such' (*Modern Eucharistic Agreement* (SPCK, London, 1973), p. 60).

46. Theodore of Mopsuestia (d.428), *Patrologia Graeca*, 66, col. 714, quoted in the encyclical *Mysterium Fidei*, 45.

47. Cyril of Jerusalem (d.386), *IVe Catéchèse mystagogique*, 1–2, in *Sources chrétiennes*, 126 (1966), pp. 135–7. This metabolism does not prevent Cyril from speaking a few sentences later of the body as 'given under the *form* of the bread' and of the blood 'given under the *form* of the wine' (ibid., p. 137), for the gift and the presence are here in the signs.

48. A eucharistic neologism of St Ambrose himself; cf. R. Johanny, op. cit., p. 120.

49. Ambrose of Milan, *Des Sacrements*, IV, 14–15, in *Sources chrétiennes*, 25 bis (1961), pp. 109–11.

50. *Irénikon*, 1959, pp. 161–4.

51. *Ceci est mon corps*, p. 35; see also pp. 32 and 33.

52. *Irénikon*, 1959, pp. 160–1.

53. ibid., p. 158.
54. ibid., p. 161. Leenhardt develops the eschatological point of view in connection with the cup: *Le Sacrement de la Sainte Cène* (Delachaux et Niestlé, Neuchâtel, 1948), pp. 39–48. As Durrwell says, 'At least in our own time, the relation between the eucharistic bread and this final term, the glorified Christ, is unique; this one bread *is sanctified in the Spirit by a total concentration upon Christ*, assumed by the *eschaton* so closely that Christ becomes its immediate *sub-stantia*, the underlying reality of this bread in which it subsists. The Eucharist is the full realization of Christo-centricism, the *effect of an absolute reduction to the centre*, the anticipation in our world of what is proper to the realities of the Kingdom in which Christ is "all in all things" ' ('Eucharistie et Parousie', in *Lumen Vitae*, 26 (1971), pp. 117–18).
55. *Des Mystères*, 53, in *Sources chrétiennes*, 25 bis (1961), p. 189.
56. Cf below, pp. 147–56.
57. *De fide orthodoxa*, in *Patrologia Graeca*, 94, col. 1141.
58. Cf above, p. 111.
59. *Des Sacrements*, in *Sources chrétiennes*, 25 bis, p. 111.
60. *S. Aurelii Augustini, Textus Eucharistici selecti, Florilegium patristicum*, fasc. XXXV (H. Lang, Bonn, 1933), p. 17.
61. ibid., *Sermo*, 272, p. 22. Similarly, cf. also pp. 8–10.
62. Faustus of Riez (d.500), no doubt Bishop of Provence, a strong opponent, moreover, of Augustine's teaching on grace but a true disciple on eucharistic questions.
63. An expression that is neither Augustinian nor Pauline: salvation is gratuitous.
64. *Easter Sermon*, in *Patrologia Latina*, 67, col. 1053. This passage is quoted from the French translation of J. M. Scheeben's *Die Mysterien des Christentums, Les mystères du christianisme* (DDB, Paris, 1948), p. 509. Scheeben, pp. 506–9, makes fruitful use of the incorporation of Christians in Christ for explaining the true nature of transubstantiation.
65. Durrwell, *L'Eucharistie Présence du Christ* (Paris, 1971), pp. 62–5, who accepts this terminology, nevertheless regrets its neglect of eschatology. See also the reservations of E. Pousset, 'L'Eucharistie: présence réelle et transsubstantiation', in *Recherches de Science religieuse*, 1966, pp. 200–1. V. Warnach synthesizes trans-finalization, trans-signification, and even trans-functionalism, in 'La réalité symbolique de l'Eucharistie', in *Concilium*, 40 (1968), pp. 86–7. The trans-functionalism referred to here is completely different from that of which M. Xhaufflaire writes. In *Feuerbach et la théologie de la sécularisation, Cogitatio fidei*, 45 (Le Cerf, Paris, 1970), the latter advocates, under the term 'trans-functionalization', an uncompromising political reduction of the Church to the service of 'socialized' man, already existing or still to come. See, for a similar view, 'Christianisme critique et vie religieuse', in the *Supplément (Vie spirituelle)*, 94, (1970), pp. 352–(379)–84. Warnach uses 'trans-functionalization' to mean *the use, entirely redirected by the Eucharist, to which are put the bread and wine changed into the body and blood of Christ*. On 'trans-signification', see also W. Beinert in *Theologisches Jahrbuch*, 12 (1969), p. 278, and more particularly, in the same volume, O. Semmelroth, 'Eucharistische Wandlung', pp. 302–14. C. Duquoc, 'Signification

sacrementelle de la "Présence" ', in *Revue des sciences philosophiques et théologiques*, 53 (1969), believes that the notions of trans-signification and trans-finalization 'describe a dialectic immanent in the symbol rather than the basis of this dialectic, envisaged in the earlier concept of transubstantiation' (pp. 427–8).

66. The encyclical *Mysterium Fidei* (in *Documentation catholique*, 1965, cols. 1633–51) is dated 12 September 1965. W. Beinert, art. cit., p. 273, shows that the purpose of this encyclical of Paul VI was solely to emphasize the importance of the concept of transubstantiation, and not to hinder legitimate research. The same writer deals accurately with the circumstances in which the encyclical appeared (ibid, pp. 267–8). See also 'Diskussion um die Realpräsenz', in *Herder Korrespondenz*, 19 (1965), pp. 517–18.

67. *Documentation catholique*, 1965, col. 1645.

68. O. Semmelroth, art. cit., p. 307, speaks of an *Entweder oder*, 'either-or', method, and rightly rejects it. Things have to be held together, not kept apart. For inept analogies, see W. Beinert, art. cit., pp. 278–80, where he refers to several: the change in the value of food or drink when they pass from the shop to the table at which friends are entertained; the importance of human 'presence' when there is a true relationship and not merely rubbing shoulders in a bus. Such examples, offered by P. Schoonenberg or L. Smits, fall far short of the completely different originality of the eucharistic Presence. Charles Davis, 'L'intelligence de la Présence réelle', in *Théologie d'aujourd'hui et de demain* (Le Cerf, Paris, 1967), pp. 153–79, is rightly critical of this 'reification' and correctly emphasizes that we should look on the bread as 'in a special way linked to man'; even so, he leaves the reader dissatisfied.

69. *Documentation catholique*, 1965, col. 1946.

70. H. B. Green, 'The Eucharistic Presence: Change and/or Signification', in *Downside Review*, 83 (1965), pp. 32–48, shows that the necessary synthesis of the two points of view can be effected. It is this synthesis, we believe, of symbolism and metabolism which defines the sacramentality proper to the Eucharist, and which governs our whole approach in this problem. See also, on the same lines, Edouard Schillebeeckx, *Die eucharistische Gegenwart*. Similarly, Père de Lavalette in 'Transsubstantiation et transfinalisation', in *Etudes*, November 1965, p. 574; and Jean Mouroux in *Faites ceci en mémoire de moi* (Aubier, Paris, 1970), p. 125.

71. Mouroux (see note 70) follows this up; and so, even more fruitfully, Durrwell (note 65).

72. 'Through whom, Lord, you unceasingly create all things, vivify them, and give them to us': from the Canon of the Roman Mass.

73. *Le Milieu Divin*, pp. 113–15 *passim*; *The Divine Milieu*, pp. 102–4 *passim*. 'In Christ we live, and move, and have our being' is the characteristically Teilhardian and strictly Christological adoption of a thought taken from a Greek poet of the sixth century BC, which St Paul used to the Athenians in his address on the Areopagus (Acts 17:28). 'The divine immensity', says Teilhard again, in *Le Milieu Divin*, p. 112 (*The Divine Milieu*, p. 101), 'has transformed itself for us into *the omnipresence of christification*', which, in his view, is inseparable from the Eucharist itself.

74. *Le Milieu Divin*, p. 35; *The Divine Milieu*, p. 32.

75. See above, notes 54 and 71. V. Warnach is most explicit, in *Concilium*, 40 (1968), pp. 88–90; he quotes a fine phrase from Schillebeeckx on the 'sacramental parousia' in *Die eucharistische Gegenwart*. See also B. Welte and his comments on an article by L. Scheffsky, 'Die materielle Welt im Lichte der Eucharistie', in *Aktuelle Fragen zur Eucharistie*, ed. M. Schmaus (Munich, 1960), pp. 156–80 and 184–90; also, Semmelroth, Ratzinger, *Theologisches Jahrbuch*, 1969, pp. 309, 298 (the latter, too, in his article 'Himmelfahrt', in *Lexikon für Theologie und Kirche*); so Pousset, in *Recherches de Science religieuse*, 1966, p. 203; and J. M. Tillard's very important *L'Eucharistie Pâque de l'Eglise*, ch. II, 'Le corps eucharistique du Seigneur', *Unam sanctam*, 44 (Le Cerf, Paris, 1964), pp. 54–105, written, however, from an entirely historical point of view. We are still, so far as I know, without an organic synthesizing which stresses what might now be called 'the point of no return' in the relation between Eucharist and Resurrection.

76. Carlo Colombo, at present rector of the Catholic Faculty of Milan *Teologia, filisofia e fisica nella dottrina della transustanziazione, Scuola cattolica*, 83 (1955), pp. 123ff.

77. C. Vollert, 'Controversy on Transubstantiation', in *Theological Studies*, 22 (1961), pp. 422–5. There are useful suggestions in J. Ratzinger, 'Das Problem der Transsubstantiation und die Frage nach dem Sinn der Eucharistie', in *Theologische Quartalschrift*, 147 (1967), pp. 129–59: 'What happens', he asks in particular of transubstantiation, 'when nothing physical or chemical happens?' This is, pre-eminently, the preliminary question which makes it plain that the Eucharist belongs to the met-empirical order of the Resurrection.

2. THE GAP WIDENS

1. On this revival of Platonism of which Plotinus (d.270), contemporary and at first fellow-pupil of Origen (d.254), was the initiator in Alexandria, see Louis Bréhier, *La philosophie de Plotin* (Boivin et Cie, Paris, 1928).

2. This passage from *In Joannem*, II, IV, 20, is translated by Olivier du Roy, *L'intelligence de la foi en la Trinité selon saint Augustin, Genèse de sa Théologie trinitaire jusqu'en 391*, Etudes Augustiniennes, 1966, pp. 101–2. On the importance of Neoplatonism in St Augustine's conversion and in particular the discovery of the Word and of Christ, see ibid., pp. 53–106.

3. 'Still' because the break with biblical anthropology was already so marked that it was then impossible to see its consequences.

4. Louis Bouyer, *L'Eglise de Dieu, Corps du Christ et Temple de l'Esprit* (Le Cerf, Paris, 1970), p. 41.

5. Aimé Solignac, 'Notes à la Traduction française des Confessions', in *Bibliothèque Augustinienne*, vol. 13 (D.D.B., Paris, 1962), pp. 100–12, and particularly pp. 145–9.

6. *Confessions*, VII, X, 16, in *Bibliothèque Augustinienne*, vol. 13, pp. 615–17.

7. *Sermo*, 361, in *Patrologia Latina*, 39, col. 1602.

8. *Sermo*, 272, in *Patrologia Latina*, 38, col. 1246.

9. *In Joannem*, L, 13, in *Corpus Auctorum Christianorum*, vol. XXXVI, p. 439.

10. See above, pp. 83–4.

11. Dom Maïeul Cappuyns, *Jean Scot Erigène* (d. *c.* 877), *Sa Vie, son œuvre, sa pensée* (D.D.B., Louvain and Paris, 1933).

12. Later he asked 'how our Lord Jesus Christ, to whom the Father has entrusted the judgement, could be patient of a local or temporal movement, after his humanity had been exalted in the unity of his divinity above all times and all places and all that can be said or thought' (*De divisione naturae*, 1, V, 38, in *Patrologia Latina*, 122, cols. 994b and 997a). Erigena was to have a great influence on the 'spiritualism' of Ratramnus and Berengar, although neither of them was to follow him in his doctrine of the ubiquity of the body of Christ. On that point both remained loyal Augustinians; while they strongly emphasized the incorruptibility of the glorified body, they clung tenaciously to its localization in heaven, as we shall be seeing. On the eucharistic thought of Scotus Erigena, see Josef Geiselmann, *Die Eucharistielehre der Vorscholastik* (Paderborn, 1926), pp. 36–44. This, with Père de Lubac's *Corpus mysticum*, 2nd ed., has been our main source for the history of eucharistic doctrine.

13. *Epistola*, 187, on Christ's words to the good thief: 'This day thou shalt be with me in Paradise' (*Patrologia Latina*, 35, cols. 835–6). Augustine's difficulty in avoiding the *separatism* of two natures is evident. This prevents him also from understanding how in Christ the divinity is the very principle of a *new mode of the being* of his humanity and so of his body, not changed but nevertheless *transnaturalized* in relation to our world. That is why the Resurrection is conceived by Augustine as a *local transference of the body* 'into heaven', whereas it is in reality a *transfiguration of Christ's relation to the world*, as we have already shown.

14. Hans Jorissen, *Die Entfaltung der Transsubstantiationslehre bis zum Beginn der Hochscholastik* (Münster, 1965), pp. 4–6. See also Karl Adam, 'Zur Eucharistielehre des helligen Augustinus', in *Theologische Quartalschrift*, 112, (Tübingen-Stuttgart, 1931), pp. 490–536, which restates the ideas put forward in an earlier article with the same title published in Paderborn in 1908.

15. Henri de Lubac, *Corpus mysticum*, p. 150. We should note, too, that while the considerable difficulty of correct representation did not prevent Augustine from stressing the spiritual realism of the *effects* of the Eucharist, neither did it prevent the opponents and supporters of Berengar, for example, from asserting that 'the bread and wine of the altar were, after the consecration, the body and blood of the Lord' (Dom Cappuyns, article 'Bérenger de Tours', in *Dictionnaire d'histoire et de géographie ecclésiastique* (Letouzey), p. 401).

16. His *De corpore et sanguine Domini*, written against Paschasius Radbertus, his abbot at Corbie, has been edited by J. N. Bakhuizen van den Brink (Amsterdam, 1954).

17. Jean de Montclos, *Lanfranc et Bérenger, La controverse eucharistique du XIe siècle* (Louvain, 1969). The *De sacra coena adversus Lanfrancum* of Berengar of Tours has been edited by W. H. Beekenkamp (The Hague, 1941). While the crisis of the ninth century was contemporaneous with the Carolingian renaissance, that of the eleventh century coincided with the Gregorian renaissance, and Berengar was to see his name associated with that of Hildebrand, the future Gregory VII.

Among his opponents were also: Alger of Liège (d.1131) and Guitmond of Aversa (d.1095). Lanfranc was born at Pavia and became abbot of Bec, where he had Guitmond of Aversa as a pupil. He died as Archbishop of Canterbury, while Guitmond, who had been born in France, was to become a bishop in Italy. That men should move around in this way tells us much about 'Gregorian' Europe. The story of this complicated controversy has not yet been fully clarified. An English historian, quoted by Montclos, p. 22, calls it a 'morass'. I need hardly point out that we are treating it here from a strictly limited point of view: the place of the Resurrection in the dispute about the Eucharist.

18. Dom Jean Leclercq, *L'amour des lettres et le désir de Dieu, Initiation aux auteurs monastiques du Moyen Age* (Le Cerf, Paris, 1957), pp. 179–217, with an explicit reference, p. 201, to Ratramnus on the lines we are exploring.

19. Martin Grabmann, *Geschichte der Katholischen Theologie seit dem Ausgang der Väterzeit* (Freiburg-im-Breisgau, 1933), p. 29. The school of Chartres had been founded by Fulbert of Chartres (d.1028). Among his pupils Berengar had the future St Bruno.

20. J. H. Fahey, *The Eucharistic Teaching of Ratramne of Corbie* (Mundelein, Illinois, 1951), analysed by H. Weisweiler in *Scholastik*, 28 (1953), pp. 622–3, takes it as certain that Ratramnus distinguished two bodies in Christ. The problem is without doubt more complicated. Ratramnus was not, it would appear, speaking of things as they are in themselves, but of things as they are according to 'their appearance to man' (J. de Montclos, op. cit., p. 451).

21. On this, see J. Geiselmann, *Die Eucharistielehre*, pp. 290–9.

22. The order in which the various contributions appeared is as follows: Paschasius Radbertus, Abbot of Corbie, brought out his *De corpore et sanguine Domini* in 831. This made it the first comprehensive exposition of the Eucharist. In 844 the Emperor Charles the Bald asked Ratramnus, a monk of Corbie and a theological opponent of Radbertus, to set out his views on the Eucharist. Ratramnus then wrote his own *De corpore et sanguine Domini*. In 856 Radbertus addressed a celebrated letter on the same subject to a monk of Saint-Riquier, Frédugard. Radbertus's two texts are published by Bede Paulus in the *Corpus Christianorum, Continuatio Mediaevalis*, XVI (Turnhout, 1969). Only the second, the letter, which we cite as *F*, was a direct reply to Ratramnus.

23. Ratramnus, *De corpore et sanguine Domini*, c.VII, VIII, X, pp. 34–5.

24. Radbertus, in Paulus, III, 1–5, p. 23. He considers the Eucharist primarily from the point of view of its *efficacy* rather than its structure.

25. Ratramnus, *De corpore et sanguine Domini*, c. IX, p. 35.

26. J. Geiselmann, *Die Eucharistielehre*, p. 149, compares the eucharistic definitions of Ratramnus and Raban (d.856), one of Radbertus's German opponents, Archbishop of Mainz. Only Radbertus asserts the coincidence *in truth* of what *faith believes* and what the *things themselves become*. The other two hold that there is a *dualism* between the two orders.

27. Radbertus, Paulus, III, 24–9, p. 24. In an ancient expression, which is difficult to date, but which is a true reflection of patristic thought, the relation between the two natures in Jesus Christ is distinctly called 'the sacrament which must be able to resist dissolution' by a separation

in Christ of God and man, cf. Denzinger and Schönmetzer, *Enchiridion Symbolorum* (Herder & Herder, Freiburg, 1963), n. 355, p. 124. St Bonaventure was later to speak of the 'sacrament of the Incarnation', in III 1, a 2, 9, ad 1 (Quaracchi, 1917, vol. III, p. 21).

28. Isidore of Seville (b. *c.* 560, d.636) stands as one of the cultural peaks of Visigothic Spain. His *Etymologiae*, the fruit of a real concern for an encyclopedic synthesis, were immensely successful in his own day, and later were to serve as one of the most important links between the Middle Ages and antiquity. J. Fontaine, *Isidore de Séville et la culture classique dans l'Espagne wisigothique, Etudes Augustiniennes*, 2 vols., 1959. His definition of sacraments, very much on the Augustinian model, had considerable influence on medieval theology. 'There is sacrament in a celebration', explains Isidore, 'when the act done has no other meanings except that of *signifying* what must be received in a hallowed spirit' (*Etymologiarum*, 1.VI, c. xix, 39, in *Patrologia Latina*, 82, col. 255c).

29. P. Radbertus, XIX, 10–15, in Paulus, pp. 101–2.

30. id., *F*, 41–9, in Paulus, p. 146.

31. id., IX, 6, in Paulus, p. 52.

32. XXI, 29, in Paulus, p. 110 (*F*, 886).

33. *F*, 116.

34. *F*, 228.

35. X, 25–8, in Paulus, p. 66. The idea comes from St Augustine. Thus in his *Sermon on Psalm 40* : 'He died', says Augustine, 'but his name has not perished; rather has he been sown; he died, but as a grain of corn dies – struck by death, it forthwith reappears as harvest' (*Patrologia Latina*, 36, col. 453).

36. V, 24, in Paulus, p. 32.

37. *F*, 668, in Paulus, p. 166. Here Radbertus is quoting St Augustine's *In Joannem*, 26, 19.

38. *Sensualiter* is difficult to translate; the adverb means at the least that the body of Christ is so real that the Eucharist in some way transforms it into *an object of sense*. This is contradictory of the sacrament, and merited Berengar's Pauline rejoinder: 'Even though we once regarded Christ from a human point of view, we regard him thus no longer' (2 Cor. 5 : 16) (*De sacra coena adversus Lanfrancum*, c. XXXVII, in Beekenkamp p. 110). This declaration had been imposed by the same Cardinal Humbert who headed the Roman mission at the time of the break with Constantinople in 1054.

39. '*Quia incorruptibilis et insecabilis*' (*De sacra coena*, in Beekenkamp, p. 161). He speaks also of '*corpus indesecabile*' (ibid., p. 66).

40. So Peter Lombard (d.1160), who was to refute a sensualist conception of the sacramental presence by re-adopting Berengar's argument of the incorruptibility of Christ's body (*Sentences*, 1, IV, dis.XII, c.II–IV, de fractione panis (Quaracchi, 1917, p. 810)). See St Thomas, 3a, 77,7, ad 3. Jean de Monclos, *Lanfranc et Bérenger*, has well noted the slowness of the progress made during this period (pp. 460f., 470f.).

41. This is still only the first reappearance of Aristotle, with the categories (analysis of propositions); the second, in the twelfth century, introduced the *Analytica* (the science of the syllogism); only the third, at the beginning of the thirteenth century, was metaphysical. Yves Congar,

article 'Théologie', in *Dictionnaire de théologie catholique*, XV, 1 (1946), cols. 359–60.

42. Cappuyns, op. cit., p. 403. For Berengar's teaching in his co-called second period (after 1059), see Geiselmann, *Die Eucharistielehre*, pp. 331–65.

43. Jean Leclercq brought out in the *Revue Bénédictine*, 57 (1947), pp. 213–14, an unpublished piece by Guitmond of Aversa, in which it is said that in the Eucharist, and in virtue of God's omnipotence, the accidents subsist independently of their proper substance. 'Technically speaking', and as early as at the end of the eleventh century, this is the doctrine of transubstantiation. On Alger of Liège, see Jean de Montclos, *Lanfranc et Bérenger*, pp. 464–70. On the specific influence of Lanfranc, see ibid., pp. 451–4.

44. Text translated in Dumeige, *La Foi catholique*, no. 726. Berengar was forced to sign the declaration in 1079, and this he did in Rome itself during the pontificate of Gregory VII. For further details, see Cappuyns, op. cit., pp. 395–6. On the origin of the term 'substance', see J. de Montclos, op. cit., pp. 232–4. Cf. *Downside Review*, April 1973, pp. 101ff.

45. J. de Montclos, op. cit., pp. 475–6. We are grateful to the author for valuable comments communicated to us in writing, which we have taken into consideration in discussing this nice question of the eucharistic teaching of Berengar and Ratramnus.

46. Jean de Montclos is careful in emphasizing this point in relation to the dispute between Lanfranc and Berengar, and puts 'Aristoteliansim' in quotes, pp. 445–9.

47. H. de Lubac, *Corpus mysticum*, pp. 168–72.

48. J. de Ghellinck, 'L'Entrée d'*essentia, substantia*, et autres mots apparentés dans le langage médiéval', in *Bulletin de Cange*, 16 (1942), in particular pp. 88–112. For a long time in classical Latin and in medieval usage, the word *substantia* centred on the notions of patrimony, wealth or property. Concrete in its origins, the speculative development of the word came late, and was moreover open to reversal.

49. J. A. Jungmann, *Missarum solemnia*, III, p. 321. It was under this name that the feast specially dedicated to the Eucharist came into the liturgical cycle during the Middle Ages (E. Dumoutet, *Le Christ selon la chair et la vie liturgique au Moyen Age* (Beauchesne, Paris, 1932), pp. 129–44). On the relation between devotion to the Eucharist and the Berengarian crisis, see the same writer's *Le désir de voir l'Hostie et les origines de la dévotion au Saint-Sacrement* (Beauchesne, Paris, 1926), pp. 26–8.

50. H. de Lubac, *Corpus mysticum*, pp. 172–3. It appears that Berengar would have been able to accept the phrase '*salva sua substantia*' in speaking of the body of the risen Christ in heaven, but not of the bread and wine at the altar (J. de Montclos, op. cit., p. 147, n. 4).

51. *Sermon 71*, in *Patrologia Latina*, 38, col. 453. We remember the famous '*Crede et manducasti*' ('Believe and you have eaten') of *In Joannem*, XXV, 12, C.C.XXXVI, p. 254. On this, see H. de Lubac, *Corpus mysticum*, pp. 154–61.

52. Geiselmann, *Die Eucharistielehre*, pp. 38–9.

53. H. de Lubac, op. cit., pp. 183–8. For its use by Berengar, see *de Coena*

Domini, in Beekenkamp, p. 163.

54. 'You are denying the truth of the flesh and blood' was the reproach made to Berengar (H. de Lubac, op. cit., p. 238).

55. The neo-Manicheanism which began to be rife in the south of France and which taught a contempt for the flesh was not calculated to lessen suspicions of language which from the eucharistic point of view could seem too 'spiritualist' (H. de Lubac, op. cit., p. 181). On the theological importance of the Pauline concept of 'spiritual body', see G. Martelet 'Le mystère du corps et de l'Esprit dans le Christ ressuscité et dans l'Eglise', in *Verbum caro*, 12 (1958), no. 45, pp. 31–53.

56. 'Who sits at the right hand of the Father' was the wording of the 1079 declaration. Dumeige, *La Foi catholique*, no. 726.

57. H. de Lubac, *Corpus mysticum*, p. 247.

58. ibid., p. 269.

59. ibid., p. 27.

60. ibid., p. 275

61. Yves Congar, *The Mystery of the Church* (Geoffrey Chapman, London, 1960), mentions St Thomas, pp. 97–117.

62. H. de Lubac, *Corpus mysticum*, pp. 128–35. The analogy of the human body, understood in the sociological sense of the *body politic*, was to dominate fourteenth-century ecclesiology, and even more the theology of the post-Tridentine period. It has become a commonplace to blame Bellarmine in this connection. In fact, the 'juridification' of the notion of Church is much earlier, and goes back to the Gregorian reform in the eleventh century. We see it in the form of titles such as 'Spouse' (asserting her liberty in relation to the temporal power) and 'Mother' (and therefore with authority over her children) (Yves Congar, *L'Eglise de saint Augustin à l'époque moderne* (Le Cerf, Paris, 1970), pp. 107–112). On earlier ecclesiology, which emphasized the aspect of 'communion' (in relation to the Eucharist), see the same author's *L'ecclésiologie du Haut Moyen Age* (Le Cerf, Paris, 1968), pp. 86–90, where he is in full agreement with H. de Lubac in *Corpus mysticum*.

63. The quotation is from Raoul Ardens (d. c. 1100), as published and studied by J. de Ghellinck, in connection with the first use of the word 'transubstantiation', in *Recherches de Science religeuse*, 1911, pp. 570–2.

64. As St Thomas explains, *Summa Theologica*, 3a, 75, 7, 1⁰, where he refers to Mark 7:31–3.

65. ibid, 3⁰.

66. op. cit., 3a, 75, 4, and the whole of question 76 on the presence of Christ in the sacrament. For an overall understanding of St Thomas's eucharistic thought, see Dom Anscar Vonier, *The Key to the Doctrine of the Holy Eucharist* (Burns & Oates, London, 1925). For all the depth of St Thomas's eucharistic synthesis, one cannot but wonder at the underlying concept of the *risen body* implied in the following answer: If we do not receive Christ in his own form in the Eucharist, but under the veil of the *accidents* of bread or wine, the reason, says St Thomas, is that 'the eating of human flesh and the drinking of human blood is not customary to men but shocking' (3a, 75, 5 (echoing 75, 6)).

67. *Sermon sur le culte dû à Dieu*, Carême de saint Germain 1666, *Oeuvres oratoires*, Lebarq (D.D.B., Paris, 1892), vol. 5, p. 115.

68. op. cit., 3a, 3, 7.

69. For the strictly theological point of view, see Paul Vignaux, *Nominalisme au XIVe siècle* (Vrin, Montréal and Paris, 1948).

70. H. de Lubac, *Surnaturel, Etudes historiques,* in the series *Théologie,* no. 8 (1946), p. 277.

71. ibid., p. 278.

72. Pierre Duhem, *Le Système du Monde, Histoire des doctrines cosmologiques, Platon à Copernic,* vol. VI (Hermannet Cie, 1954), on *Guillaume d'Ockam et l'occamisme,* pp. 600–1.

73. Duhem, op. cit., p. 729, notes this in connection with Buridan's system (d.1358). The 'merit' of nominalism, from this point of view, is that it got rid of the dogmatism of Aristotle, and made possible a 'positivism' from which modern science would be able to emerge. Similar comments in Francis Rapp, *L'Eglise et la vie religieuse en Occident à la fin du Moyen Age, Nouvelle Clio,* 25 (P.U.F., Paris, 1971), 'Le Procès de nominalisme', pp. 342–8. A well-balanced general judgement of nominalism.

74. I had Pierre Bayle (d.1706) in mind, even more than Voltaire (d.1778). Paul Hazard, *The European Mind* (1680–1715) (Hollis & Carter, London, 1953), pp. 99–115, and, on the Rationalists and the denial of miracle, pp. 119–179.

75. The *Summa* of St Thomas was widely read in the fourteenth century, and in the fifteenth his thought was to find a most valuable interpreter in Capreolus (d.1444), to be followed in later centuries by other celebrated commentators, Cajetan (d.1534), John of St Thomas (d.1644), the Carmelites of Salamanca (seventeenth century) and very many others. See M. Grabmann, *La Somme Théologique de saint Thomas* (Bloud et Gay, Paris and Liège, 1925), pp. 52–60.

76. For the doctrine of justification, in particular, as taught by the nominalists, see H. A. Obermann, *The Harvest of Medieval Theology, Gabriel Biel and Late Medieval Nominalism* (Harvard University Press, Cambridge, Mass., 1963), pp. 255–61. See also Joseph Lortz, *The Reformation in Germany* (Darton, Longman & Todd, London, and Herder & Herder, New York, 1968). For the influence of nominalism on Luther, see Louis Bouyer, *Du Protestantisme à l'Eglise,* 2nd ed., *Unam Sanctam,* 27 (Le Cerf, Paris, 1955), pp. 164–7; Joseph Lortz, Erwin Iserloh, *Kleine Reformations-geschichte* (Herder & Herder, Freiburg, 1969), pp. 34–5; Rapp, op. cit., pp. 335–6, 342–5.

77. Held in 1215: in the decree against the Albigensians it uses the word 'transubstantiation'.

78. James F. M. McCue, 'The Doctrine of Transubstantiation', in *Harvard Theological Review,* 1968, pp. 403–6. Duns Scotus (d.1308) thus restates the three views that were still openly discussed at the beginning of the thirteenth century by such men as Peter of Capua (ibid, p. 390).

79. He proposed to speak not only of 'transubstantiation' but also of 'transaccidentation and so avoid affirming that an accident is the body of Christ' (*De Captivitate Babylonica Ecclesiae Praeludium* (1520), translated in *Reformation Writings of Martin Luther,* trans. B. L. Woolf, vol. I (Lutterworth Press, London, 1952), p. 229).

80. See James F. M. McCue, art cit., pp. 413–17.

81. So L. Smits (see below, p. 236, note 84, for his writings on Calvin), in a small book entitled *Fragen um die Eucharistie,* the substance of

which is summarized in *Herder Korrespondenz*, 19 (1964), p. 518.

82. James F. M. McCue, art. cit., p. 419.

83. *Institution de la religion chrétienne*, ed. J. D. Benoît (Vrin, Paris, 1961), IV, XVII, 14, vol. 4, p. 388. On the circumstances of its publication, first in Latin in 1536, and in its final French form in 1559, see Jean Cadier, *The Man God Mastered* (Inter-Varsity Fellowship, London, 1960), pp. 58–75.

84. Luchesius Smits, *Saint Augustin dans l'oeuvre de Jean Calvin*, vol. 1 (Assen, 1958), pp. 259–65. Harnack accused Calvin of having taken his eucharistic teaching from Ratramnus; cf. Geiselmann, *Die Eucharistielehre*, p. 179. Whether Harnack was historically justified or not, there is no doubt but that the Reformed Churches and the Anglicans of the seventeenth and eighteenth centuries were greatly interested in both Ratramnus and Berengar, as witness the editions of Ratramnus published during that period. On this, see J. N. Bakhuizen van den Brink, *Texte établi d'après les manuscrits, et Notice bibliographique* (Amsterdam, 1954), pp. 62–128. We know that G. E. Lessing (d.1781), the celebrated editor of Reimarus (above, p. 213, note 13), edited Berengar's answer to Lanfranc in 1770; W. H. Beekenkamp, *Berengarii Turonensis de sacra coena adversus Lanfrancum* (The Hague, 1941), Praefatio, note 1.

85. On Calvin's eucharistic teaching, see François Wendel, *Calvin, The Origins and Development of his Religious Thought* (Collins, London, 1963), pp. 329–355; Joseph Ratzinger, 'Das Problem der Transsubstantiation und die Frage nach dem Sinn der Eucharistie', in *Theologisches Jahrbuch*, 12 (1969), pp. 283–6 (with some pages on Luther also). But, most important, Max Thurian, *The Eucharistic Memorial*, vol. 2, pp. 110–24.

86. *Institution de la religion chrétienne*, IV, XVII, 12, p. 387.

87. Above, pp. 124–8.

88. He puts it so in *Letter* 187 in *Patrologia Latina*, 33, col. 836. A little before, Calvin, convinced that here he was touching upon a point essential to faith, had also said, 'It is not Aristotle but the Holy Spirit who teaches that the body of Jesus Christ, after having risen from the dead, remains in his own "local habitation", and is received into heaven until the last day' (*Institution de la religion chrétienne*, IV, XVII, 28, p. 409.

89. *Institution de la religion chrétienne*, IV, XVII, 28, p. 413. Both in Calvin and in St Augustine we find the concern with the problem of 'as' ('as God', 'as man'), which divides the nature instead of considering their *union*.

90. ibid.

91. M. Thurian, *The Eucharistic Memorial*, vol. 2, p. 118. The author has been charged (T. Süss in *Revue des sciences philosophiques et théologiques*, 53 (1969), p. 446) with himself reintroducing the Lutheran doctrine of the ubiquity of Christ – but not, to my mind, justifiably. It is true, however, that a more fully worked out theology of the body is undoubtedly necessary. Such a theology will have to show that the relation of the glorified Christ to our world is *constitutive* of the identity of the Lord, and that his true nature, *presupposed* by the Eucharist, will be *revealed* only in the parousia. The *body* of Christ, as mystery of the Resurrection, is part of faith; but it must be thought out by theology. It may well be true, as T. Süss writes again (ibid.),

that 'the traditional problem of the real Presence is the very precise problem of overcoming a spatial gap, between Christ raised to the right hand of God and the community united somewhere on earth for the eucharistic celebration' (p. 441); but it is also true that one of theology's urgent tasks is really to outflank this problem, on the ground that it rests upon an imaginary gap, and, so far as possible, to enable all Christians to shake it off for good.

92. *Institution de la religion chrétienne*, IV, XVII, 12, p. 387.
93. Above, pp. 86–9.

3. A MISUNDERSTANDING CORRECTED

1. Y. Congar, ' "Pneumatologie" ou "Christomonisme" dans la tradition latine?', in *Ecclesia a Spiritu Sancto edocta*, (Duculot, Gembloux, 1970), p. 45. T. M. R. Tillard already regards this question as 'of minor importance' at the end of a good scriptural and patristic summary in 'L'Eucharistie et le Saint-Esprit', in *Nouvelle revue théologique*, 90 (1968), pp. 363–87.

2. Boris Bobrinskoy, 'Présence réelle et communion eucharistique', in *Revue des sciences philosophiques et théologiques*, 1969, p. 403 : 'First of all,' he writes, 'let us make it quite clear that the problem of the relation of the Holy Spirit to the Eucharist is far wider than the no longer important question of the epiclesis.'

3. Archimandrite Pierre L'Huillier, 'Théologie de l'epiclèse', in *Verbum caro*, 53 (1960), p. 322.

4. The reference is to the prayer *Veni sanctificator omnipotens*. On this, see Jungmann, *Missarum Sollemnia*, II, p. 342.

5. The question was asked by Nicolas Cabasilas (d.1363), the famous Byzantine theologian, in connection with the *Te Supplices* of the Roman Mass, in his *Commentary on the Divine Liturgy* (SPCK, London, 1960). Jungmann, on the other hand, would see a *consecratory epiclesis* in the prayer *Quam oblationem*, already known to St Ambrose (*Missarum Sollemnia*, III, pp. 102–6). To end this account of Latin equivalents of the Eastern epiclesis, we may add that Jungmann sees in the two prayers *Te Supplices* and *Supra quae* an *epiclesis of communion*, or an invocation to the Holy Spirit, praying that he may grant us worthily to assimilate the riches of the Eucharist (*Missarum Sollemnia*, III, pp. 155f.).

6. Théodore Strotmann, 'Pneumatologie et liturgie', in *La liturgie après Vatican II, Unam sanctam*, 66 (Le Cerf, Paris, 1967), pp. 289–312.

7. This was known as *monarchianism* : meaning the preponderance of the Father and the subordinate, not to say secondary, character of the Son and the Spirit (*Nouvelle histoire de l'Eglise*, vol. 1 (Le Seuil, Paris, 1963), pp. 138–9).

8. This was Arianism : the error of Arius of Alexandria (d.336), who refused to say that the Word was God, because he is begotten of the Father. Arianism was condemned at Nicaea in 325 (ibid., vol. 1, pp. 390–1).

9. Rejecting consideration of the personal merits of the minister in the administration of the sacraments, St Augustine formulated the celebrated golden rule of sacerdotal ministry in Western theology: 'Paul baptizes, Peter baptizes, Christ baptizes.' Cf. *In Joannem*, 7–CC.XXXIV, p. 57. On Donatism, see *Nouvelle histoire de l'Eglise*, vol. 1, pp. 285–6.

Congar has given a magnificent exposition of St Augustine's sacramental theology, emphasizing its pneumatology. Introduction to vol. 28 of the works of St Augustine in the *Bibliothèque Augustinienne* (D.D.B., Paris, 1963), pp. 86–117. On later distortions, and the ultimately somewhat juridical character of the theology of the sacerdotal ministry in the West (this last further encouraged by the Great Schism of the fourteenth century), see Louis Saltet, *Les réordinations* (Gabalda, 1907), pp. 289–368.

10. *Nouvelle histoire de l'Eglise*, vol. 2, *Le Moyen Age* (Le Seuil, Paris, 1968), pp. 128–9. The problem is one of deciding how to understand the eternal procession of the Spirit: from the Father *and* from the Son (the Latin attitude in the filioque) or from the Father *through* the Son (the 'Greek' attitude). For a treatment of this problem as now irrelevant, see Paul Evdokimov, *Le Saint Esprit dans la Tradition orientale* (Le Cerf, Paris, 1969).

11. Y. Congar, ' "Pneumatologie" ou "Christomonisme" ', p. 48.

12. In this context the two words hardly differ in meaning. Johannes Betz, *Die Eucharistie in der Zeit der griechischen Väter*, I, 1, p. 223.

13. *De fide orthodoxa*, in *Patrologia Graeca*, 94, cols. 1153, 1154.

14. On the iconoclastic crisis, see *Nouvelle histoire de l'Eglise*, vol. 2, pp. 109–23. On the theological argument against the iconoclasts, the article 'Epiclèse' by Salaville, in *Dictionnaire de théologie catholique*, V, 251.

15. And so Nicolas Cabasilas, for example (see above, n.5): 'And that now [the Word of consecration spoken by Christ] uttered by the priest, by reason of being uttered by the priest, has this efficacy, this is nowhere taught; for the creative word is not acting either . . .' (*Commentary on the Divine Liturgy.*

16. Dumeige, *La Foi catholique*, nos. 731–3. Cf. J. Gill, *The Council of Florence* (Cambridge University Press, London, 1959).

17. The Greek word used here is *metaballein*, whence the English 'metabolism'. The Council of Trent speaks of 'conversion'; see above, pp. 105–8.

18. Quoted by Bouyer, *Eucharist: Theology and Spirituality of the Eucharistic Prayer*, p. 288.

19. ibid., p. 296.

20. *De fide orthodoxa*, in *Patrologia Graeca*, 94, cols. 1158–42.

21. G. C. Smit, 'Epiclèse et théologie des sacrements', in *Mélanges de sciences religieuses*, 1958, pp. 124–32.

22. Salaville, article 'Epiclèse', in *Dictionnaire de théologie catholique*, V, 294.

23. Cyprien Kern, 'En marge de l'Epiclèse', in *Irénikon*, 1951, p. 169.

24. By epicleses of appropriation we mean those which ask the Spirit that we may become worthy recipients of the spiritual treasures of the Eucharist; we distinguish these from the epicleses of consecration (as they are called) which ask the Holy Spirit, after the recital of the Institution (the anamnesis) to *consecrate* the offerings. On the epicleses of appropriation, see below, pp. 185–6.

25. L. Bouyer, op. cit., p. 310, and the whole passage, pp. 310–14, which harmonizes the two.

26. Y. Congar, 'L' "Ecclesia" ou communauté chrétienne sujet intégral de l'action liturgique', in *La liturgie après Vatican II*, pp. 241–82.

On this phraseology, see B. D. Marliangeas, ' "*In persona Christi*", "*in persona Ecclesiae*" : Note sur le développement de l'usage de ces expressions dans la 'Théologie latine', in *La liturgie après Vatican II*, pp. 283–8.

27. A. Chavasse, 'Epiclèse eucharistique dans les anciennes liturgies orientales. Une hypothèse d'interprétation', in *Mélanges de sciences religieuses*, 1946, pp. 197–206. The writer is correct in seeing that the epiclesis raises a question of ministry, but is mistaken in looking in the *clearly expressed intention* for what should be sought in the *office mercifully assisted*.

PART III

1. RESURRECTION AND REAL PRESENCE

1. 'The Word took on flesh that we might be able to receive the Holy Spirit. God made himself bearer of our flesh that man might be able to become bearer of the Spirit' (*De Incarnatione*, in *Patrologia Graeca*, 26, col. 996.

2. *De fide orthodoxa*, in *Patrologia Graeca*, 94, col. 1141. Cf. above, p. 114.

3. The quotation, somewhat abbreviated here, is from Père de Lubac, in *The Splendour of the Church* (Sheed & Ward, London and New York, 1956), p. 92.

4. See below, p. 163.

5. Above, pp. 39–47.

6. *Early Writings*, p. 127. (Our italics)

7. ibid., p. 155. It will be remembered that it is of communism that Marx says that 'as the fulfilment of naturalism it=humanism, as the fulfilment of humanism=naturalism : it is the *true* solution of the conflict between man and nature, between man and man, the true solution to the struggle between existence and essence, between objectification and affirmation of self, between freedom and necessity, between individual and species. It is, and claims to be, the answer to the riddle of history.' We can understand how communism has been called a secular Christianity.

8. Above, pp. 82–90.

9. Here Teilhard adds a footnote: 'And, it may be added, in perfect analogy with the mystery of the first Christmas which (as everyone agrees) could only have happened between Heaven and an Earth which was *prepared*, socially, politically and psychologically, to receive Jesus.'

10. 'But not, of course, sufficient in itself!' (Note by Teilhard).

11. 'The Heart of the Problem', in *The Future of Man*, pp. 267–8.

12. 'The Phyletic Structure of the Human Group', in *The Appearance of Man*, p. 171.

13. Michel Foucault, *Les mots et les choses, Une archéologie des sciences humaines* (Gallimard, Paris, 1966), p. 359.

14. Jean Lacroix, *Le Monde*, 18 November 1958.

15. 'The Singularities of the Human Species', in *The Appearance of Man*, pp. 268–9.

16. *Human Energy*, p. 159.

17. 'Introduction to the Christian Life', in *Christianity and Evolution*

(Collins, London, and Harper & Row, New York, 1969), pp. 155–6.

18. Here reference should be made to Christ's 'informing' action, in the most modern sense of the word, of providing the 'information' that determines a programme. Christ is in fact the 'programme' set up for ever for the world by the Resurrection, a 'programme' of eschatological suppression of the effects of sin, of entropy and death, of our finiteness.

19. Marcel Legaut, *Introduction à l'intelligence du passé et de l'avenir du christianisme* (Aubier, Paris, 1970), p. 27.

20. In an unpublished MS. Joseph Moingt writes: 'Christ's actions at the Supper signify the *work* by which the Father of a family feeds his children, taking from nature the things that are needed for their nourishment. And his sufferings on the cross make manifest, as the martyrs understood so admirably, the work by which Christ reduces his body to wheat. The nourishment of the Eucharist continues all this work in us, transforming our mortal flesh into flesh assured of resurrection.' On this notion of Christ's *work* during his Passion, which is an Ignatian idea, see G. Fessard, *La dialectique des Exercises* (Aubier, Paris, 1956), pp. 157–60.

21. 'The Priest', in *Writings in Time of War*, p. 207.

22. See N. M. Wildiers, Introduction to *Hymn of the Universe*.

23. *Le Christique* (1955), unpublished. From his own angle, the Abbé Monchanin has put forward views that harmonize perfectly with Teilhard's: 'At the parousia the universe which, through the Church, is already Body of the risen Christ, will be manifest as such to the whole Church and to every one of its members, no longer under the restriction of even the absolute ritual sign, but without any restriction whatsoever. The Eucharist which magnetizes the universe will transubstantiate it' (quoted by H. de Lubac in *Images de l'abbé Monchanin* (Aubier, Paris, 1967), p. 143).

24. *Le Milieu Divin*, p. 115; *The Divine Milieu*, p. 104.

25. Gregory of Nyssa, *Catechetical Oration*, XXXVII, 7 and 8.

26. J. P. de Jong, 'Epikleses und Mischungsritus nach Irenäus', in *Jahrbuch für Liturgiewissenschaft*, 1965, p. 29, speaks of men's 'symbolic alphabet'.

27. *Modern Eucharistic Agreement*, p. 29.

2. THE EUCHARIST AND THE GENESIS OF MAN

1. Henri de Lubac, *Corpus mysticum*, pp. 231–3.

2. Jean Mouroux, *Faites ceci en mémoire de moi*, pp. 90–1.

3. Joseph Robert, 'Faites cela en mémoire de moi', in *Lettre*, 125 (1969), pp. 18–44.

4. Gérard Philips, *Seminarium*, 1 (Rome (Vatican), 1970), p. 7.

5. Hugo Rahner, SJ, *Greek Myths and Christian Mystery* (Burns & Oates, London, 1963), pp. 29ff.

6. Walter Kasper, 'Accents nouveaux dans la compréhension dogmatique du service sacerdotal', in *Concilium*, 43 (1969), p. 25.

7. Guy Goureaux, 'Le marasme de l'Eglise en France', in *IDOC International*, 39 (1971), p. 53.

8. James 2 : 2–5.

9. *Lettre*, 120–1 (1968), pp. 1–3.

10. Jean Cardonnel, after *Le Monde*, 8 August 1970.

11. Maurice Bellet, *Christus*, 69 (1971), p. 49.

12. Jean Mouroux, op. cit., p. 88; Tillard, *Eucharistie purification de l'Eglise pérégrinante*, in *Nouvelle revue théologique*, 1962, pp. 449–74, 579–97.

13. Edgar Haulotte, 'Le mouvement de l'Esprit dans les Actes des Apôtres', in *Vienchrétienne*, 127 (1970), p. 11, goes so far as to speak of the 'economic dimension of the relation to the risen Christ'.

14. Above, p. 38.

15. Adalbert Hamman, *Vie liturgique et vie sociale* (Desclée, Paris, 1969), pp. 307–8.

16. Cosmao, in *Le Monde*, 3 June 1971.

17. Decree on the Apostolate of the Laity, 8, 3 and 4, in *The Documents of Vatican II*, pp. 498–9.

18. '*Immaculata ex maculatis*': Ambrose of Milan, *Expositionis in Lucam*, 1.17, in *Patrologia Latina*, 15, col. 1540C.

19. *Sermo*, 5, 6–8, in *Patrologia Latina*, 36, cols. 57–9 (quoted by Urs von Balthasar in *Le visage de l'Eglise, Unam sanctam* SL (1958), p. 77).

20. *Lumen Gentium*, 14, in *Documents of Vatican II*, p. 33.

21. Louis Bouyer, *Eucharist: Theology and Spirituality of the Eucharistic Prayer*, p. 174.

22. ibid., pp. 284–5.

23. ibid., p. 264

24. ibid., p. 169. All these prayers belong to what we have called earlier, p. 238, note 24, 'epicleses of appropriation', and whose importance is now evident.

25. *Adversus Haereses*, IV, 18, 5 (*Against the Heresies*, vol. II, p. 40). Nicolas Cabasilas (d.1371), 'La vie en Jésus-Christ', trans. Broussaleux, in Supplement to *Irénikon*, 1932–4, c.IV, note 24, 'Les effets de l'Eucharistie', pp. 97–138, to which I have been greatly indebted in this section.

26. The idea was first put forward by Oscar Cullman, 'Le culte dans l'Eglise primitive', in *Cahiers de l'actualité protestante*, 8 (Delachaux et Niestlé, Neuchâtel, 1944), p. 18, and has often been elaborated since – recently by Medard Kehl, quoted above, p. 206, note 15.

27. *Adversus Haereses*, III, 19, 1 (*Against the Heresies*, vol. I, p. 133).

28. Gregory of Nyssa, *Catechetical Oration*, XXXVII.

29. Cyril of Alexandria, in *Patrologia Graeca*, 77, 1021B.

30. Octave of Easter (eighth-ninth centuries), in P. Bruylants, *Les oraisons du Missel romain*, vol. 11 (Mont-César, Louvain, 1952), p. 246, from which all these prayers are quoted, though they will be found, of course, in the Roman Missal.

31. op cit., pp. 45–6.

32. Post-communion for the Sunday within the Octave of the Epiphany, ibid., p. 320.

33. ibid., p. 255.

34. ibid., p. 329.

35. Formerly the fifteenth Sunday after Pentecost, ibid., p. 189.

36. Defined by Henri Piéron, *Vocabulaire de la Psychologie* (P.U.F., Paris, 1951), as 'individual capacity to experience feelings and emotions'; and, more exactly, by Foulquié and Saint Jean, *Dictionnaire de la langue philosophique* (P.U.F., Paris, 1962), following Pradines's comments, as '. . . experience feelings of pleasure and pain'. In psychoanalytical language, which is directly derived from German psychological language,

as noted by Laplanche and Pontalis, *Vocabulaire de la psychanalyse*, under the word, 'affect' means 'every affective state, painful or pleasant, vague or qualified, whether presented in the form of a massive discharge or of general tonality'. Writing from a strictly philosophical point of view, Emmanuel Levinas, *Totalité et Infini, Essai sur l'extériorité* (The Hague, 1961), pp. 88–114, deals with affectivity in the sense in which we use it here, as being the very shape of the subject in the world.

37. The phrase is borrowed from J. de Waelhens, and sums up what we were trying to understand earlier, pp. 39–47.

38. Post-communion for Saturday of the second week in Lent, Bruylants, op. cit., p. 287.

39. Prayer for the feast of St Clotilda, 3 June.

40. op cit., p. 327.

41. 'The Mass on the World' (1923), in *Hymn of the Universe*, pp. 20–34 *passim*. Although the passages are not annotated separately, they all run on in their correct order.

Index

abortion, 40

Absolute, the, 75, 85-6

absoluteness in man, 55, 56-7

action, human, 54, 55-6; liturgical notion, 101-2

activity, 83, 195, 219

Adam, 167, 169; first and second, 164, 167, 171, 189, 198

Adam, Karl, 230

affectivity, 192-3, 241-2

agape, 24, 184

Albigensians, 235

Alger of Liège, 134, 231, 233

Ambrose, St, 223, 237; on Church, 184-5; on Eucharist, 110, 113-14, 134, 226

anamnesis, 103; and Christ's act in Eucharist, 171-2; consecration, epiclesis and, 151-4; value of words, 155; Western subordination of epiclesis to, 151-2

annihilation, 141

anthropocentrism, 51, 167, 168; Teilhard's neo-, 205

anthropogenesis, 164

anthropology, 13, 212; of the body, 94, 120-1, 143; and influence of dogma of Incarnation, 46; and man's irreducibility in the world, 55-6; of the Resurrection, 59, 67-8, 82; social, 36

Aragon, Louis, 19-20

Arianism, 150, 237

Aristotle, 44, 134, 137, 208, 232, 235

Arsac, Jacques, 203

Ascension, the, 94, 218, 223

Athanasius, St, 160, 239

Augustine, St, 128, 130, 131, 134, 158, 229; on Baptism and Eucharist, 114, 227; and Calvin, 143-4; on Church, 131, 184-5, 232; on glorified body of risen Christ, 124-8, 230; on God, 123; on holiness of Christians, 184-5; on meaning of Gospel, 68; and

Neoplatonism, 122-4, 229; on sacerdotal ministry, 237-8; on sign, 19, 203; spiritualism and Eucharist, 135, 230, 233

Bachelard, Gaston, 45, 209, 213

Baciocchi, J. de, 108, 109-10, 111-12, 226

Bakhuizen van den Brink, J. N., 230, 236

Baldwin of Canterbury, 225

Balthasar, H. Urs von, 190, 208, 220, 223, 241

baptism, 104, 114; Donatists and, 150

Barbotin, E., 205, 206, 214

Barreau, Jean-Claude, 222

Barth, Karl, 213, 218

Barthélemy-Madaule, M., 210

Basil, St, liturgy of, 151, 153

Bayle, Pierre, 235

Beccari, R., 208

Beekenkamp, W. H., 230, 236

bees, 42, 205

Beinert, W., 224, 227, 228

Bellarmine, Cardinal Robert, 234

Bellet, Maurice, 240

Benoît, J. D., 236

Benoit, P., 223

Benvéniste, E., 205, 225

Berengar of Tours, 127, 128, 129, 131, 132, 133, 161, 230-1, 232, 236; and notion of substance, 133-4, 135, 145, 224, 233, 234

Bergounioux, F. M., 205

Bergson, Henri, 52, 210-11

Betz, J., 225, 238

Beuron, abbey of, 99

Biel, Gabriel, 141

biology, 49, 50

bipedalism, 41

Blondel, Maurice, 213

Bobrinskoy, B., 225, 237

body, human, an access to things, 192, 242; action and passion in, 83; and

metaphors, 43

metaphysics, 138-9, 159

metapsychology, 50

Metzger, Witmar, 208

ministry, apostolic, 197, 199-201; episcopal, 200; priestly, 197, 200, 201, 237-8, 155-6

miracles, 62, 63-4, 138-9, 214

modernism, 61

Moingt, Joseph, 240

Moltmann, J., 219

monarchianism, 150, 237

Monchanin, Abbé, 240

Monod, Jacques, 209, 210; on entropy, 211

Montclos, Jean de, 230, 231, 232, 233

Morendo, Bruno, 210

Mounin, Georges, 205

Mouroux, Jean, 228, 240, 241

Mühlen, Heribert, 219

multiple, the, 50, 51

murder, 40

Musurillo, H., 203

mutilation, 40

Mysterium Fidei, encyclical, 116-17, 119, 228

mystery, concept of, 101-2, 224

mystical Body, 137

nature, man and, 40, 163; symbolism of bread and wine, 31-3; symbolism of Creator in, 31-3, 39

needs, basic human, 37, 40

neg-entropy, 53-4, 211, 219; man structural and relative, 83; Resurrection of Christ absolute, 83-4, 93, 163

Neoplatonism, 46, 122-4, 135, 229

neurology, developmental, 44, 208

neuroses, 48

Nirvana principle, 50-1

nominalism, 139-41, 235

noogenesis, 53

Obermann, H. A., 235

Offertory, Teilhard on, 194

Origen, 44, 45, 229

Orthodox Christians, *see* Eastern Church

orthopraxis, 181

palaeontology, 41

Pankow, Gisela, 207

Pannenberg, Wolfhart, 215-16, 218

parousia, 28, 79, 84, 88, 89, 93, 94, 107, 146; Augustine and, 126; and Eucharist, 117-19, 177; and history, 164, 165-6; 'sacramental', 229; Teilhard on, 164, 195; world and, 163-4, 170, 173, 175-6, 177

Pascal, Blaise, 51, 172, 210

Pasch, Christ's, 171-2; man's spiritual, 171-3; trans-cultural, 171

Paschasius Radbertus, 230, 231, 232; on Eucharist and realism of Incarnation, 128, 129-30, 231; on real Presence, 161; on Resurrection and body of Christ, 131-3

passivity, 83, 195, 219

Passover, 109

Paul, St, 79, 84, 136, 228; on apostolic ministry, 197-8; and appearances of Christ, 68, 218; on Christ in creation, 112; on Christ as man's ultimate identity, 172-3; on Christ as mediator, 24, 208; and Christ as symbol, 23-4; 'Christ in you the hope of glory', 13, 101, 165; on the Christian, 170; and communion with all things, 195; concept of 'spiritual body', 161, 234; and 'cup of the new covenant', 97; dominion of Christ over all things, 74, 83, 142, 167; on expression of God in universe, 26; hermeneutics and, 62; on invocation of Jesus, 147; on Lord's Supper, 37-8, 117, 131, 161; on man's spiritual sacrifice, 170-1; and 'putting on Christ', 189; and Resurrection, 60, 80, 222; on resurrection in general, 77, 82, 217; on revelation of Spirit, 84-5; on second and last Adam, 171; on Spirit of Christ, 102; and spiritual body of Christ, 161

Paul VI, pope, 38, 116-17, 206, 228

Paulus, Bede, 231, 232

Pelletier, A., 214

Pentecost, 198

Perroux, François, 38, 206-7

personality, 192

Peter, St, 93, 147, 198

Peter of Capua, 235

Peter Lombard, 232

Petre-Quadens, O., 208